D0242367

General Editors

Steven Connor and Thomas Healy

214322

University Centre Barnsley

Engendering Fictions

The English Novel in the Early Twentieth Century

Lyn Pykett

Professor of English,
University of Wales, Aberystwyth

A member of the Hodder Headline Group

LONDON

First published in Great Britain 1995 by
Edward Arnold, a division of Hodder Headline PLC,
338 Euston Road, London NW1 3BH
175 Fifth Avenue, New York, NY 10010

Co-published in the United States of America by
Oxford University Press Inc.,
198 Medison Avenue, New York, NY 10016

British Library Cataloguing in Publication Data
A catalogue entry for this book is available from the British Library

Library of Congress Cataloging-in-Publication Data
Pykett, Lyn.
Engendering fictions : the English novel in the early twentieth
century / Lyn Pykett.
    p.   cm. — (Writing in history)
Includes bibliographical references and index.
ISBN 0-340-64577-6. — ISBN 0-340-56277-3 (pbk.)
    1. English fiction—20th century—History and criticism.
2. Gender identity in literature.   3. Authorship—Sex differences.
4. Sex role in literature.   I. Title.   II. Series.
PR888.G35P9   1995   94-48338
823'.91209—dc20   CIP

ISBN 0 340 56277 3 PB

Typeset in 10/12 Sabon by Scribe Design, Gillingham, Kent

Contents

General Editors' Preface

The title of this series intimates the reciprocal relations of writing and history that its contributors seek to encourage: literature acting as history and history acting in literature. Writing in History aims to write history back into the practices of literary study, at a time when the demands made by literary and cultural theory on the time and attention of student and teacher alike may effectively have written history out of the picture. But the history that this series aims to write back in is neither a simple alternative nor antidote to 'theory'; rather, it is the reasoned consequence of the heightened levels of theoretical awareness and debate within literary studies.

The series title points to an enlarged conception of the historical embeddedness of all forms of writing, whether literary or non-literary, a conception of writing not merely as the register of history, but as itself a form of historical event, action and effect. According to this view of the relations between writing and history, there is no particular value in the distinction between the worldly purposes of legal, religious, medical, scientific, or political writing and the literary writing which W. H. Auden gloomily concluded 'makes nothing happen'. The writing in 'Writing in History', is more verb than noun, more process than product. To read historically is to catch writing in the act: to watch it happening.

The phrase 'writing in history' is meant to remind the authors and readers of these books that the understanding of history is always itself determined by historical conditions; determined both in the negative sense that we are limited by who we are, and what our condition enables us to see, and also in the positive sense that our limited perspective is what makes possible the renewal and discovery of different relations to the past. In the writing of history, we are always partly writing the stories of our relations to the past.

The last years have seen an explosion of guides to theory which enable students to question most aspects of literary study. Surprisingly, though, there has been no concerted attempt to inform them of the changes in history and literary history: e.g. the rethinking of ideas of period, the greater prominence given to social and cultural history, and the emergence of new areas of focus such as gender history. This series gives students of literature access to recent ideas about history and involves them in measuring their implications for critical practice. Writing in History refuses to allow history to be imagined either as existing only in writing, or as a retrieval of the past as background to literary expression. Using exemplary work to explore key interactions between writing and history, the series makes accessible their complexities and the critical excitement they generate in reconsidering literary and historical experience. Each book exemplifies the varieties of theoretical methodologies and histories available, and challenges the conventions of traditional literary history.

One of the most acute difficulties for students confronting new issues of writing in history has been the unfamiliarity and inaccessibility of many of the texts studied and discussed. Writing in History helps overcome some of this difficulty by providing an appendix to each volume, in which difficult to obtain material (such as trial transcripts, sermons, popular literature, political pamphlets, medical writing, journalism, or chronicles and historical writing) is reproduced in full or in longish extract. This appendix offers a complementary reader, where the book's arguments can be tested and where texts difficult for students to locate may be compared with those more frequently studied.

Steven Connor and Thomas Healy
London

♈

Abbreviations

PREFATORY NOTE

This book, like others in the present series, is designed to act as a source-book as well as providing its own argued account of a particular moment of writing in history. I have, therefore, tried to provide in the text sufficient citation from contemporary sources to enable readers not only to test the validity of my own arguments, but also to begin to construct alternative accounts of their own. I have also provided an Appendix of extracts from both late nineteenth and early twentieth-century sources, which provide additional examples of the discourses of gender and gendered discourses which I explore in the main part of the book.

For ease of reference, and in order to avoid a plethora of endnotes, I have, wherever possible, incorporated references into the text. Works which are cited frequently in the main body of the text are referred to by an abbreviation, a page reference, and, where necessary, a volume number given in parenthesis in the text. A full list of abbreviations appears below. All other references in the following chapters are given in the endnotes, where I provide a full bibliographical description for the first reference in each chapter. Thereafter op. cit. is used for works by authors who only have one work cited in the chapter in question, and a short title is given where two or more works by a particular author are cited. For all references given in the endnotes, the place of publication is London, unless otherwise indicated.

In order that the Appendix can be used separately as well as in conjunction with my own text, I provide a reference following each extract. In the case of works which are cited more than once I have given a full bibliographical reference following the first extract and a shortened reference thereafter.

ABR	Wyndham Lewis, *The Art of Being Ruled* (London: Chatto & Windus, 1926)
B&B	Wyndham Lewis, *Blasting and Bombadeering* (1937; rev. edn, London: John Calder, 1982).
CDML	Virginia Woolf, 'Craftsmanship', in *The Crowded Dance of Modern Life*, ed. Rachel Bowlby (Harmondsworth: Penguin, 1993)
CE	Virginia Woolf, *Collected Essays*, ed. Leonard Woolf (4 vols.; London: Hogarth Press, 1966–7)
CSS	E. M. Forster, *Collected Short Stories* (Harmondsworth: Penguin, 1954)
D.	Max Nordau, *Degeneration* (New York: D. Appleton, 1895), ed. George Mosse (1968; rev. edn pbk edn 1993, Lincoln, Neb.: University of Nebraska Press)
DVW	*The Diary of Virginia Woolf*, ed. Anne Olivier Bell and Andrew McNeillie (5 vols.; London: Hogarth Press, 1977–84)
F.	D. H. Lawrence, *Fantasia of the Unconscious* (1923; Harmondsworth: Penguin, 1971)
FD	Daniel Pick, *Faces of Degeneration: A European Disorder, c. 1848–1918* (Cambridge: Cambridge University Press, 1989).
GM	Bonnie Kime Scott, *The Gender of Modernism* (Bloomington, Ind.: Indianapolis University Press, 1990)
HE	E. M. Forster, *Howards End* (Harmondsworth: Penguin, 1941)
IS	Edward Carpenter, *The Intermediate Sex: A Study of Some Transitional Types of Men and Women* (London: Swan Sonnenschein, 1908)
LCA	Edward Carpenter, *Love's Coming-of-Age: A Series of Papers on the Relations of the Sexes* (Manchester: Labour Press Society, 1896)
LL	*The Letters of D. H. Lawrence*, ed. James T. Boulton *et al.* (7 vols.; Cambridge: Cambridge University Press, 1979–93)
M&W	Havelock Ellis, *Man and Women: A Study of Secondary Sexual Characteristics* (1894; London: Scott, 1904)
MWA	Wyndham Lewis, *Men Without Art* (Cassell, 1934)
P.	Dorothy Richardson, *Pilgrimage* (1915–35; 4 vol.; London: Virago, 1979)
PG	Mona Caird, *Pathway of the Gods* (London: Skeffington & Son, 1898)
Px	*Phoenix*, ed. E. D. McDonald (London: Heinemann, 1936)
Px II	*Phoenix II: Uncollected, Unpublished and Other Prose Works by D. H. Lawrence*, ed. W. Roberts and H. T. Moore (London: Heinemann, 1968)
R.	D. H. Lawrence, *The Rainbow* (Harmondsworth: Penguin, 1949)
RO	Virginia Woolf, *A Room of One's Own* (1928; Harmondsworth: Penguin, 1967)

S&C   Otto Weininger, *Sex and Character* (first English translation, 1906; London: Heinemann, 1912)

SH   Sigmund Freud and Joseph Breuer, *Studies in Hysteria* (Harmondsworth: Penguin, 1991)

WD   *A Writer's Diary, Being Extracts from the Diary of Virginia Woolf*, ed. Leonard Woolf (London: Hogarth Press, 1953)

WE   *A Woman's Essays*, ed. Rachel Bowlby (Harmondsworth: Penguin, 1992)

WSPU   Women's Social and Political Union

$\upharpoonright \Upsilon \upharpoonright$

Introduction: Writing in History

It takes a great deal of history to produce a little literature ... [and] ... it needs a complex social machinery to set the novelist into action.[1]

This book explores the contexts of early twentieth-century English fiction. The terms in which I have formulated this project need a word or two of explanation. I have chosen to focus on 'English' fiction, not 'British' fiction, nor even 'fiction in English', despite the fact that for much of the second half of the twentieth century there has been widespread critical agreement that the major works of English-language fiction in the early twentieth century (indeed, some would say in the entire century) were produced by an American (Henry James), a Pole (Joseph Conrad), and an Irishman (James Joyce). I have chosen not to revisit the 'great tradition' represented by these male exiles and *émigrés*. This is not because I want to establish an alternative canon of the literature of 'our island race', but partly because I want to focus on alternatives to what has become the dominant tradition of international modernism, and partly because I want to examine some of the ways in which the specific socio-historic conditions of turn-of-the-century England produced the kinds of writing that emerged in the early decades of the twentieth century. In short I focus on English fiction because it is precisely an English cultural formation that I wish to examine. 'Early twentieth century' is preferred to 'modern' or 'modernist' in my title, even though I shall be describing and analysing the formation of a variety of modernisms, and arguing for the modernism of Dorothy Richardson, Virginia Woolf, and D. H. Lawrence, each of whom I discuss in some detail in later chapters. I have preferred the wordier formation partly because I do not wish to begin by begging the

question of whether there was 'ever really an English modernism',[2] and
partly because it refers (albeit slightly vaguely) to a particular historical
period. 'Modern' and 'modernist', on the other hand, refer to a concept
or concepts whose meaning is subject to change.

At some point in the first decade of the twentieth century a new age
dawned in England; the moment or movement of 'modernism' was said
to have arrived. As in more recent times, England was a latecomer to this
European community which traded in new ideas and aesthetic forms, and
also acted as a 'front' for entrepreneurial Americans. The English, as ever,
were reluctant Europeans, unwilling to obey the central directives emanat-
ing from (in this case) Paris – in Walter Benjamin's phrase, 'the capital of
the nineteenth century'.[3] The aim of this book is to re-examine the history
of the dawning of this new age of modernism, and to explore its relationship to certain nineteenth-century discourses: discourses about women,
discourses about gender, and other discourses which I shall argue are
organized in gendered terms. My concern, ultimately, is to locate the
fiction of the first decades of the twentieth century in a somewhat longer
historical perspective and a broader discursive context than those in which
it has customarily been viewed, and to explore its sometimes problematic
relationship to modernism.

The important role of women writers in the making of literary
modernism has been recognized for some time now, and I shall want to
emphasize this in my own study. However, this is not my central purpose.
For reasons which I sketch in briefly below (and which I develop in the
following chapter), I do not simply want to add women to the canon of
modernism. Moreover, this is not a work of gynocriticism. My main
concern is not with women writers, but rather with the issue of gender,
and the history (or histories) of gender – the history of thinking about
gender, and also the history of gendered forms of thinking and representation. This book aims to explore a range of contesting and contradictory
discourses on gender, discourses on 'woman', the feminine, and feminism,
and, especially, discourses about the political and aesthetic representation
of 'woman' or women. In my reinvestigation of the history of early twentieth-century English fiction I shall re-examine turn-of-the-century debates
about the feminine in fiction, and the practice of gendered writing in the
context of what I shall argue is a late nineteenth-century crisis of representation. This crisis of representation was linked both to a crisis of definition of gender, and to the gendered discourses of degeneration and
renovation which pervaded late nineteenth- and early twentieth-century
culture.

This re-examination of the historical moment of the development of
early twentieth-century English fiction, and of the history of the discursive formation within which it was constituted inevitably challenges
dominant definitions of modernism – the modernism of what Raymond
Williams described as the 'selective tradition'.[4] I aim to challenge the

claims of both self-professed modernists, and their later academic appro-
priators, that the 'making it new' of modernism represents a complete
break with the past, and particularly with the nineteenth century. Instead
I shall suggest that the moment of modernism is formulated in terms of
a late nineteenth-century discourse of rupture. The projected transcendence of history found in the works of what has come to be regarded as
canonical high modernism can be seen as an attempt to build a new order
from the ruins of a masculine history – a degenerative (for some a
feminized) state which prefigures its own end.

Readers of a book in a series entitled 'Writing in History' might reason-
ably expect its author to offer some explanation of the general project.
What kind of history is being undertaken? What view of history is being
offered? What relationship is being suggested between writing and history,
and history and writing? One of the most obvious points that this book
makes about writing in history is the relationship which it, itself, reveals
between the writing subject in history and the subject of history. I am
writing in history, and the kinds of questions I want to ask, the kinds of
patterns I discern, the issues and images that I prioritize, are to a very
great extent produced by my own historical situation at another *fin de
siècle*, some twenty-five years into yet another flowering of feminism and
all the destabilizing and reconfiguring of sex and gender roles which have
followed in its wake. As Peter Widdowson has argued, 'every historical
moment "writes" the literature it wants to read largely by way of the
ceaseless flow of ephemeral monographs and collections of critical essays'
which 'challenge and fracture' earlier versions of an author (or, one might
add, a cultural formation) and construct 'yet another partial version,
derived from different historical and ideological determinations'.[5]   My
own project falls within these determinations, in so far as the kinds of
questions it asks are – sometimes explicitly, sometimes implicitly – shaped
by current theoretical and political concerns. However, I have also tried
to recognize the pastness as well as the continuing presence of the past,
and to maintain a historical distance: to recognize that the writers of this
period had their own questions and, more particularly, their own answers.
I have strenuously tried to avoid judging them by late twentieth-century
standards of political progressiveness or political correctness. I hope that
I have avoided simply shaping them to my own ends. For this reason,
among others, I have used supporting quotation more fulsomely than is
perhaps the norm. Like other books in this series, this one is designed to
act as a sourcebook as well as an argument about or an account of a
particular moment of writing in history. I have tried to provide sufficient
documentation to enable readers to produce different accounts from my
own. I have chosen not to consign the bulk of the documentation to the
Appendix because I want to avoid, as far as possible, constructing a
background/foreground model of the relationships between texts and their
contexts.

Throughout this study I have sought to return the writing of the early twentieth century to history. The history of canonical high modernism has been a story of the removal of the 'great works' of modernist 'literary' writing from the material and historical conditions of their production, and from their relationship with other texts (not just 'literary' texts) which surrounded them, and of their insertion into the timeless ideal order of the 'modern tradition'. T. S. Eliot, himself a participant in the history that I am seeking to rewrite, provided the theoretical justification for this process of canon-formation and the form of literary history that it underwrites in 'Tradition and the Individual Talent' (1919), in which he claimed that the true poet is the man [sic] who extinguishes his own personality and writes 'with a feeling that the whole of the literature of Europe . . . has a simultaneous existence and composes a simultaneous order'.[6] My intention, on the contrary, is to continue that interrogation of the universalizing idealism of the Eliotean model and of other traditional paradigms of literary history which feminist literary historians in particular have undertaken in recent years. I also hope to illuminate some of those areas of blindness which arise from the professional, disciplinary organization of literary studies, especially its tendency towards period specialization. Thus I attempt to explore and analyse a range of different kinds of writing, and not just that writing that has been filtered through the sieve of those definitions of the literary which emerged with the development of institutionalized literary studies in the twentieth century. As I suggested earlier, I am seeking to avoid using or constructing a background/foreground model of the relationship between ('literary') texts and their (non-literary or discursive) contexts. Rather my concern is with a discursive formation that is constituted by the whole range of the texts of a culture. Similarly, I am not seeking merely to locate the historical 'background' of early twentieth-century texts in certain nineteenth-century 'contexts', but again I am concerned with exploring the contours of a discursive formation which spans the late nineteenth and early twentieth centuries. In short I am working with a more localized (less overarching and less totalizing) variant of Michel Foucault's concept of the 'episteme', which he defines in *The Archeology of Knowledge* as:

> the total set of relations that unite, at a given period, the discursive practices that give rise to epistemological figures . . . The episteme is not a form of knowledge . . . it is the totality of relations that can be discovered for a given period, between the sciences when one analyses them at the level of discursive regularities.[7]

By focusing on the 'discursive regularities' (which can involve disjunctions as well as continuities) of a range of writings from the 1880s to the 1930s, I shall hope both to demonstrate the operations of a particular discursive formation, and also to suggest something of the significance and complexity of its history.

This study takes its lead from recent interrogations (from a variety of theoretical and methodological perspectives) of the validity of periodizing a culture through such arbitrary entities as centuries, or the reigns of monarchs. Nevertheless it will also demonstrate the potency of ends and beginnings, however arbitrary. There is no doubt that the approaching end of the nineteenth century and the beginning of a new century to a large extent generated images of degeneration and renovation. Both individuals and societies became entangled in metaphors, and sometimes acted fatally on the strength of them.

My project has been both to look at historical questions through the reading of literature (defined here as the written representations of a culture), and to look at writing in general, and 'literary' (that is to say aesthetically self-conscious and culturally valued) writing in particular as part of history. Literary texts (whether one is using literary in the broader or narrower of the senses indicated above), like other cultural practices are 'not simply derived from an otherwise constituted social order', but are themselves 'major elements in its constitution'.[8] Written texts are just as much historical events as are the Peasants' Revolt or the passing of the Reform Act: they are just different sorts of events, discursive events. The following pages attempt to investigate a chapter in the history of discourse. Clearly I think that such a history is both interesting and worth undertaking. However, I should make clear at the outset, what I hope the ensuing pages will demonstrate, that I do not believe that we exist in a purely discursive universe, and that, as Derrida puts it in *Of Grammatology*, 'il n'y a pas d'hors-texte',[9] usually (mis)translated as 'there is nothing outside of the text'. As Valentine Cunningham has recently argued:

> [T]he world is in a continuous state of rhetoricization; the real is never not a matter of rhetoric, writing, story, never not sailing through (and sometimes becalmed in) the tropics of discourse; but still, the historical *realium* is also never not just a construction in a text – not ever, and especially not in the worlds of power and victimization, of colonizing and persecution, where ideology impacts on the body, and bodies are tortured, minds deformed, men and women ... subjugated.[10]

1

Rethinking Modernism

I shall begin with the vexed question of 'modernism'. In the twentieth century 'the modern' and 'modernism' have come to stand for 'a particular set of practices and ideologies of representation' as well as a 'specific historical experience',[1] both of which are thought to be peculiar to the twentieth century. However, the Victorians, much maligned by their modern successors, also thought of themselves as moderns, latecomers constantly scanning a rapidly changing physical and social world in an attempt to make sense of the signs of their times. Similarly the eighteenth-century literary scene was enlivened by (among other things) graphic accounts of the struggle between the Ancients and the Moderns. As Richard Poirier has pointed out:

> It is the privilege of any people at any time in history to claim that they are living in the 'modern age', in the sense of the Latin *modo*, just now or lately, and works that by any prevailing standards prove to be unconventional or especially difficult have been called 'modernist' since at least the seventeenth century.[2]

'Modern' has a long and complex history, but in the twentieth century 'the modern', 'modernity', and 'modernism' have become particularly problematic terms. These terms, and the debates about them, are themselves aspects of the contexts which I wish to examine.

As Virginia Woolf observed – 'with greater boldness than discretion' – in her talk to the Heretics in Cambridge on 18 May 1924, 'in or about December, 1910, human character changed' ('Mr Bennett and Mrs Brown', WE 70). This change is said to have inaugurated a new age in British fiction: the age of the modern. The date, 1910, may have been heretical or arbitrary as Woolf acknowledged, but the idea of a rupture and a new beginning at some point around the beginning of the twentieth century was not. This idea was part of a new orthodoxy which has been remarkably enduring. The idea of modern/ist rupture is perpetuated in the newer (post-structuralist) orthodoxy which also plots literary history in terms of a radical change in the conceptualization of human character and its representation in fiction: in the beginning (i.e. the nineteenth century) was the classic realist text with its hierarchy of discourses ordered by an authoritative (and probably authoritarian) omniscient narrator (or author), and then the author died, human character was dispersed across a range of subjectivities, and narrative structure entered free flow.

The foregrounding of a particular date in Woolf's account marks the struggle of the modern as a wrestling with, and ultimately a discarding of, the immediate past. Her narrative is one of generational conflict in which the preceding generation of Edwardians is superseded and surpassed. However, Woolf's concept of modernity is, as it were, spatial as well as temporal. It not only sets a limit to the past, but it also marks off the 'modern' Georgians from those of their contemporaries who were still working (compromisingly, as Woolf would have it) with the old and 'inadequate' tools of fiction. Both of these ways of marking off the modern from the pre- or non-modern have tended to work against certain kinds of historical understanding of the English fiction (and perhaps also of European and American literature more generally) of the early part of the twentieth century. Although Woolf's lecture attempts to develop a concept of the modern that has a local habitation and a name, here, now (1910 or 1924), and in England, most influential accounts of the modern or of modernism transcend the local and the particular. If modernism is a historical category, it belongs to the master narratives, to the history of the *Zeitgeist* or spirit of the age. Most standard accounts of modernism represent it as a crisis formation, an aesthetic response to a moment of rupture, to a breakdown in the Western (to use a slightly anachronistic way of labelling European and American) social and cultural order.[3]

As David Trotter has recently pointed out, modernism has 'acquired an explanatory, or causative, function' and has 'come to signify a cultural event or force which, at a particular "moment", in Europe and the Americas, *determined the way in which writers wrote*'.[4] Modernism is thus not simply a matter of when, but also a matter of what and how.

WHEN WAS MODERNISM?

Modernity or modernism isn't something we've just invented. It's something that comes at the end of civilizations. ('Do Women Change?', Px II 540)

Historians of modernism have displayed a positively Victorian preoccupation with the question of origins. Malcolm Bradbury, in *The Social*

Context of Modern English Literature (1971), agrees with Virginia Woolf
that 1910 has a certain plausibility as the founding year of English
modernism. Not only did human character change in 1910, but a new
monarch ascended the throne, inaugurating the Georgian age. The year
1910 was also a key date in the death of the past, as George Dangerfield
rather floridly noted:

> The year 1910 ... is actually a landmark in English history, which
> stands out against a particular background of flame. For it was in
> 1910 that fires long smouldering in the English spirit suddenly flared
> up so that by the end of 1913 Liberal England was reduced to ashes
> ... the true, pre-war Liberal [*sic*] – supported, as it still was in 1910,
> by Free Trade, a majority in Parliament, the ten commandments and
> the illusion of Progress – can never return. It was killed, or killed
> itself, in 1913.[5]

The year 1910 was also a landmark in aesthetic history. It was the year
of the Post-Impressionist exhibition at the Grafton Galleries. However, as
Bradbury notes, there are numerous other dates in contention. There is a
certain chronological neatness about 1900, and it is also the year in which
Nietzsche died and modern physics was born with Planck's quantum
theory. It is also an important moment in the development of modern
psychiatry, as the year in which Freud's *Interpretation of Dreams* was
published. Henry James, on the other hand, located the beginning of the
modern age in 1914, the beginning of the great divide constituted by the
First World War: 'The plunge of civilization into this abyss of blood ...
that so gives away the whole long age during which we have supposed
the world to be ... gradually bettering.'[6] While D. H. Lawrence affirmed
that 'It was in 1915 that the old world ended.'[7]

Michael Levenson, in *The Genealogy of Modernism* (1984), offers quite
a different originating date, and indeed sees the moment of modernism very
precisely as delimited by the arrival of Ezra Pound in London in 1908 and
the publication of T. S. Eliot's *The Waste Land* and W. B. Yeats's *Late
Poems* in 1922. Levenson's dating of the inception of modernism coincides
rather neatly with the account given by Pound himself (in 1937) of the way
in which 'In the dim mainly forgotten backward of 1908 and 1910 a few
men in London groped toward the "revolution of the word" '.[8] Frank
Kermode had opted for rather similar dates to Levenson's in his earlier essay
on 'Modernisms', arguing that 'anybody who thinks about what modernism
now means will rightly look more closely at the period between 1907 and,
say, 1925'. Kermode settled on these particular dates after considering an
alternative starting-point for modernism in the literature of the 1890s.

> If there was a persistent world-view of [modernism] ... we should
> have to call [it] apocalyptic; the modernism of the Nineties has a
> recognisable touch of this, if decadence, hope of renovation, the

sense of transition, the sense of an ending or the trembling of the veil, are accepted as its signs. At such times there is a notable urgency in the proclamation of a break with the immediate past, a stimulating sense of crisis, of an historical licence for the new.[9]

Kermode's ultimate rejection of the 1890s as merely 'precursors' of modernism, and his preference for the years 1907–25 as delimiting the period of modernism proper, seem to me to be closely connected to his concern with 'what modernism *now* means' (emphasis added) in the 1960s, and with his own sense of modernism as a continuing presence and project, as an aesthetic and intellectual issue in relation to which writers and critics must situate themselves. As we approach the turn of another century, we have come to view the matter differently. 'This is a time', as Frederic Jameson has noted, in which 'at least in part owing to what is called postmodernism, there seems to be renewed interest in finding out what modernism really *was* ... and in rethinking that now historical phenomenon in new ways'.[10] In this book I will follow a number of recent literary historians, writing from quite different theoretical perspectives, who have returned to the possibility of the different definitions of modernism offered by Kermode's alternative dating of the moment of modernism in the 1890s. I am thinking here of the rethinking of modernism undertaken by feminist literary historians and theorists such as Ann Ardis (*New Women, New Writing*, 1990) and Marianne DeKoven (*Rich and Strange: Gender, History, Modernism*, 1991), who see turn-of-the-century fiction as the seed-bed of a 'modernist formal practice' which 'emerged unevenly within a general period, roughly 1890–1910',[11] or Elaine Showalter (whose view I share), for whom modernism emerges from the 'sexual anarchy' of the *fin de siècle* (*Sexual Anarchy*, 1991). Peter Keating (*The Haunted Study*, 1989) and more explicitly David Trotter (*The English Novel in History, 1895–1920*, 1993) are extremely sceptical about the theories and practices of feminist literary historians, but nevertheless they agree with them in placing the beginning of the moment of modernism in the turn-of-the-century period. In fact, both Keating and Trotter display a healthy scepticism about the usefulness of the term 'modernism'. Keating recalls 'the long-running critical debate on when exactly "Modernism" can be said to begin, or, sometimes, whether it can ever be said to have begun at all'.[12] More radically, Trotter argues that, while the term is useful for its 'descriptive function', its 'explanatory or causative function' and its 'evaluative function' are 'a blatant mystification'.[13]

WHAT WAS MODERNISM?

It has been notoriously difficult to provide definitive answers to the questions of when, where, and what modernism was. In answering the question of what modernism was, Eugene Lunn, like many other historians of modernism, defines it as a reaction-formation. It is a set of 'multiple revolts against traditional realism and romanticism'.[14] Lunn offers a general outline of the key characteristics of modernism which would probably command broad assent: aesthetic self-consciousness or self-reflexiveness; simultaneity, juxtaposition, or montage; paradox, ambiguity, and indeterminacy or uncertainty; 'dehumanization', and the disappearance or dispersal of the integrated individual human subject. To these characteristics Raymond Williams added a specific relationship (which is more than simply a particular response) to the city. There are 'decisive links', he argued, 'between the practices and ideas of the avant-garde movements of the twentieth century and the specific conditions and relationships of the twentieth-century metropolis'.[15]

The answer to the question '*what* was modernism?' is, in fact, complexly intertwined with the answer to the question '*when* was modernism?'. Moreover, the answers to both questions also depend on who is asking them and when. 'Modernism' is variously: an aesthetic programme, a self-conscious artistic movement, a retrospective descriptive category, a way of periodizing literary history, and/or a means of constructing a canon of value. The 'moment' of modernism is thus difficult to fix. If, as Malcolm Bradbury has argued, (English) modernism constitutes a paradigm shift, it is a paradigm shift both *in* the history of literature, and in the way in which literary history has been constructed mainly, but not exclusively, in the universities. The moment of modernism is, according to Bradbury, a moment in which 'there occurs a marked change in the temper and texture of English artistic culture',[16] which may have begun at any point between the late 1880s and 1915 and which came to end in 1922 (according to Michael Levenson), or continued until round about 1930 (according to Bradbury and McFarlane), or 1940 (according to Ricardo Quinones in *Mapping Literary Modernism*, 1985). Alternatively (or additionally) the moment of modernism is the moment of its construction as a rigorously exclusionary category of value in the twentieth-century academy, as *the* canonical form of early twentieth-century literature; a moment in which one particular form of aesthetic practice, a practice committed to particular kinds of formal and linguistic experimentation, was privileged above others; a moment in which a restricted group of texts and authors was removed from the complex social and cultural specificities of history and located in that transcendent ideal order of the literary tradition described (or invented) by Eliot in 'Tradition and the Individual Talent'; a moment in which a particular 'discipline of reading'[17] was established by 'the intellectual hegemony of Eliot, Leavis, Richards and the New Critics'.[18] In this latter sense, the moment of modernism is a prolonged one in which a hegemonic version of literary history and value is first produced and then reproduced by a literary academy committed to working constantly over the same relatively small group of texts. Interestingly, this academic process of categorization and exclusion replicates the preoccupation with boundaries, and anxieties about the erosion of boundaries which are characteristic of those literary texts which have conventionally been labelled 'modernist', but which are also found in a wide variety of other late nineteenth and early twentieth-century cultural forms, as I hope to show in the chapters that follow.

THE GENDER OF MODERNISM

Modernity entails a certain valorization of the feminine.[19]

Modern writing has been precisely bound up with the question of female language and feminine discourse.[20]

One result of the growing importance of feminist literary history and theory in universities has been to focus attention on the exclusionary nature of the category of modernism. If modernism can be said to have a gender, then the gender of canonical Anglo-American high modernism was clearly masculine; it was, as Pound put it, 'a few men' who groped towards that ' "revolution of the word" ' which defined what has come to be regarded as the dominant tradition of literary modernism. Women were notably, even notoriously, absent from the record of the modern tradition. As Bonnie Kime Scott,[20] has pointed out, 'fewer than nine' of the 948 pages of Ellmann's and Feidelson's 1965 collection, *The Modern Tradition*, were allocated to women writers (*GM* 7). (George Eliot and Virginia Woolf were the two who slipped through the net.) The exclusivity of the male pantheon has proved extremely resistant to female infiltration. As recently as 1984 Pound, T. E. Hulme, Ford Madox Ford, Wyndham Lewis, and T. S. Eliot were the key figures in Michael Levenson's revisionary genealogy of modernism. Joyce, Lawrence, and Virginia Woolf (for a long time modernism's singular female anomaly) are said to loom on the periphery.

The revisionary feminist history of modernism has addressed its masculinism in a variety of ways. The most obvious, but by no means the least problematic, strategy has been that of adding women writers to the modernist canon. The feminist presses have performed an important service here, as they have in so many periods and areas of writing, by reprinting the work of a number of neglected or forgotten turn-of-the-century and early twentieth-century women writers. The providing of new contexts in which to re-view this work, and important reassessments of it, have been undertaken by, among others, Susan Squier (ed.) in *Women Writers and the City* (1984), Shari Benstock in *Women of the Left Bank: Paris 1900–1914* (1986), Gillian Hanscombe and Virginia Smyers in

Writing for their Lives: The Modernist Women 1910–1940 (1987), and
Bonnie Kime Scott's anthology *The Gender of Modernism* (1990). As
always, adding women to the picture changes that picture in subtle and
quite far-reaching ways. However, the main problem with this strategy is
that it has tended to leave in place, rather to interrogate, the 'traditional',
hegemonic conceptualization of the modern as a particular kind of 'revolution of the word'. It also continues to valorize one particular set of formal
practices above all others, an aesthetic practice committed to 'abstraction
and highly conscious artifice, taking us behind familiar reality, breaking
away from familiar reality, breaking away from familiar functions of
language and conventions of form . . . the shock, the violation of expected
continuities, the element of de-creation of crisis'.[21]

Two other revisionary strategies by feminists reconceptualize modernism
and its gendering, but do so in paradoxical, even contradictory ways. The
first interrogates canonical high modernism, and, perhaps, attempts to
dislodge it from its prominence in the academy, by exposing and exploring its masculinism. For example, Sandra Gilbert's and Susan Gubar's
monumental *No Man's Land* explores the phallic language and misogyny
of Pound, Eliot, Lawrence, Wyndham Lewis, and other male modernists.
Gilbert and Gubar foreground the importance of women's hitherto
unacknowledged contribution to modernism, but they also describe
modernism as a battle of the sexes, and as a 'reaction-formation' against
women and the feminine. Although Gilbert's and Gubar's sex-wars
metaphors become rather tedious, their view that 'a reaction-formation
against the rise of literary women became not just a theme in modernist
writing but a motive for modernism'[22] is suggestive, and is one to which
I shall wish to return.

A second strategy attempts to recuperate modernism for a variety of
feminist and left positions by refuting or sidestepping the view that
modernism is either a masculine or masculinist formation. On the
contrary, this strategy reconceptualizes modernism as a feminine formation by viewing twentieth-century (and even late nineteenth-century)
formal and linguistic experimentation through the linguistic theories of
Julia Kristeva, Luce Irigaray, and Hélène Cixous. The disruption of hierarchical syntax, and dislocation or abandonment of a consistent, unitary
point of view and linear time which are characteristic of modernist form,
are also central components of what these and other theorists have
described as a 'feminine aesthetic' or *écriture féminine*. Similarly, a
'foregrounding of the pre-Oedipal or aural features of language', and a
'formal decentredness, indeterminacy, multiplicity, and fragmentation',[23]
are seen as characteristic of both modernist and 'feminine' writing. Thus,
irrespective of the gender of its author, the form of a modernist text is
said to be anti-patriarchal, feminine, and radical.[24] Thus, according to
Stephen Heath, the feminine discourse of the modern text emerges 'as a
challenge to the "male" and "female" which are the very terms – the

places – of that identity, as a challenge to the very principle of sexual identity, the whole fix of "sexuality" '.[25] This recuperative strategy seems to me to be problematic in a variety of ways. First, in its privileging of form and textuality, it would appear to represent a variant of the modernist and New Critical separation of the 'verbal icon' from the complex social and cultural world in which it is produced. Second, it implicitly reproduces the Eliotean separation between the (wo)man that suffers and the mind which creates. Third, it requires us to believe that, irrespective of the avowed politics of its author, and irrespective of any overtly 'conservative' statement (at the risk of understating the force of the right-wing views of many male modernists) which a modernist text might make, its disruptive form is 'subversive'. Perhaps most problematic of all, it is rather difficult to accommodate the Kristevan view of the language of modernism as a feminine language of flow and flux with the tendency of some rather important male modernists (Ezra Pound and T. S. Eliot, and D. H. Lawrence, for example) to castigate the offensiveness or incoherence of women and of feminine language.

I have taken this detour through the histories of modernism because, as I have already suggested, the moments of the production and institutional reproduction of modernism were and are important elements of the contexts in which early twentieth-century fiction was produced and continues to be reproduced. Another purpose of the detour has been to emphasize that gender issues have played a crucial part in the production, reproduction, and recent reconfiguring of modernism – in short, to emphasize that modernism was constructed (and has continued to be reproduced) on the terrain of gender. It will be the central argument of this book that anxieties about gender, discourses on gender, and gendered discourses of various kinds, all of which have their origins in the late nineteenth century, were central to the production of modernist, as indeed of all forms of early twentieth-century fiction in England. The next two chapters will begin to outline these anxieties about gender and some of the gendered forms of crisis thinking in which and from which early twentieth-century English fiction was formed.

|2|

Gender, Degeneration, Renovation: Some Contexts of the Modern

THE TURN-OF-THE-CENTURY GENDER CRISIS

The nineteenth-century women's movement, in fighting to improve the legal, political and social position of women, necessarily challenged prevailing socio-cultural definitions of femininity and masculinity. The gender order was placed under spotlights and a furious debate on what it meant to be a real man, a real woman, ensued.[1]

We may not know exactly what sex is; but we do know that it is mutable, with the possibility of one sex being changed into the other sex, that its frontiers are often uncertain, and that there are many stages between a complete male and a complete female.[2]

During the Eighties and Nineties of the last century . . . [m]en became women. Women became men. Gender and country were put in doubt. The single life was found to harbour two sexes and two nations . . . [It was] an age in which there seemed to be three sexes, an age tormented by genders . . . by the 'he' and the 'she' and the 'who' of it all.[3]

As numerous feminist literary historians have pointed out, the turn-of-the-century period was one of gender crisis. This gender crisis was, in part, a social crisis which impinged directly on the ways in which people lived their lives. It was the latest phase of longer-term changes in social and familial roles, particularly those of women, and in relations between men and women. The gender crisis was also a crisis of representation; it was a crisis in both the representation of gender and in the gender of representation. I shall seek to suggest throughout this study that, both as a crisis in social experience and as a crisis in representation, the turn-of-the-century gender crisis was an extremely important part of the social and intellectual formation in which (and by which) early twentieth-century fiction was produced. Modern woman (and hence modern man), modern marriage, free love, the artistic aspirations of women, female eroticism, these were 'the fundamental themes of the late-Victorian dissolution'.[4] It was precisely these issues, and, indeed, the whole context of the late-Victorian dissolution with which self-consciously modern novelists engaged – from H. G. Wells, Ford Madox Ford, E. M. Forster, and D. H. Lawrence to May Sinclair, Virginia Woolf, Dorothy Richardson, and Rebecca West.

The *fin de siècle* gender crisis, or, more accurately, the series of crises around the issue of gender, manifested itself most obviously and clamorously in the ongoing debates about women and the feminine. The turn-of-the-century campaigns of feminists and their male sympathizers for fuller educational, social, and political opportunities for women kept the question of 'woman', her biological and emotional nature, and her familial and social roles in the forefront of public attention. The question of woman and the woman question had, of course, been among the most important social, philosophical, and biological questions since the middle of the nineteenth century. For much of the last two decades of the nineteenth century and the first two decades of the twentieth century the controversies and divisions over the 'Votes for Women' campaigns gave a new force to long-running, wide-ranging, and heated debates about *how*, and *by whom*, women might best be represented in the political sphere. These debates about the representation of women, or of those more numinous and essentialist concepts 'woman' and 'the feminine', also extended beyond the discourse of politics into the discourses of law, medicine, and literature (especially, as I shall show, in the theory and practice of fiction). The representation of 'woman' and/or the feminine was also central to the emerging 'new sciences' of anthropology, sex psychology and sexual pathology, and psychoanalysis, and may be linked to the 'hysterization of women's bodies', a 'threefold process' which Michel Foucault, the French historian of sexualities, has hypothesized as occurring in the eighteenth and nineteenth centuries:

> whereby the feminine body was analysed . . . as being thoroughly saturated with sexuality . . . integrated into the sphere of medical practices, by reason of a pathology intrinsic to it . . . [and] . . . placed in organic communication with the social body (whose regulated fecundity it was supposed to ensure), the family space (of which it

had to be a substantial and functional element), and the life of children (. . . by virtue of a biologic-moral responsibility lasting through the entire period of the children's education): the Mother, with her negative image of 'nervous woman', constituted the most visible form of this hysterization.[5]

Inevitably, given that femininity is habitually defined as the other of the masculine in Western culture, the prolonged nineteenth-century focusing on the 'Woman Question' also put masculinity into question. By the 1890s there was widespread evidence of a crisis of gender *definition*. Scientists, social scientists, journalists, poets, novelists and literary critics all addressed themselves to the question of what precisely was meant by the term 'man' or 'woman', and indeed what it meant to be a man or a woman in the modern age. They became extremely preoccupied with the question of gender boundaries, which they anxiously searched for and explored, and policed and reinforced, or blurred and undermined according to inclination. For progressive thinkers this was a time of interesting fluidity. Writers such as Havelock Ellis (one of the founders of the new 'sex science') began to interrogate the naturalness of sex/gender categories, and to explore the role of society in constructing those categories.

> We have to recognise that our present knowledge of men and women cannot tell us what they might be or what they ought to be, but what they are, under the conditions of civilisation. By showing us that under varying conditions men and women are, within certain limits, indefinitely modifiable, a precise knowledge of the facts of the life of men and women forbids us to dogmatise rigidly concerning the respective spheres of men and women. (*M&W* 441)

The most dramatic examples of the crisis of gender definition and representation at the *fin de siècle* were the New Woman (and her sisters the Wild Woman and Revolting Daughter),[6] and the homosexual or decadent. Both of these figures challenged traditional gender boundaries, and both were at the centre of public attention (and were the focus of moral panics) in the mid-1890s. In fact (and contrary to the opinion of those contemporary commentators who asserted that the New Woman had disappeared from view by 1896), the New Woman remained a prominent figure in the early twentieth century, and makes several important appearances in fiction. Elizabeth Robins's *The Convert* (1907) and H. G. Wells's *Anne Veronica* (1909) are both New Woman novels; Miriam Henderson, the heroine/centre of consciousness of Dorothy Richardson's *Pilgrimage*, is a New Woman, as are the Schlegel sisters in Forster's *Howard's End*. The New Woman also appears in several of D. H. Lawrence's novels, including *Sons and Lovers* (1913), *The Rainbow* (1915), and *Women in Love* (1920), and in Virginia Woolf's *The Voyage Out* (1915) and *The Years*

(1937). However, 1894 was the New Woman's *annus mirabilis* with the staging of Sydney Grundy's play *The New Woman*, the addition of several widely reviewed novels to the growing body of New Woman fiction, and the appearance of a number of articles naming and exploring the phenomenon, many of them provoked by the exchange between Sarah Grand and 'Ouida' in the *North American Review* in the spring of that year.[7] On the other hand, 1895 was the year of that other main *fin de siècle* challenger of conventional sex-gender definitions – the homosexual. In that year the trials of Oscar Wilde were the occasion of a very public display of the homosexual, who was, at this point, still in the process of being named and defined as a type possessing a separate sexual identity.

The New Woman, as represented in fiction and in journalistic accounts, was a creature of contradictions. She reproduced and was produced by a complex network of social tendencies and anxieties. The New Woman was represented, by turns, as either a cause or a symptom of cultural disintegration and social decline, or as the cure for current social ills. To her detractors the New Woman was both unfeminine and hyperfeminine. She was 'mannish' in dress, as she was in her overdeveloped mind and her underdeveloped, flat-chested, lean-hipped body. In short, she was, in Eliza Lynn Linton's phrase, 'a curious inversion of sex'.[8] It is worth pondering Linton's choice of words here. The use of the term 'sexual inversion' by Linton, a noted anti-feminist, alerts us to the remarkable consonance in the discourse of subversive or dissident gender types. The terms in which conservative thinkers castigated the New Woman are often barely distinguishable from those in which the new sex psychologists described the lesbian or, indeed, the homosexual,[9] and in which even progressive thinkers (like Edward Carpenter) described feminists.

> The women of the new movement are naturally largely drawn from those in whom the maternal instinct is not especially strong; also from those in whom the sexual instinct is not preponderant. Such women do not altogether represent their sex; some are rather mannish in temperament; some are homogenic . . . inclined to attachments to their own, rather than to the opposite sex; some are ultra-rationalising and brain-cultured . . . to [some] Man's sex-passion is a mere impertinence, which they do not understand, and whose place they consequently misjudge. (*LCA* 66–7)

Paradoxically, however, the 'mannish' New Woman was also said to display an excess of 'femininity' in her overdeveloped feelings. Here 'femininity' denotes the affectivity, heightened capacity for nervous stimulation, or susceptibility to emotion which were seen as essential attributes of the normal woman throughout the period under discussion. 'The dearer, tenderer emotions of the true woman',[10] which, properly channelled, should become the sisterly, wifely, and, above all, motherly affectivity of the normative 'womanly woman', became, in the New Woman, self-directed, excessive, and degenerate. She was said to display 'an intense and morbid consciousness of the ego,'[11] and the sexual self-consciousness of the erotomaniac.[12] In this latter guise the New Woman has much in common with her contemporary, the *femme fatale*, another version of the threateningly sexualized woman.

While to her detractors she was the negation or perversion of womanhood, to some of her supporters the New Woman was the perfection of womanhood, and indeed of humanity. For Sarah Grand, for example, in the *North American Review*, the New Woman was the spiritualized mother of the race and the herald of a new dawn, who would save society by feminizing it. Far from being an erotomaniac, the New Woman, as represented by those whose feminism had been developed around the social-purity campaigns against the Contagious Diseases Acts and the 'white-slave trade' of prostitution (such as Frances Swiney, Blanche Leppington, Sarah Grand, Elizabeth Wolstenholme Elmy) was a chaste adherent of 'psychic love';[13] she was committed to bringing about a sexual revolution through making coarse animal man more like 'Woman', his moral and spiritual superior.

The homosexual – that other disrupter of conventional gender boundaries and the natural, social, and moral order which those boundaries supported – was, like the New Woman, first named (at least in English) in the 1890s. The word 'homosexual' was coined in 1869, by Karoly Benkert (a Hungarian), and became part of the English debate on sexual pathology and sexual identity with the translation of Krafft-Ebing's *Psychopathia Sexualis* in 1892. Another similarity which the homosexual shared with the New Woman was that he was represented, paradoxically, not only as a figure who traversed and disrupted traditional gender boundaries, but also as one in whom 'normal' gender categories were polarized. The homosexual was represented as 'effeminate' or feminized, or alternatively as hypermasculine, the Whitmanesque manly comrade, admirer of, or admired for, virility. This apparent contradiction became an integral part of the discourse on homosexuality which emerged in England in the 1890s. On the one hand, Edward Carpenter, Henry Havelock Ellis, and John Addington Symonds (like their German counterparts Karl Ulrichs and Magnus Hirschfeld) saw the homosexual as a sexual invert,[14] and hence, incidentally, saw homosexuality as an innate condition. On the other hand, the homosexual was represented, not as a 'gender bender', in whom masculine and feminine characteristics combine to form a third, or intermediate sex, but as the epitome of gender differentiation, embodying the most highly developed form of masculinity. The contradictory nature of the discourse on homosexuality is evident in the fact that Carpenter and others seem to have subscribed to *both* of the views I have just outlined.

The discourse on homosexuality was as much productive of gender crisis as produced by it. As Foucault and others have argued, the formation of a distinct homosexual identity (or of a range of homosexual identities) in the 1890s gave the homosexual a subject position from which to speak. The self-display of the decadents, the Wilde trials and various other sexual scandals of the *fin de siècle*, and the widespread discussion of homosexuality in the writings of the sex psychologists (complete with case studies) had the effect of putting the homosexual on display and putting a range of alternative masculinities into circulation. This became an important dimension of the gender crisis in which the writers (especially the male writers) of the first decades of the twentieth century wrote, and which they had to negotiate. It is, to take one of the most obvious examples, extremely important in D. H. Lawrence's construction of the male and his representation of masculinity. Lawrence's proximity to his 1890s' predecessors can be seen especially clearly in the discarded Prologue to *Women in Love*. The Prologue's description of Birkin's compulsive attraction to handsome men has a very close resemblance to the confessional case studies of 'inverts' and homosexuals found in the sex-psychology literature.[15]

Oscar Wilde, arguably England's most famous homosexual, was also an 'aesthete' and a 'decadent', whose public flamboyance, private sexual behaviour (made very public by his trial), and artistic practice (also on trial in 1895 as Regenia Gagnier and Ed Cohen have shown)[16] all challenged middle-class social norms. In common with his fellow decadents, Wilde's sexual behaviour and artistic theory and practice challenged both the natural and social order and the gendered terms by means of which they were articulated and represented. He rejected a 'masculine' commitment to production, and espoused a 'feminine' role of decorative idleness; his homosexuality was a rejection of 'natural masculinity' and was 'contrary to mainstream notions of "productive" or "purposive" sexuality';[17] his aestheticism ('art for art's sake') was a rejection of the purposive, and also of the commodification of culture, and of the mechanized mass culture of the modern epoch. This latter aspect of the Wildean project was replicated in both E. M. Forster's and D. H. Lawrence's rejection of bourgeois materialistic culture, and in the way in which literary modernism defined itself as mass culture's other.

Aestheticism, decadence, and homosexuality (considered to be more or less synonymous terms in the 1890s) have been seen by some commentators as responses to or reactions against the New Woman. Thus Fraser Harrison sees the decadents associated with *The Yellow Book* as early casualties of the sex wars that were to dominate the coming century. 'Unnerved and unbalanced' by the 'threats and demands represented by the ever accelerating movement towards female emancipation on all fronts', the decadents are offered as evidence of a crisis in masculinity.[18] Harrison's account of homosexuality as one of a range of escape-routes taken by the endangered artistic male in the face of the onslaughts of the mannish New Woman has a certain dramatic force, and is, of course, reproduced in a number of novels and short stories in the period covered by this book.[19] It is also, to an extent, reproduced in Gilbert's and Gubar's plotting of early twentieth-century literary history in terms of a sex war in their *No Man's Land* volumes. However, Harrison's account needs to be read sceptically as having greater metaphoric than analytic power. Linda Dowling has argued very persuasively that the New Woman and the decadent were neither opposites nor 'antagonistic principles intent on each other's destruction', but were engaged in a very similar challenge to the social order: 'literary critics and reviewers persistently identified the New Woman with the decadent, perceiving in the ambitions of both a profound threat to established culture.'[20]

The decadent, the homosexual, and the New Woman were not formed *by* each other, but were produced *in relation to* each other, from the same complex of social anxieties and within the same network of discourses, or ways of thinking about and representing masculinity and femininity. In other words, whether for them or against them, those who attempted to represent the New Woman and the decadent or homosexual in writing (or in visual images for that matter) could only do so within a discourse of sexual difference in which particular human characteristics and forms of behaviour were gender marked, but in which the gender terms were contradictory, unstable, and fiercely contested. It is on this shifting ground, and from these struggles, that the novel of the early twentieth century was produced.

SPEAKING FOR WOMAN, WRITING WOMAN OUT

As we have seen, the crisis in the representation of gender was not confined to the representation of femininity, but it tended to become focused on this particular issue. In the late nineteenth century and throughout the early decades of the twentieth century the question of *how* woman (the generic form of essential feminity) or women should be represented was clearly very closely linked to the question of *who* represents woman/women. As I have already suggested, the developing scientific culture of the nineteenth century provided a range of very authoritative discourses which claimed to speak about woman (the general category), and, by extension, about and for women. At the end of the century the new sex science and the emergent theory and practice of psychoanalysis were added to the Darwinian and neo-Darwinian biological and medical sciences concerned with the representation, classification, and sometimes modification of woman/women. I shall return to neo-Darwinism and the

English sex science in later sections; for the moment I will glance at two episodes in the turn-of-the-century representation of woman/women: Joseph Breuer's and Sigmund Freud's *Studies on Hysteria* (1895, translated 1909), which, among other things, announces the birth of psychoanalysis, and Otto Weininger's *Sex and Character* (1903, translated 1906), a *fin de siècle* peroration which is suffused not so much with a 'sense of an ending' as with the ending of sense. These two German language texts have a twofold interest in the context of the present study. First, their preoccupations, and the figures and rhetorical strategies which they employ are symptomatic of that *fin de siècle* 'dissolution' which, I suggest, is an important constitutive element of the cultural formation within which the fiction of the early twentieth century was produced. Second, in their English translations (and diffused and mediated through reviews and discussions), both texts had a wide currency amongst intellectuals and artists in the early decades of the twentieth century.

Studies on Hysteria is a key text not only in the history of psychoanalysis, but also in the representation of women's subjectivity; one might even argue that it claims to represent a distinctive form of feminine subjectivity. The *Studies on Hysteria* is a book of many stories, one of which is the story of the 'discovery' of psychoanalysis, one of those systems of knowledge which is conventionally held to define modernity, and to mark off the twentieth century from its pre-modern past. As is well known, Breuer's patient, Anna O, discovered what she called the 'talking cure' when she realized that, under the influence of hypnosis (induced by her doctor), by telling stories – recounting daydreams, narrating the history of her symptoms – she could talk those symptoms away. The story (the plot?) of *Studies in Hysteria* is the story of how the male doctors, and ultimately Freud – who dominates the volume – by acting as the mediators and orderers of Anna's story, transform it into the story of how they discover a 'psychotherapeutic procedure' (*SH* 68).

Starting with Anna O, the male doctor presses a series of female patients into telling their stories, and then takes those stories back in order to tell other stories: the story of the origins of the aetiology of a particular disorder, hysteria; the story of sexuality; the story of femininity itself. Like his patients, who have to be hypnotized into narration, Freud represents himself as a somewhat reluctant storyteller. Thus, he notes uneasily in his account of the case of Elizabeth von R:

> It still strikes me myself as strange that the case histories I write should read like short stories and that, as one might say, they lack the serious stamp of science. I must console myself with the reflection that the nature of the subject is evidently responsible for this, rather than any preference of my own ... The fact is that local diagnosis ... lead[s] nowhere in the study of hysteria, whereas a detailed description of mental processes such as we are accustomed

to find in the works of imaginative writers enables me, with the use
of a few psychological formulas, to obtain at least some kind of
insight into the course of that affection. (*SH* 231)

Freud's stories combine the characteristics of *fin de siècle* experiments in
the short story with what we have come to see as modernist techniques.
They are fragmented and embedded, made up of moments and sketches.
Each case history contains a series of layered and intersecting, but
ultimately diverging, narratives: the episodic and fragmented narratives of
the self-observing speaking subject – the pseudonymous woman who is
also the object of the analytic gaze of the male doctor; the observing and
ordering speaking subject, Freud. The case histories are also organized
around different narrative times. There is, for example, the long time-
scheme which is the duration of the treatment. There is also the short
time-scheme found in the series of different narrative presents contained
in the diary-like entries which document each encounter between doctor
and patient. Then there is the time-scheme which extends back beyond
'story time', the time-scheme which includes the pre-history of the woman
(i.e. the story of her experiences before the onset of her hysterical
symptoms). The story of her pre-history as recounted by the female patient
is in one sense a nineteenth-century story of the search for origins, but its
form is distinctively modern, even modernist: an impressionistic narrative
triggered by associations, which emerges in a dislocated, non-linear
fashion. Each case history also contains two versions of an after-history:
the first, provided by Freud's later interpolated glosses on the patient's
stories and the story of the treatment; the second, found in the brief
allusive references to the patient's life after the conclusion of the treatment. Finally there is the history of the treatment, viewed retrospectively
in the concluding discussion section.

The case histories can be seen as contests about narrative, about *whose*
story is being told and *what* story is being told. The female patients are
not in control of their own stories, which emerge as a series of fragments
which they shore against their ruins. In any case, these women from 'an
educated and literate social class' (*SH* 47) are only empowered as story-
tellers through the mediation of the male doctor. The doctor, on the other
hand, aspires to be a masterly narrator in the mould of the omniscient
narrator of the nineteenth-century novel. He seeks to order all the different narratives and subsume them to his own, but the stories keep running
away from him; his narrative is full of lacunae and unanswered questions.
This contest becomes an increasingly prominent aspect of the post-
Freudian novel.

In 1903, eight years after the publication of *Studies on Hysteria*, another
German publication claimed to give 'a definitive solution to the feminine
problem'. Otto Weininger's *Sex and Character* (according to its prefatory
publisher's note) undermines the 'data' of contemporary debates 'concern-

ing the emancipation of women, sexuality, the relation of woman to culture' (S&C, v). It does this, as the Freudian case studies seek to do, by making woman yield up her secret, namely that '[the] meaning of woman is to be meaningless'. Like Luce Irigaray, a more recent theorizer of the feminine,[21] Weininger saw woman as 'Ce sexe qui n'en est pas un' ('This Sex which is not one'):

> Women have no existence and no essence; they are not, they are nothing. Mankind appears as male or female, as something or nothing. Woman has no share in ontological reality, no relation to the thing-in-itself, which in the deepest interpretation, is the absolute, is God. (S&C 286)

Weininger's extraordinary misogynistic and anti-Semitic diatribe no doubt owes much to his own mental state; *Sex and Character* is possibly the longest suicide note in history. However, it is worth looking at more closely, since it is a cultural symptom as interesting and significant as the symptoms it attempts to represent and diagnose. Weininger's antipathetic representation of the Jew as feminized and degenerative provides a particularly clear example of that obsession with the Jew, and, sometimes, outright anti-Semitism which was to become an important component of the discourse of literary modernism. More importantly, for the purposes of my present argument, Weininger rehearses and recirculates many of the arguments about the New Woman that I have already examined. Like many of his English counterparts he thought that a 'woman's demand for emancipation and her qualification for it are in direct proportion to the amount of maleness in her' (S&C 64). Weininger went further than most by attributing the desire for emancipation to a woman's 'deep-seated craving to acquire a man's character' (S&C 65). He shared the progressives' view of the constructedness of gender characteristics and sexuality: 'We may suppose the existence of an ideal man, M, and of an ideal woman, W, as sexual types, although these types do not actually exist. Such types not only can be constructed, but must be constructed' (S&C 7). Like the English sex scientists, Weininger argued that human beings have a 'fundamental bisexuality' and inhabit a 'permanent bisexual condition' (S&C 7), an idea that many turn-of-the-century feminists found very liberating. Nevertheless, ultimately Weininger's idea that most human beings combine masculine and feminine characteristics was based on the view that masculinity constituted the originary and normative state.

One of the most interesting aspects of Weininger's account of femininity is his articulation of what was often only implicit in most nineteenth-century accounts: that woman is a wholly sexual creature, to be defined entirely in terms of sexual relations and the reproductive function. The dangers of the company kept by those recent French theories of the feminine which celebrate the female body and an autonomous female sexuality become alarmingly clear when one reads in Weininger that a woman 'is nothing but sexuality, because she is sexuality itself ... man possesses sexual organs; her sexual organs possess woman' (S&C 92).

Weininger's treatise provides a broader cultural context in which to locate and understand both the tone and the substance of various turn-of-the-century representations of gender. For example, Weininger's conception of universal bisexuality together with his privileging of the masculine is clearly part of the discursive framework in which Virginia Woolf formulates her contradictory ideas on androgyny. Weininger also provides another example of that remarkable coherence of the discourse on gender that I noted earlier. Although Weininger's text will strike most late-twentieth century readers as extraordinarily reactionary, several turn-of-the-century progressives made selective use of his theories, and operate with the same terms. The feminist Florence Farr, for example, uses Weininger's terminology, and argues that it is 'very difficult to classify temperaments without alluding to Weininger's Sex and Character'.[22] Similarly the feminist sympathizers Ellis and Carpenter work with the same categories as the misogynist Weininger, but they assign them a different value. As I shall suggest in a later chapter, the convolutions of Sex and Character, and especially its transvaluation of sex/gender characteristics, throws particularly interesting light on Lawrence's rhetoric of gender, and hence on the changing rhetoric and subject-matter of his fiction. The degree to which Lawrence works with and reworks a late nineteenth-century discourse on gender becomes clear when one compares his pronouncements on, and representation of, the male and the female with Weininger's: 'The male lives consciously, the female lives unconsciously' (S&C 102); 'Man is infinitely more mysterious, incomparably more complicated [than woman], (S&C 212); 'Man is form, woman is matter' (S&C 293); 'The power of giving form to chaos is with those in whom the most universal memory has made the widest comprehension possible; it is a quality of masculine genius' (S&C 120).

DEGENERATION

One epoch of history is unmistakably in its decline, and another is announcing its approach. There is a sound of rending in every tradition, and it is as though the morrow would not link with today. Things as they are totter and plunge, and they are suffered to reel and fall, because man is weary, and there is no faith that it is worth an effort to uphold them. (D. 5–6)

At the end of the nineteenth century both the New Woman and the homosexual (and indeed the 'masculinity' and 'femininity' in relation to which they were defined) were represented in terms of the discourse of evolution, which had provided one of the most powerful explanatory models of the latter half of that century. Within the terms of the model of biological evolution developed by Darwin and his followers, both the New Woman and the homosexual were represented either as freakish sports of nature – regressive or degenerative forms – or, conversely, as highly evolved types. Similarly, a Darwinian model of social evolution represented them as either symptoms of cultural degeneration and decadence, or as forms of resistance to cultural crisis and as points of cultural renewal and regeneration. The contradictory discourse within which the New Woman and the homosexual were produced and reproduced belongs to what the nineteenth-century biologist Edwin Lankester described as *Degeneration: A Chapter in Darwinism* (1880). This 'chapter', begun in the 1880s, was still being written, and was a context for writing, into the 1930s. Indeed, it is one of the central arguments of this book that this chapter of degeneration, and the gendered language in which it was written, were key components of the discourse of rupture and the crisis formation within which literary modernism, and early twentieth-century fiction (whether or not it was self-consciously modernist), were produced.

The Darwinian model of biological evolution by a process of natural selection, or survival of the fittest, was initially seen as a progressive model: simple forms developed into complex, the primitive into the civilized. However, Darwin's initial equation of evolution with progress was questioned by his successors, and indeed by Darwin himself, who came to think that the 'fittest' for survival, and the most adaptive inherited characteristics, might not necessarily be the highest, most complex, nor most civilized. As Darwin's disciple, Lankester observed:

> It is clearly enough possible for a set of forces such as we sum up under the head 'natural selection' to so act on the structure of an organism as to produce one of three results, namely these: to keep it in *status quo*; to increase the complexity of its structure; or lastly, to diminish the complexity of its structure. We have as possibilities either Balance, or Elaboration, or Degeneration.[23]

Lankester was particularly interested in emphasizing and exploring the last-mentioned possibility: that under the 'general laws of evolution' mankind is 'as likely to degenerate as to progress'. This questioning of the inevitability of progress, the suggestion that mankind might not 'necessarily have arrived at a higher and more elaborated condition', but might be 'drifting, tending to the condition of intellectual Barnacles',[24] raised fundamental questions about man's position in the order of things. The disturbing implications of those questions, and the language of degeneration and regeneration in which they were formulated, resonate through much of the fiction of the first decades of the twentieth century.

If the evolutionary model in Darwin's *The Descent of Man* was, in the first instance, progressive, it was also hierarchical. Moreover, like many other explanatory models in the nineteenth century, the evolutionary model was organized around a particular concept of gender, and also around particular concepts of class and race. The Darwinian model also helped to reinforce those concepts of gender, class, and race by which it was itself produced. Thus, according to the Darwinian schema, organisms and animals evolve from simple or lower to complex or higher forms. Human beings represent the highest point on the evolutionary scale. However, men are held to be both physically and intellectually more highly developed than women, the upper classes than the lower, and the white races than the 'primitive' or 'savage' dark races. George Romanes refers to this evolutionary hierarchy of class and race in *Mental Evolution in Man* (1889):

> When we come to consider the case of the savages, and through them the case of prehistoric man, we shall find that, in the great interval which lies between such grades of mental evolution and our own, we are brought far on the way toward bridging the psychological distance which separates the gorilla from the gentleman.[25]

In fact more than half of *The Descent of Man* is concerned less with the differences between the gorilla and the gentleman, than with exploring the differences between the human male and the human female, and with making the case for the superior development of the (white) male. However, as is the case with so much nineteenth-century thinking about gender (or gendered forms of thinking), evolutionary discourse is contradictory. Woman is said to be inferior to man because her development has been arrested at a lower point on the evolutionary scale, and she is, therefore, a simpler, more primitive form. On the other hand, man is held to be superior to woman precisely because he has retained some important 'primitive' characteristics – for example, physical strength and mental toughness – from 'the long ages of man's savagery'. Man is thus, paradoxically, both more highly evolved (and hence more civilized) and more 'savage' (and hence less civilized, or more primitive) than woman; woman is simultaneously both less highly evolved and less savage than man.

The progressive and hierarchical imperatives of Darwinian evolutionary theory informed much of the social theory of the mid-Victorian period. They were also of particular importance in the formation of the new discipline of anthropology, which was to play such an important part in mapping the mental world of the modernists, particularly in reconfiguring the relationship between the primitive or savage and the civilized. Nineteenth-century anthropology studied the societies and customs of modern 'savages', not as separate cultures quite distinct from European culture, but as 'survivals', or relics of past cultures, from which European culture had evolved/progressed, and which could give insight into the course of man's (i.e. European man's) development. This study of 'primitive' cultures proved extremely useful to the European domination of the 'dark races' in the Age of Empire. Put simply, the anthropological 'knowledge' developed by pioneering anthropologists such as Sir John Lubbock, E. B. Tylor, and others, and taken up by 'popularizers' and antiquarians such as Andrew Lang and J. G. Frazer,[26] was a form of power which not only demonstrated the evolutionary superiority of the white races over those who were thus 'known' and classified, but also served as a legitimating model for colonization.

However, this progressive, evolutionary construction of the dark races and dark places of the world as primitive survivals worked in complex and conflicting ways, which undermined as well as supported the colonizer. In constructing Africa as the Dark Continent, the nineteenth-century sciences created not only a theatre for the civilizing endeavours of highly evolved European man, but also a test of his civilization; the Dark Continent represented both a challenge and a threat, a space in which the primitive might be civilized, or in which the civilized might regress or degenerate. Africa was figured as the most savage place remaining in the world, a primitive, pre-civilized domain, a darkly mysterious feminine space into which a culture's fears and fantasies (especially its fears and fantasies about the fragility of 'culture') were projected. As Edward Said has shown, 'Orientalism' was produced and has functioned in a very similar way.[27] The conflicts and contradictions of the nineteenth-century construction of the dark races and dark places of the world as civilization's Other had a continuing importance as integral elements of that rethinking of the relationship between nature and culture, the instinctive and the rational, the conscious and the unconscious, which were central to early twentieth-century definitions of the modern. Indeed the nineteenth-century construction of Africa, the Orient, and the dark races as the locus of the primitive, non-rational Other of Western culture, and as a metaphor for the mysterious inner territories of the human psyche, has been seen by many recent critics as one of the central components of literary modernism. It is also an important element in fiction from *Heart of Darkness* to *Women in Love* and *A Passage to India*.

The chapter of degeneration described in Lankester's book on Darwinism began with biology but extended its scope to embrace the social organism. It also provided a framework for understanding and representing social and historical processes. By the end of the nineteenth century and throughout the early decades of the twentieth century, social, literary, and psychological debates were dominated by the language of degeneration, and by the question of whether modern European society was progressing or declining; whether 'in general we are getting on, and if so where we are going to' (to use the words of John Ruskin which C. F. Masterman borrowed for the epigraph to *The Condition of England*, 1909); whether society was becoming more or less civilized; whether it was becoming over-civilized or reverting to barbarism; whether modern civilization was in itself a form of decline or barbarism, as Edward Carpenter suggested in *Civilisation: Its Cause and Cure* (1889) – a 'kind of disease', a 'temporary alienation from true life'.[28] These debates on the meaning and direction of culture and civilization constitute a key component of the cultural formation to which Dorothy Richardson, Virginia Woolf, and D. H. Lawrence, and the other twentieth-century writers discussed in later chapters, belong. Their fiction and their thinking about fiction were pervaded by the language of evolution, regression, and degeneration, and also by a counter-discourse of regeneration and renovation.

By the turn of the century, the theorization and analysis of both modern and 'primitive' societies were increasingly informed by the concepts of degeneration and regression. As Daniel Pick demonstrates in his important book on the subject, *Faces of Degeneration*, the language of degeneration pervaded late nineteenth- and early twentieth-century culture. It was a general European phenomenon, and extended well beyond its originating field of the natural sciences to inform 'much wider representations of culture' (*FD* 5), even extending to the conceptualization of language itself. Indeed it was in the area of language that degeneration theories made a particularly profound impact on both nineteenth- and early twentieth-century writers. Degenerationist thinking about language was clearly an important element in the formation of the linguistic theories which underwrote literary modernism.

The 'revolution of the word', which, according to Ezra Pound, was produced by a group of male writers working in London between 1908 and 1910, seems to have emerged in relation to two conflicting models of the history of language, each of which assigns a different status and valuation to the word. On the one hand, degenerationist thinkers like Richard Chenevix Trench and J. C. Hare[29] plotted a model of linguistic 'development' as a process of decline from an originary linguistic vitality. According to this model, there was in primitive language a direct and vital, even quasi-magical, relationship between the signifier and signified: 'every word was a metaphor, the naming of a presence, the acknowledgement of a wonderful encounter.'[30] Modern language, on the contrary, lacked the magic of this immediacy and vitality. It had degenerated into a set of conventions, it was a collection of dead metaphors. In short, the degeneration of language was a matter of the failure and the loss of the power of the word. However, according to the other major strand of degenerationist thinking, the decline of language was a process of decomposition in which power was ceded *to* the word. A couple of late nineteenth-century descriptions of a linguistic decadence in which writing decomposes to the word will serve both to illustrate the theory of language decline, and also, perhaps, to suggest the very different valuation of the 'anarchy among the atoms' which modernist writers would offer. The first is Paul Bourget's description of decadent language, which is quoted by Havelock Ellis. 'A style of decadence is one in which the unity of the book is decomposed to give place to the independence of the page, in which the page is decomposed to give place to the independence of the phrase, and the phrase to give place to the independence of the word.'[31] The second is Friedrich Nietzsche's account of a decadent style, which seems to entertain the possibility that the independence of the word might be a route back to linguistic vigour and vitality.

> Decadence [is] characterized by the fact that in it life no longer animates the whole. Words become predominant and leap right out of the sentence to which they belong, the sentences themselves trespass beyond their bounds, and obscure the sense of the whole page, and the page in its turn gains in vigour at the cost of the whole – the whole is no longer a whole. This is the formula for every decadent style: there is always anarchy among the atoms, disaggregation of the will.[32]

It was, however, in the area of social and cultural analysis and prognostication that the rhetoric of degeneration made its most obviously dramatic impact. At the turn of the century degenerationist thinking was a key element in the analysis and theorizing of both the modern-type and modern society. From the late nineteenth century onwards there was an 'avalanche' of books, pamphlets, and articles on 'social evolution, degeneration, morbidity and perversion' (FD 20). Among these were Lombroso's *Criminal Man* and *The Female Offender*, Lankester's *Degeneration*, Krafft-Ebing's *Psychopathia Sexualis*, Edward Carpenter's *Civilization: Its Cause and Cure*, Havelock Ellis's *The Criminal* and *The Problem of Race-Regeneration*, and Max Nordau's *Degeneration*. One might even add Breuer's and Freud's *Studies in Hysteria*, since it too, engages with the degeneracy of its female case studies. In all of these works degeneration is discussed 'as an empirically demonstrable medical, biological or physical anthropological fact' (FD 20).

The most notorious and sensational of these books is Max Nordau's *Degeneration*, which, despite (or because of) its eccentricity and extremism, is becoming increasingly widely recognized as an important source for understanding turn-of-the-century debates about art and society, and the rhetorical terms in which they were constructed and conducted. First published in Germany in 1893, it was translated into English in 1895 and went through at least seven impressions in its first year. Nordau's massive, verbose, and reactionary tome was widely discussed in English newspapers and periodicals, and received front-page treatment in the popular press at the time of Oscar Wilde's trial. It also attracted a lengthy and spirited reply from George Bernard Shaw in an article published in the American paper *Liberty* (in 1895). The reverberations of Nordau's contribution to the degeneration debate were still being felt in 1908 when Shaw's essay was reissued with an explanatory preface as *The Sanity of*

Art: An Exposure of the Current Nonsense about Artists Being Degenerate. The tone and even some of the terms of Nordau's hysterical attack on modern art and society can also be detected in the social and literary criticism of D. H. Lawrence.

Nordau's intemperate book is a cultural pathology of the *fin de siècle.* More particularly, it is a 'wholesale denunciation of tendencies in modern art – particularly in literature'.[33] It is among the first of a long line of books attacking the wilful difficulty, obscurity, and self-indulgent, self-referentiality of modern art. *Degeneration* diagnoses the culture of contemporary Europe as diseased, and energetically applies itself to classifying and analysing its various illnesses. It is a 'long and sorrowful wandering through the hospital' which is constituted by 'the upper stratum of the population of large towns' (*D.* 531). Nordau sees 'the prevalent feeling of the age' as being one 'of imminent perdition and extinction' (*D.* 2), the product of fatigue, nervous exhaustion, and hysteria. He reserves his greatest scorn for the upper classes and also for (decadent) artists whose behaviour and work threatened gender boundaries. Among his main examples are mystics and symbolists for whom 'the highest development of morality consists in renouncing sexuality and transforming oneself into a hybrid hermaphrodite' (*D.* 222).

In effect, Nordau describes a civilization which is in the process of becoming unhealthily feminized through the abandonment of 'traditional discipline' and proper masculine restraint, particularly in the area of aesthetic representation. In fact, many of the characteristics which Nordau attributes to the degenerate are those which, as I show in the next chapter, were attributed to modern woman, and especially (by unsympathetic English reviewers) to modern women writers: 'unbounded egoism', 'impulsiveness', 'emotionalism' (*D.* 18), a 'predilection for inane reverie', 'mysticism' (*D.* 20), 'suggestibility' (*D.* 26), 'erotomania'. The degenerate is either *like* a woman, or he likes women too much. Both Wagner and Ibsen, for example, are castigated as examples of the degenerate as woman worshipper (*D.* 412). When they are not like women, degenerates are like savages (and hence feminized by a different route). They are 'atavistic' cultural survivals, or they have regressed to a more primitive state in which 'they utter monosyllabic cries, instead of constructing grammatically and syntactically articulated sentences', they 'draw and paint like children', and 'confound all the arts, and lead them back to the primitive forms they had before evolution differentiated them' (*D.* 555. See Appendix vi).

Nordau's book is a fascinating (if infuriating) example of the use of a gendered language of degeneration for representing the strange disease of modern life. Havelock Ellis uses a similar lanaguage when he describes 'our complex modern civilisation' as 'feminine' in *Man and Woman* (*M&W* 448); so does D. H. Lawrence in some of his fiction and much of his discursive writing in the 1920s. *Degeneration* is also an intervention in the (gendered) debate about the meaning of modernity, and one which combines an interesting, and often contradictory mixture of modernist and anti-modernist rhetoric. Despite (or perhaps because of) the hysteria of Nordau's rant about modern 'cant', his representation of the modern condition, and even the imagery he uses, is itself proto-modernist and anticipates the wrestlings with modernity of Pound, Eliot, Lawrence, and Forster among others. Nordau's pronouncements on the regressive utterances of degenerate artists (quoted above) also anticipate Julia Kristeva's view of modern writing as a feminine, semiotic babble – although, of course, Nordau attributes quite a different (i.e. negative) value to the flow of modern writing. Indeed, Nordau's description of modern painting is replicated in the negative response of respectable London to Roger Fry's first Post-Impressionist exhibition in 1910, as seen, for example, in Sir William Blake Richmond's anxieties about its emasculating potential:

> For a moment there came a fierce feeling of terror lest the youth of England . . . might be contaminated here. On reflection I was reassured that the youth of England, being healthy in mind and body, is far too virile to be moved save in resentment against the providers of this unmanly show.[34]

For Nordau, as for many anti-modernists, modernity in the arts was itself a psychopathology, and at the same time an obsession with the psychopathological, the subjective, and the deviant. Nordau condemns as degenerate the art that dispenses with the 'established order, which for thousands of years has satisfied logic [and] fettered depravity' (see Appendix i). He dismisses as decadent that art of the modern age that is self-consciously new or experimental, or just self-conscious. Yet he does so in language which itself deploys what was to become part of the rhetoric of modernism: the discourse of degeneration and regeneration. In the first extract reproduced in my Appendix, Nordau, like many of the modernists against whom he railed, figures degeneration as a necessary prelude to renovation and a new beginning. The *fin de siècle* condition which he describes is also an *aube de siècle*: 'One epoch of history is unmistakably in its decline, and another is announcing its approach.' Like the Futurists and the Vorticists (although from a rather different perspective), he represents the present as a time of smashing and crashing, of chaos and confusion, in which there is a new role for art. Similarly, where Virginia Woolf was later to hear the 'melancholy' but, in her view, necessary sound of the 'smashing and the crashing . . . the sound of breaking and falling . . . and destruction' ('Mr Bennett and Mrs Brown', *WE* 80), Nordau heard the 'sound of rending in every tradition' as 'things as they are totter and plunge'.

Nordau's attack on the erosion of tradition as both symptom and cause of modern dissolution remained current in the responses to modernist experiment in the first decades of the twentieth century. For example, A. M. Ludovici, writing of the 'anarchy of the Futurists' in 1914, employs the terms of Nordau's pathology of the modern:

This anarchy in painting and sculpture is only a forecast of what the most disintegrating and most dissolvent influences of modern times are accomplishing and will ultimately try to achieve in every other department of life . . . [I]t behoves all those who, like myself, realise this condition as a danger, to do everything in their power to stand firm, and to resist the attack, which one day will be general, upon all the most valued institutions of orderly life . . .[35]

Throughout the greater part of *Degeneration* Nordau appears to be an adherent of the 'bob-sled or "down we went" theory' of civilization[36] espoused by many modernist writers. However, in his final chapter he draws back from this position, suggesting that degeneration is only a phase or chapter, and not the twilight of civilization: 'humanity is not yet senile . . . it can recover itself' (D. 540). Nordau offers a way out of the waste-land of modern society by a curiously contradictory move in which modern society ceases to be a wasteland, either as a result of the inevitable disappearance of degenerates (who are by definition too weak and insuf-ficiently adaptive to survive), or by degenerating to the point of dissolu-tion and subsequent renovation. The latter possibility is figured in a Lawrentian rhetoric of breaking through the husk which will bring forth new life – 'Humanity resembles a vast torrent of lava, which rushes . . . in constant activity. The outer crust cracks into cold, vitrified scoriae, but under this dead shell the mass flows, rapidly and evenly, in living incan-descence' (D. 540). Nordau also envisages the possibility that mankind will either give up the idea of 'progress', or, by adapting to modern condi-tions, make its accommodation with what Forster (in *Howard's End*) was to call the 'world of telegrams and anger':

The end of the twentieth century, therefore, will probably see a gener-ation to whom it will not be injurious to read a dozen yards of newspapers daily, to be constantly called to the telephone, to be thinking simultaneously of the five continents of the world, to live half their time in a railway carriage or in a flying machine . . . It will know how to find its ease in the midst of a city inhabited by millions. (D. 541)

DEGENERATION, THE MASSES, AND MODERNITY

The spectre of the 'city inhabited by millions' invoked by Nordau in the last quotation linked together the disparate strands of the turn-of-the-century discourse of degeneration. Nordau focused on the degenerate individual or group (the decadent artist, the mystic, the egomaniac, and his followers), and Lombroso and Havelock Ellis focused on the degenerate type (the criminal, the prostitute, the sexual deviant), but a fear of the urban mass is their shared subtext. This fear became the dominant concern of both liberal and conservative commentators in the 1890s and in the first decades of the twentieth century. Two aspects of turn-of-the-century representations of the modern urban masses are particularly important for our understanding of early twentieth-century fiction in England. The first, which is a general European phenomenon, is the way in which the urban mass became *the* distinguishing characteristic of the modern condition, and also a motive for modernism. The second is the way in which the urban masses became the focus for a range of anxieties about a specifically British (or, more accurately, English) decadence or degeneration.

During this period, as Daniel Pick has noted, there was 'a general shift from notions of the individual degenerate ... towards a bio-medical conception of crowd and mass civilization as regression' (*FD* 222). In the work of Gustave Le Bon in France and Graham Wallas in England,[37] the crowd became a 'sociological category in the understanding of society' and a 'commentary upon modernity itself' (*FD* 223). Quite independently of any particular examples of mass disorder (e.g. particular strikes or riots), the crowd was reconceptualized as 'constant irrationality', a 'permanent fact of degeneration and regression' (*FD* 223). This conceptualization of the crowd remained an important part of the twentieth-century discourse on cultural crisis. Thus Ortega Y Gasset, writing on *The Revolt of the Masses* in the 1930s, describes 'mass man' as 'a primitive who has slipped through the wings on the age-old stage of civilization'.[38] The discourse on the crowd, like almost every other aspect of the cultural formation I am examining, is a gendered discourse. The crowd is a feminine space: 'like women it goes at once to extremes', and is notable for the 'simplicity and exaggeration of [its] sentiments.'[39]

Just as the 'amorphous body of the crowd' (*FD* 223) was seen as the locus of degeneration and atavism, so too the amorphously proliferating culture of the masses (or culture *for* the masses) was seen as both the locus and the cause of cultural degeneration and the decline of civilization. Again, the debate about the growth of mass culture was conducted in gendered terms. From at least the middle of the nineteenth century, as I have suggested elsewhere, mass-produced, commodified cultural forms were habitually defined as feminine by the gendered discourse of cultural criticism.[40] The idea 'that mass culture is somehow associated with woman while real, authentic culture remains the prerogative of men'[41] became even more pronounced with the expansion of mass culture at the turn of the century. The proliferation of writing and of outlets for writing in this period continued that process of fragmentation and stratification of the literary market that had been going on throughout the nineteenth century. The gap between the 'literary' creation and 'the debased reading-matter

being produced for mass entertainment'[42] was growing ever wider, and
new organs of literary opinion and a new discipline of literary criticism
were being formed in order to police the boundaries of 'Literature' and
prevent infiltration or invasion by the forces of mass entertainment. As
we shall see in later chapters, the negotiation and/or re-establishment of
the boundaries between a feminized mass culture and a masculinized high
art (as well as a contest over the meaning and implications of the 'masculine' and 'feminine' in writing) were central concerns in both the writing
of literature and writing about literature in the early twentieth century.
Indeed, as several critics have recently argued, the project of the male (and
some of the female) modernists, with its commitment to difficulty and
indirection (among other things), can be seen as a reaction formation
constituted by fears of the engulfing femininity of a formulaic, commodified, and vulgarized mass culture.[43]

The fear of the crowd and anxieties about the invasive degenerative
forces of mass culture were yet another version of the pervasive fear of
the feminine in late nineteenth- and early twentieth-century culture; a fear
of woman which is also 'a fear of nature out of control, a fear of the
unconscious, of sexuality, of the loss of identity and stable ego boundaries
in the mass'.[44] A fear of the feminine is also found in the 'condition-of-
England' and/or 'condition-of-Empire' commentaries of the late nineteenth
and early twentieth centuries – for example, in the seventeen volumes of
Charles Booth's *Life and Labour of the London Poor* (1889–1903),
Seebohm's and Rowntree's *Poverty: A Study of Town Life* (1901), C. F.
Masterman's *From the Abyss* (1902), and Jack London's *The People of
the Abyss* (1903) and *Glimpses into the Abyss* (1906). Medical and
cultural debates of the late nineteenth century were fuelled, on the one
hand, by the need to preserve the manliness of the Imperial race, and, on
the other, by anxieties about racial decline, contamination by foreign influences, and feminization (see Appendix vii). The ignominious episode of
the Boer War (1899–1902) served to confirm longer-term fears that
Britain's Imperial ambitions were imperilled by the regression and atavism,
or by the physical and moral degeneracy, of what Kipling called the 'town-
bred masses'. On the other hand, critics of Empire saw the Imperial project
itself as potentially barbarizing, rather than (as its proponents did) as
taking 'masculine' progress to the primitive (and hence feminized) dark
races. This dialectic is seen in numerous fictional narratives of regression
in the Dark Continent, from Rider Haggard's *She* to Conrad's *Heart of
Darkness*.

Anxieties about physical degeneracy and atavism were particularly
evident in the gloomy aftermath of the South African War, in the vigorous debates conducted in the press and in the government reports which
were commissioned to determine whether or not it was the case that 'the
whole labouring population of the land are at present living under conditions which make it impossible that they should rear the next generation

to be sufficiently *virile* to supply more than two out of five men effective for the purposes of either peace or war'.[45] In seeking to address this question, some liberal reformers 'discovered' a degenerate and barbarized populace at the 'Heart of Empire', as C. F. Masterman titled the book of essays he edited in 1901. Masterman's representation of the degenerate 'New Town type' is worth quoting at length, since it brings together several important strands of the discourse on the crowd, mass culture, and the degenerative modern condition:

[The New Town type] is physically, mentally, and spiritually different from the type characteristic of Englishmen during the past two hundred years. The physical change is the result of the city upbringing in twice-breathed air in the crowded quarters of the labouring classes. This as a substitute for the spacious places of the old, silent life of England; close to the ground, vibrating to the lengthy, unhurried processes of Nature. The result is the production of a characteristic *physical* type of town dweller: stunted, narrow-chested, easily wearied; yet voluble, excitable, with little ballast, stamina or endurance . . . Upon these city generations there has operated the now widely spread influence of thirty years of elementary school teaching. The result is a *mental* change; each individual has been endowed with the power of reading, and a certain dim and cloudy capacity for comprehending what he reads. Hence the vogue of the new sensational press, with its enormous circulation and baneful influence; the perpetual demand of the reader for fiercer excitement ('more chops, bloody ones, with gristle!') from his papers; and the strenuous competition of the papers, in their fight for his patronage, each to become the most clamorous, lurid and dreadful.[46]

In short, the New Town type is a feminized degenerate: 'voluble', 'excitable', a half-educated sensation-seeker. This figure reappears in a range of different incarnations in much of the fiction of at least the first two decades of the twentieth century. The 'cunning' and 'etiolated' schoolboy Williams, who tests Ursula Brangwen's social sympathies to destruction in *The Rainbow*, is one such example of the working-class degenerate, and Forster's Leonard Bast is another variant of the 'city generations'.

Masterman and his fellow liberals were looking for political and economic solutions to what they rightly perceived to be a serious social and economic problem, but nevertheless they formulated the problem in the usual gendered terms. Elsewhere both the problem and solution were formulated in terms of gender, and, more precisely, in terms of the erosion of traditional gender categories, and the need to reinforce them. One suggested cure for the physical and moral degeneracy of town-bred boys was physical development and the cultivation of manliness via the Scouting ethos.

Robert Baden Powell's *Scouting for Boys* (1908) is a fascinating cultural document in this context. Its project is cultural renovation and the underpinning of Empire. Its subtext is degeneration and feminization. Its method is the inculcation of manliness, and the proper moral, social, and physical development of boys.

> The nation is showing signs of illness. We can diagnose it as 'bad citizenship'. We know the kind of remedy to apply, namely education of the rising generation in 'character' ... It is by such a 'snowball' movement that we may hope to take a really useful part in bringing strength, both moral and physical' to our Empire.[47]

In order to overcome his physical degeneracy, his suburban over-civilization, or his New Town barbarism, and become a worthy servant or leader of Empire (depending on whether he was working class or middle class), the Scout was to learn the skills of the savage: survival, navigating unknown terrain, identifying and tracking animals. But he was also to transcend his savagery, direct his hooligan impulses to responsible ends, and most important of all gain entrance to a nation-wide system of male bonding that would preserve the social status quo both at the Heart of Empire and in its furthest outposts.

Baden Powell emphasizes male-bonding and the development of masculinity as the cure for a degenerative individual and social condition whose cause was not just 'feminization' but *women*. The diagnosis was, and is, a familiar one; it has been made with extraordinary regularity since the 1890s, and its most recent version can be seen in the moral panic about the family that has arisen in our own *fin de siècle*. The physical deterioration of the race, and the 30 per cent decline in the birth-rate between 1870 and 1910 (about which there was much anxiety), were both attributed to the neglect or refusal of their 'natural' maternal function by women, especially women who organized themselves together and 'invaded' the public sphere to campaign for birth control, widened educational and employment opportunities, the reform of relations between the sexes, the reform of marriage customs and the divorce laws, and, of course, the vote. 'The race must degenerate', wrote Karl Pearson in 1894, 'if greater and greater stress be brought to force woman during the years of child-bearing into active and unlimited competition with men.'[48]

Feminism, like femininity, feminization, and effeminacy, was figured by its opponents as disruptive of the class and gender hierarchies which sustained the nation's vigour and its Imperialist ambitions. Those who espoused the woman's cause were seen as threatening the natural and social order with incalculable upheaval and destruction. As Eliza Lynn Linton warned her readers in the 1890s:

> The franchise for women would not simply allow a few well-conducted, well-educated, self-respecting gentlewomen to quietly

record their predilection for Liberalism or Conservatism, *but would
let in the far wider flood of the uneducated, the unrestrained, the
irrational and emotional.*[49]

Arabella Kenealy, a member of the Eugenic Society, put the anti-feminist
case in even more forceful terms:

> Nature marvellously prescient in all her processes, has provided that
> the sexes, by being constituted wholly different in body, brain and
> bent, do not normally come into rivalry and antagonism in the fulfil-
> ment of their life roles. Feminism disrupts this complementarity of
> the sexes. The result of women's competition with men was the
> development of 'mixed type', more or less degenerate, structurally,
> functionally and mentally, which imperil the race.[50]

In short, feminism and female assertion generally (both forms of 'sexual
inversion') were seen as both proceeding from and as producing a disruption of 'natural' gender boundaries and hierarchies; they were both the
cause and the symptom of degeneration.

RENOVATION

The feminist – like her counterparts the New Woman, the physically (and
morally) degenerate male, and the homosexual – was represented in
contradictory ways at the turn of the century. She was figured as both a
symptom and a cause of degeneration and decline, but she was also a key
figure in a counter-discourse of renovation, often utopian in form, which
represented a brave new world which would come into being through
redefinitions of gender and of relations between the sexes. The convolutions of the discourse on feminism and the discourses of feminism, their
intersection with the discourse of degeneration and renovation, the contradictory ways in which the feminine and the feminized were represented,
and the different values which were assigned to what is marked 'feminine'
or 'masculine' are all fascinating in themselves. They are also particularly
important for my present purposes because, together, they constitute the
complex and contradictory network of ideas which pervaded the culture
within which early twentieth-century novelists were formed, and with
which their writings engaged. An understanding of the contradictions of
these intersecting but competing discourses will, for example, throw some
light on Forster's representation of gender and his philosophy of personal
relations. It will also provide a framework in which to read D. H.
Lawrence's contradictory representation of woman and women, of
male–female relationships, and of the male and female principles. An
exploration of the gendered nature of these discourses, and particularly of

the contradictory and contesting ways in which they represent woman and femininity, will also offer a useful perspective on Virginia Woolf's and Dorothy Richardson's attempts to interrupt what they saw as the masculine tradition, and to theorize and practise a feminine form of writing. In this section I will look at the convolutions and intersections, and continuities and discontinuities of four important renovatory formations: the new moral order of the social-purity feminists; the new personal and social order envisaged by the sexual radicals Havelock Ellis and Edward Carpenter, both of whom were associated with the socialist Fellowship of the New Life; the feminists and modernists associated with the *Freewoman* in its successive incarnations as the *New Freewoman* and the *Egoist*; and, finally, a masculinist counter-discourse of renovation which emerged in the post-First World War period.

NEW WOMAN, A NEW ORDER, AND THE NEW MAN

The New Woman envisaged by liberal reforming feminists and socialist feminists at the turn of the century differed in several respects from the New Woman of the late nineteenth-century social-purity feminists (to use a convenient shorthand term). Liberal reforming feminists aimed to redefine woman and the feminine by developing a philosophy of individual rights. Like socialist feminists they insisted on a woman's rights over her own person and property, and on women's equality with men in the social sphere via education, increased employment opportunities, and political enfranchisement. Their emphasis on a woman's right to choose whether, when, and how frequently she should become a mother envisaged a feminine identity and a female sexuality that was not defined solely in terms of reproduction and maternity. This redefinition of the feminine and of woman was seen as the basis of a transformation of women's lives, and of society in general.

On the other hand, the social-purity feminists, as I indicated in the opening section of this chapter, redefined femininity by appropriating traditional gender stereotypes and deploying them, in militant fashion, apparently against the patriarchal order. The social-purity feminists' version of the New Woman has some striking resemblances to the womanly woman of the anti-feminists. She is the *magna mater*, the Universal Mother, who will preside over the birth of a New Order in which both men and women will be regenerated. The renovatory rhetoric of this strand of feminist thinking is evident in this utopian prediction from Elizabeth Wolstenholme Elmy.

The time is fast coming when men having learnt purity and women's courage, the sexes shall live together in harmony, each other's helpers towards all things high and holy; no longer tyrant and victim, oppressor and oppressed, but, hand in hand, eye to eye, heart in heart, building up that nobler world which shall yet be.[51]

The new moral order envisaged by the social-purity feminists would be brought into being first by women's recognition, development, and assertion of their own special nature as the mothers of the race, and, second, by women's transformation of men, from whom the New Woman must 'banish the brute'.[52] The crucial gender redefinition in this particular renovatory model is the redefinition of masculinity and male sexuality. Men, whom the social-purity feminists saw as (in their normal social state) aggressive, selfish, and prone to 'unbridled sensuality',[53] must become spiritualized. In short, men must become more like women. 'It is only as men recognise the supreme unselfishness and sublime abnegation of motherhood that they will themselves rise to a higher plane of ethical evolution and emerge from self-centred masculine individualism to a far loftier discipline of a tender sympathetic Altruism.'[54] Male brutishness continued to be an issue for the suffragists in the pre-war period. In 1913 the Women's Social and Political Union (WSPU) conducted its suffrage campaign under the slogan of 'Votes for Women and Purity for Men'. Similarly the desire to extend women's traditional maternal role and 'womanly' values into the public sphere, which had long been a part of 'spiritual' or social-purity feminism, remained a motivating force for a substantial group of early twentieth-century suffragists. Writing in *Votes for Women* in 1908, Emmeline Pethick-Lawrence asserted the renovatory ambitions of the woman warrior: 'For the sacred ideals of the home, for the responsibility which we, as women, bear towards the children of future generations ... we must take up arms and wage this holy war of freedom.'[55] Feminists were, as ever, divided on the question of whether male brutishness and female superiority were natural, or the product of social organization. Many associated what they took to be woman's higher nature with her maternal function, others, like Olive Schreiner questioned whether 'those differences which we, conventionally, are apt to suppose are inherent in the paternal or maternal sex are not inherent', and concluded that the 'sex relation may assume almost any form on earth as the conditions of life vary'.[56]

SEX REFORM AND THE NEW LIFE

A commitment to sublime motherhood and to spiritualized sex relations were just two areas of continuity between the social-purity feminists and the 'sexual radicals' Havelock Ellis and Edward Carpenter, both, in their different ways, supporters of the women's movement. Ellis, for example envisaged that the liberation of women would lead to 'a *reinvigoration* as complete as any brought about by barbarians to an *effete and degenerating* civilization'.[57] Although the ideas of these two sex reformers have been overshadowed, for much of the latter part of the twentieth century, by the dominance of Freudian thinking on sexuality, their ideas and the debates in which they participated are a particularly important part of the context of early twentieth-century English fiction, as they were very influential in progressive intellectual and literary circles in England, and Ellis's popularizing of 'advanced thinking' and contemporary science was quite widely mediated in the broader culture. Both Ellis and Carpenter tended to adopt a prophetic stance in their writings, and to represent themselves as an advance guard fighting a battle against the ignorance and prejudice of the past. Ellis was the dominant figure in the new sex psychology of the turn of the century, and he continued to be one of the most influential writers on sexuality until his death (which coincided with the death of Freud) in 1939. He was also an energetic campaigner and journalist, and, as well as being a major popularizer of the new sex science, he was also a literary critic and commentator on the contemporary literary scene. Carpenter, a poet, lecturer, writer, and advocate and practitioner of a 'simpler life', was less widely known than Ellis, but he was influential in socialist circles, and, as Jeffrey Weeks has pointed out, aspects of his work were 'quietly absorbed . . . into the Bloomsbury emphasis on personal relationships, and inserted, through a process of influence and then rejection, into the sexual dialectic of D. H. Lawrence'.[58]

Like the social-purity feminists, both Ellis and Carpenter believed that 'the sex problem' was one of the most important problems facing modern society, and both saw the rethinking of gender roles and sex relations as a route to social renovation. In both cases this rethinking largely took place within the biologistic conception of sexuality which was formulated by the Darwinians and which continued to dominate sex science and the British psychoanalytic tradition until the 1960s. Ellis engaged in a particularly tortuous dialogue with biologism. He retained a commitment to a view of women (or, to use his preferred term, 'woman') as less variable, more childlike, and more primitive than men ('man'), and as having a greater 'affectability' and 'suggestibility' (*M&W*, *passim*). However, he also entertained the idea that these characteristics might be cultural rather than natural, and conceded in the conclusion to *Man and Woman* that 'our present knowledge of men and women cannot tell us what they might be or what they ought to be, but what they actually are under the conditions of civilisation' (*M&W* 441). Nature, however, remains the final court of appeal on the question of which sexual differences 'are not artificial, and which no equalisation of social conditions can entirely remove' (*M&W* 17).

Carpenter shared many of Ellis's conceptions of biological difference. He also saw women as more primitive, emotional, intuitive, and passive than men, and 'closer to the great unconscious processes of Nature' (*LCA* 40). Like Ellis, Carpenter also glorified motherhood, while, at the same time (as I note below), seeking to valorize a female sexual pleasure detached from maternity. Like many conservatives, the socialist Carpenter saw the New Woman as mannish and 'unmotherly', but he also saw her as potentially exercising a beneficial influence on her 'more commonplace sisters' (*LCA* 67), and thus bringing about an elevation of the practice of motherhood. Under the influence of the New Woman, he suggests, the task of motherhood 'will be carried out with a degree of conscious intelligence hitherto unknown, and which will raise it from the fulfilment of mere instinct to the completion of a splendid social purpose . . . to raise heroic as well as prosperous citizens' (*LCA* 67–8).

Despite these continuities with nineteenth-century biologism and with the ways in which the social-purity feminists represented the feminine, there were also important differences and disjunctions in the ways in which Ellis and Carpenter, on the one hand, and the social-purity feminists, on the other, conceptualized existing and future sex relations. Not least of these is the primacy which both men attached to sex. Ellis, for example, can be seen as one of the main producers of modern sexual identity in England. He anticipated the modern foregrounding of sexuality as a powerful motive force pervading the whole of life, and as *the* defining characteristic of human identity. Like Freud (with whom he disagreed fundamentally on a number of matters, but who nevertheless took aspects of Ellis's work seriously), he saw many different phenomena as having sexual origins. For Ellis, sexuality is at the centre of both individual and social life: 'it is not merely the channel along which the race is maintained and built up, it is the foundation on which all dreams of the future world must be erected.'[59] Ellis took the view – which Lawrence, at least at some points in his career, appeared to share – that sex was the key both to a fulfilling personal life and to social health. Underlying Ellis's catalogue of sexual variations and pathologies was a belief in the existence of a fundamentally healthy sex impulse which was distorted by a degenerative modern society: 'amid the sterilizing tendencies of our life the impulse of sex remains unimpaired, however concealed or despised.'[60]

Carpenter also put sex at the centre of life, as individually enriching and socially unifying. 'Sex still goes first, and hands and eyes, mouth, brain follow; from the midst of belly and thighs radiate the knowledge of self, religion and immortality.'[61] He emphasized sexual pleasure as and end in itself quite independent of reproduction. (Of course, as a homosexual Carpenter would have had pressing reasons of his own for taking this view.) In *Love's Coming of Age* he argued against the influence of the 'arbitrary notion that the function of love is limited to childbearing; and that any love not concerned with the propagation of the race must necessarily be of dubious character' (*LCA* 69). For Carpenter, regeneration rather than generation was the purpose of love. 'Regeneration is the key to the meaning of love – to be in the first place born again *in* some one else or *through* some one else; in the second place only, to be born again through a child . . . generation alone can hardly be looked upon as the primary object of conjugation.'[62] Carpenter emphasized the importance of physical sexual pleasure for individual and social health, and, at the same time, emphasized that physical union was properly a means to spiritual union and connection. Like many early twentieth-century novelists, Carpenter made something of a religion of personal relationships.

In his writings on sex and society Carpenter adopted a rhetoric of renewal. He wrote from the position of the visionary, committed to a project of enlightenment, of bringing hitherto hidden things into the fresh air and clear light of day. Carpenter's writings offer a critique of present society and its cramping of human potential, and a utopian vision of a better future. For example, echoing the degenerationists, he finds modern social conditions to be responsible for the aberrant form of femininity represented by the hysterical, over-civilized Victorian woman. Woman, he argued (apparently propounding the essentialist concept of femininity espoused by some more recent 'womanist' feminists), is 'essentially of calm, large acceptive and untroubled temperament',[63] and if, given the freedom to express herself, she would show the way to a free society.

Carpenter's utopianism is based on an evolutionary belief in progress and a belief in democracy. He figures his utopian future in terms which become increasingly familiar in the fiction of the early twentieth century; in a rhetoric of a rupture and renewal which is also a regrouping of forces. For example, the rhetoric that would shape the visionary ending of Lawrence's *The Rainbow*, with its imagery of breaking through the husks of the old forms to a new life, is already visible in the image of the new life which Carpenter set out for Walt Whitman in a letter of 1874. 'And here though dimly, I think I see the new, open life which is to come. The spirit moving backwards and forwards beneath the old forms, strengthening and reshaping the foundation before it alters the superstructure.'[64] Like Lawrence (at least in *The Rainbow*) 'Carpenter saw two sources for this new life, "woman" and "artisans" '.[65] (I would add a third source: the redefinition of gender, and of sex relations.)

Although, as I have indicated, Carpenter clearly worked with the existing gender stereotypes, he also attempted to revalue and redefine them. He had a less polarized view of gender than Ellis, and saw the masculine and feminine as the opposite ends of a continuum, in the middle of which was an 'intermediate sex'.

> It is beginning to be recognised that the sexes do not or should not normally form two groups hopelessly isolated in habit and feeling from each other, but that they rather represent the two poles of one group – which is the human race; so that while certainly the extreme

specimens at either pole are vastly divergent, there are great numbers in the middle region who (though differing corporeally as men and women) are by emotion and temperament very near to each other. (*LCA* 114–17)

These androgynous, intermediate types occupied an important role in Carpenter's 'revisioning' of the future. Conservatives in particular saw the reassertion of traditional gender stereotypes, a stabilizing of what had become fluid, as the way out of current problems. Social-purity feminists seized upon traditional definitions of femininity and sought to put them to new uses by remaking the social order as feminine. Carpenter, on the other hand, saw fluidity as the solution not the problem. In particular, the homosexual or 'uranian' who supposedly combined the physical characteristics of one sex with the emotional characteristics of the other was 'a higher type of humanity'.[66] Carpenter assigns to the uranians the role of 'reconcilers', 'connectors', 'interpreters of men and women to each other' (*LCA* 134, 115). He represents this new gender as prefiguring a possible future bisexuality that would come into being in a transformed social world. Whether or not we find this a particularly helpful way of thinking about homosexuality, it certainly helps us to understand Virginia Woolf's concept of androgyny, and the attempts to rethink gender and sex roles in the fiction of E. M. Forster and Woolf, and in the early work of D. H. Lawrence. It was this 'hermaphrodite fallacy' (*F.* 100) against which Lawrence was to react so violently in *Fantasia of the Unconscious* and some of his later fiction.

'WOMAN' OR WOMEN, FEMINISM OR MODERNISM, THE *FREEWOMAN* OR THE *EGOIST*?

It will be clear from the discussion so far that during the last decade of the nineteenth century and the first decade of the twentieth century there was a fierce contest not only over the meaning of the feminine (and consequently the masculine), but also over the meaning of feminism. This contest was as much a battle within the women's movement as it was an attack from without. The history of a short-lived but important feminist publication provides an interesting case study of the way in which the contest over the meaning of feminism, and reactions against the renovatory conceptualization of both the feminine and feminism, constituted an important site upon which literary modernism was defined. The transition of Dora Marsden's feminist magazine the *Freewoman* to Ezra Pound's modernist forum, the *Egoist*, via the *New Freewoman*, is an important moment in the formation of modernism, and one which demonstrates modernism's complex interconnections with contemporary debates about feminism, the feminine, and gender, and with the gendered discourses of degeneration and renovation that I have been discussing.

The *Freewoman* (and its successive incarnations) was an 'advanced' periodical which, like so many modernist and proto-modernist publications, made an impact and had an importance which was quite disproportionate to the size of its readership (indeed, this is almost a defining characteristic of the texts of what came to be canonical modernism). The *Freewoman: A Weekly Feminist Review* was first published in November 1911 under the editorship of Dora Marsden, who was later joined by Mary Gawthorpe, a fellow-member of the WSPU. Marsden, a former WSPU activist, had quarrelled with the WSPU over strategy, and, as Rebecca West was to recall in 1926, wanted to 'ponder on the profounder aspects of Feminism',[67] and not just the vote. Marsden announced the *Freewoman*'s publication as a moment of rupture and renewal, which 'marks an epoch ... the point at which feminism in England ceases to be impulsive and unaware of its own features, and becomes definitely self-conscious and introspective'. In the *Freewoman* the suffrage campaign is represented as belonging to a past that must be left behind for a more widely defined feminism for the New Age. Feminism is now 'the whole issue, political enfranchisement a branch issue, and the methods militant or otherwise, are merely accidentals'.[68]

From its first issue the *Freewoman*'s editorial position was defined by Marsden's individualism, a philosophic anarchism derived in part, as Michael Levenson has argued (in *The Genealogy of Modernism*), from the egoism of Max Stirner. Thus the paper was to be concerned with women not 'woman', and with individuals not a movement. It was to give spiritual freedom primacy over political freedom. Its professed aim was 'to make clear that the entire wrangle regarding women's freedom rests upon spiritual considerations, and that it must be settled as such'.[69] The *Freewoman*'s individualism and emphasis on the spirit was also an example of Edwardian vitalism, that obsession with 'life' – shared by Carpenter, Ellis, Forster, and Lawrence, among others – which was articulated as a 'demand for individual freedom and self-realization, a vague but fervent rallying cry for the poets, social rebels, and emancipated women who were fighting their way out of the drawing rooms of Edwardian England'.[70]

In distancing itself from suffragist feminism, the *Freewoman* sought both to redefine feminism and to appropriate the renovatory rhetoric of the suffragists. The 'great change which the Feminist movement seeks to bring about', claimed Marsden, 'is not merely a matter of political readjustment ... carried to success, it would accomplish a vast revolution in the entire field of human affairs, intellectual, sexual, domestic, economic, legal and political'.[71] The journal was certainly committed to a sexual revolution, and devoted a great deal of space to the issue of female sexuality and sexual pleasure. There were articles (many of which were written by followers of Ellis and Carpenter) on the relative strength of male and female sex drives, lesbianism, 'uranianism' (homosexuality) auto-eroticism, contraception, marriage, and menstruation. According to Rebecca West, the *Freewoman* 'mentioned sex loudly and clearly and repeatedly, and in the worst possible taste', and its 'unblushingness' on sexual matters was instrumental in shattering 'the romantic conception of women' as having the 'gift of perfect adaptation' (*GM* 575–6).

The individualistic redirection of feminism undertaken by the *Freewoman* (advertised in its latter stages as a 'Humanist Weekly'), became even more pronounced in its successor, the *New Freewoman*, established in June 1913 with the financial backing of one of the midwives of Poundian modernism, Harriet Shaw Weaver. The *Freewoman* had been forced to close in September 1912 when distribution problems with W. H. Smith, who disliked both its tone and subject-matter, had brought the journal's financial difficulties to a crisis. The *New Freewoman*, under the editorship of Marsden, assisted first (briefly) by Rebecca West and then by Richard Aldington, continued its predecessor's project of attempting to resolve the struggle between 'masculinism' and 'feminism'. It was adver-tised as the 'only journal of recognized standing espousing a doctrine of philosophic individualism' committed to 'lay bare the individualist basis of all that is most significant in modern movements including feminism'.[72] The proto-modernism of the *New Freewoman*'s feminism is evident in its abandoning of the collectivism of causes, which it represents as the 'titil-lation of the herd'. Even before its take-over by Ezra Pound, the project of the *New Freewoman* was remarkably like the project of Poundian and also Lawrentian modernism. Renovation and liberty are the province of strong individuals who must free themselves from the feeble and degen-erate masses.

> There is only one person concerned in the freeing of individuals; and that is the person who wears and feels and resents the shackles. Shackles must be burst off: if they are cut away from outside, they will immediately reform ... 'Causes' are the diversion of the feeble – of those who have lost the power of acting from their own nature. They are for the titillation of the herd, and a person who can act strongly should shun all Cause-ites and their works ... Accurately speaking, there is no 'Woman Movement', 'Woman' is doing nothing – she has, indeed, no existence.[73]

The rejection of the nineteenth-century discourse of 'woman' implicit in the project of the *New Freewoman* and its predecessor, and explicit in the final sentence of the above extract, appears to be a radical move, partic-ularly when viewed from the perspective of a late twentieth-century (post-modernist?) feminism which has focused on the oppressiveness of universal categories such as 'woman'. However, the *New Freewoman*'s rejection of 'woman' is less an insistence on differences within a gender category than a reinforcement of the difference between gender categories, and one which privileges the masculine term. This can be seen in the gendered language of Marsden's modernist critique of abstraction, a process which is implicitly represented as feminization. It is interesting to note that Marsden's critique of abstraction reverses the gender terms of one strand of the late nineteenth-century debate on fiction (which I discuss in the next chapter) in which abstraction and generalization are privileged as masculine positives. Thus, Marsden argues, when 'a virile people turns to thought', it creates 'a culture which promptly turns upon it to encompass its destruction'.[74] Or again: 'Our business is to annihilate thought . . . to dissolve ideas . . . Men need no ideas . . . what men need is power of Being, strength in themselves.'[75] This Lawrentian creed might have been very fruitful for the modern (male) artist, but it is more problematic for disempowered individuals, such as women, who, it might be argued, need ideas, a cause, and the strength of a group to combat a form of social organization and a way of thinking which is posited on a denial of their 'power of Being.'

Marsden's developing critique of abstract language, of (implicitly) the lack of virility of suffragette discourse, and of collectivism all tended towards the abandonment of a politics of activism in favour of a modernist 'politics' of subjectivity. During 1913 the *New Freewoman*, under the growing influence of Ezra Pound, focused less and less on the sexual revolution and more and more on the revolution of the word. Marsden's position was appropriated and taken to its logical conclusion in a letter from Ezra Pound in December 1913.

> We, the undersigned men of letters . . . venture to suggest to you that the present title of the paper causes it to be confounded with organs devoted solely to the advocacy of an *unimportant reform in an obsolete political institution* . . . We therefore ask . . . that you should mark the character of your paper as an organ of individuals of both sexes and of the individualist principle in every department of life.[76]

In the issue for 15 December 1913 the *New Freewoman* announced its change of name to *The Egoist: An Individualist Review*, a title chosen in homage to Max Stirner. Marsden offered this comment on the paper's final abandonment of feminism.

> In adopting the neutral title *The Egoist* and thereby obliterating the 'woman' character from the journal, we do not feel that we are abandoning anything there would be wisdom in retaining. The

emphasis laid on women and their ways and works was ... more in the nature of retort than of argument. 'Feminism' was the natural reply to 'Hominism', and the intent of both these was more to tighten the strings of controversy than to reveal anything vital in the minds of the controversialists.[77]

In a move that is all too familiar in early twentieth-century writing, the obliteration of 'the "woman" character' of the paper is also an abandonment of collectivism and utopianism (found in various nineteenth-century versions of feminism) in favour of an élitist privileging of those who believe themselves to enjoy intellectual freedom.

> The time has arrived when mentally-honest women feel that they have no use for the springing-board of large promises of powers redeemable in a distant future. Just as they feel they can be as 'free' now as they have the power to be, they know that their works can give evidence now of whatever quality they are capable of giving to them. To attempt to be 'freer' than their own power warrants means that curious thing – 'protected freedom', and their ability, allowed credit because it is women's, is a 'protected' ability. 'Freedom', and ability 'recognised' by permission, are privileges which they find can serve no useful purpose.[78]

The *Freewoman*'s transition to the *Egoist* is marked out in the language of gender. The journal starts with a movement from 'woman' to 'women', proceeds by shifting the focus from women to individuals, and ends with a male-defined version of the individual. By January 1914 the *Egoist* was firmly in the control of its new editor, Ezra Pound, under whose direction it was to become one of the key journals in the making of literary modernism. Under Pound's editorship the *Egoist* published critical writing by T. S. Eliot, the early chapters of Joyce's *Ulysses*, and Wyndham Lewis's agressively masculinist, Vorticist novel *Tarr*. It also became the mouthpiece for a redefinition of poetry as a form 'as much like granite as could be',[79] a poetry of 'intense frigidity' and 'distinguished aridity'.[80]

The *New Freewoman* had begun by self-consciously distancing itself from the 'woman-cause' in favour of the wider cause of feminism, and it ended by announcing history's abandonment of feminism. The key event in the *Egoist*'s account of feminism's being overtaken by history was the war. According to Marsden, the war 'brought the wordy contest about Women's Rights to an abrupt finish, and only a few sympathetic words remain to be spoken over the feminist corpse'.[81]

Some suffragist feminists, on the other hand, saw the war not as the eclipse of feminism, but as the vindication of the feminist case: it was the apotheosis of the masculine order, the result of 'woman's' lack of success in remaking man in her own image. 'This then is the world as men have made it, life as men have ordered it,' declared the *Suffragette* in 1914. 'A man-made civilization, hideous and cruel enough in time of peace, is to be destroyed . . . This great war is Nature's vengeance, is God's vengeance upon the people who held women in subjection.'[82] The 'feminist corpse' was not, in fact, dead, but it was, so to speak, dismembered. The contradictions of the *magna mater* strand of feminism were revealed when, within a year, the *Suffragette* had changed its name to the *Britannia* (October 1915), and many of the suffragettes had transformed the rhetoric of the civilizing mothers of the race into the bellicose patriotism of the mothers of empire. More importantly, however, 'the feminist corpse' was resurrected by means of women's empowerment through their contribution to the war effort and their occupation of the jobs previously undertaken by the men who had left for the battlefields of Europe.

In all sorts of ways the war to provide a difference of view, and a rhetoric of gender difference, which would have profound effects on the engendering of twentieth-century fiction. In particular, the war gave a new turn to the gendered rhetoric of degeneration and renovation that had been in circulation, and sometimes in contest, since the 1890s. From the beginning of the *fin de siècle* period, writers of all kinds and persuasions, and working in a variety of forms and registers, had been prophesying the ending of civilization in either a destructive bang or a decadent whimper – a process which would be followed, according to some prognostications, by the birth of a new epoch. The actual cataclysm of the First World War both fulfilled and complicated those prophesies. The war was variously represented as the playing-out to its deadly logical outcome of an enervated, feminized, civilization, or as the implosion of the patriarchal order in a return to barbarity. It was either the end of civilization or the birth of a new world order. In either case it gave fresh impetus to the continuing contest about the meaning and gender of degeneration and renovation.

DEGENERATION, THE FEMININE, FEMINISM, AND THE POST-WAR CRISIS OF MASCULINITY

When the literary historian of the future comes to cast his eye over our little post-war age, he will not have to go very much to the heart of the matter to detect that he is in the presence of an ethos bearing a very close resemblance to that of the Naughty Nineties. (MWA 181–2)

The connection between feminism and degeneration as one of the defining characteristics of the modern condition, which I noted in the work of some turn-of-the-century social critics, was insisted upon even more emphatically in the degenerationist rhetoric employed by many social commentators who surveyed the post-First World War period from the vantage-point of the 1920s and beyond. If the war was represented by some contemporary feminists as a crisis produced *by* the masculine order, it also constituted a crisis *in* masculinity. As Elaine Showalter has suggested, that 'most masculine of enterprises, the Great War, the "apocalypse of masculinism", feminized its conscripts by taking away their sense of control'.[83] The heightened code of masculinity that operated in wartime collapsed on its own contradictions, as numerous soldiers succumbed to hysteria or neurasthenia, conditions which had hitherto been held to be (in Showalter's phrase) female maladies. As a consequence, English psychological science (and its developing institutions of psychiatry, which were constructed on a model of radical sexual difference), 'found its categories undermined'.[84] The epidemic of nervous collapse among soldiers in the trenches undermined the validity of stoicism and emotional repression as the defining characteristics of the manly ideal, for it was not predominantly the degenerate conscripts of the urban abyss who succumbed to the 'female malady' of hysteria, but rather the flower of the nation's manly youth. Moreover, it was not just the shell-shocked, neurasthenic soldier who constituted a challenge to the dominant idea of gender difference. As William Greenslade has recently pointed out, the returning soldier was also 'a key symbolic figure in the post-1918 English novel'. The returning soldier is a liminal figure, wandering between two worlds in which traditional gender categories have become confused. 'Behind him was the unmanning trauma' of the trenches. Before him was a return to the 'feminine' world of family, and a social world of work in which women had come to play an increasingly dominant part.[85]

Although many contemporary writers attributed the crisis in/of masculinity directly to the war and to the experience of combat, the terms in which they articulated and defined this crisis are those of the *fin de siècle* discourse of gender and degeneration. The post-war crisis in masculinity was yet another phase of the longer-term crisis of gender definition which I have been discussing in this chapter. It was both produced by and, in turn, produced a great deal of anti-feminist, and indeed anti-woman rhetoric, which remained in circulation throughout the inter-war years.

The numerous books of the prolific anti-feminist, anti-democratic, and anti-modernist writer Anthony M. Ludovici provide a particularly illuminating case study of the social theory in which the cultural pessimism (or catastrophism) and misogyny of much male modernist writing is grounded, and which the feminist modernism of writers such as Dorothy Richardson and Virginia Woolf had to negotiate. Ludovici's misogyny is evident in some of his pre-war articles in such publications as the *New Age*, but it acquired a new force in the 1920s in books such as *Woman:*

A Vindication (1923), *Lysistrata, or Woman's Future and Future Woman*
(1924), and *Man: An Indictment* (1927) in which Ludovici returned again
and again to the same themes: that the modern age is an age of physical,
mental, and cultural degeneration; that feminism is simultaneously the
cause and symptom of this degeneration; that masculine degeneration is
both the cause of and caused by feminism; that the cure for degeneration
is a restitution of physical and cultural health by means of a restoration
of the 'natural' balance of power between the sexes (i.e. power should
reside with men).

Ludovici attributes all the degenerative evils that he perceives in the
modern condition – from the wearing of spectacles and the possible end
of female lactation to the prevalence of body-despising values, and from
loss of physical vigour to the loss of imperial power – to men's lack of
masculinity, and women's appropriation of 'male' power and their occupation of the male public sphere. Among the 'signs and portents' of the
degenerative modern condition which he discerns in *Lysistrata* is:

> A marked decline in the ability, versatility, and masculinity of men
> ... partly ... physical and partly ... intellectual ... [and] brought
> about on the one hand by ... cramping labour for generations, and,
> on the other, by the deliberate attempt throughout Anglo-Saxon
> civilization and its imitations to limit the notion of manliness to
> martial bravery and proficiency at sports. This has led to a loss of
> mastery over all things which is far from edifying, and has enabled
> women during the last century and recently to draw unduly
> favourable comparisons between themselves and men – which ...
> give quite a distorted view of the situation ... [It has produced] a
> movement known as Feminism ... which claims it can recruit among
> its supporters the mastery, ability, and strength to put the world
> right, and which proposes to do so by superseding men everywhere
> possible, even in his reproductive role.[86]

Described by one reviewer as 'more stimulating to serious thought on the
relation to [*sic*] the sexes than anything since Otto Weininger startled the
world with *Sex and Character*',[87] Ludovici's work perpetuates the
Weiningerian view of feminism, as a form of masculinism in women; both
men see feminism as a movement for female supremacy and the usurpa-
tion of male superiority, rather than as a movement for equality. Like the
work of most degenerationist thinkers in this period, Ludovici's is both a
diagnosis and a call to action.

> Although sex hostility may be entirely absent (which it never is) from
> the programme of the Feminists, the fact that a Feminist movement
> forms, is in itself sufficient evidence of the degeneration of the men
> among whom it forms; and since this degeneration must lead to other

and more serious consequences than the mere self-assertion of the female, it behoves all the men of a country tending to feministic development, to take stock of themselves, and to proceed with energy to arrest the dry-rot before it spreads too far.[88]

Ludovici's remedy for the degenerative dry rot that was in danger of undermining Anglo-Saxon culture was a Masculine Renaissance. He envisaged a 'regeneration of man' based on a return to the kind of man who has 'already been reared once before in these islands', the 'manly man' who displays 'will-power, leadership, mastery over the mysteries of life'.[89] This was a call to which D. H. Lawrence was to respond in much of his fictional and discursive writing in the 1920s, as I will show in my final chapter.

A similar turn to the masculine was the motive force behind Wyndham Lewis's initial championing, in *Blasting and Bombadeering*, of 'the men of 1914 . . . [that] "haughty and proud generation" . . . the Joyces, the Pounds, the Eliots' (*B&B* 252). The men of 1914, the avant-gardeists amongst whose ranks Lewis also numbered himself (at least in the pre-war period), were all 'literary sharp shooters steeped in the heroic "abstract" tradition', who were part of the 'titanic stirrings', the sounds of 'a new art coming to flower to celebrate or to announce a "new age"' (*B&B* 255), which filled Europe in the years immediately preceding the war.

Like the anti-modernist Ludovici and also many of his own associates among the male modernists, Lewis (who in his later writings repudiated literary modernism as a kind of *trahison des clercs*) saw the twentieth-century condition as one of cultural decline induced by the erosion of traditional masculine values by a process of feminization. As he wrote in the conclusion to *Paleface* (1929):

> All through the range of his complexes the contemporary White Man can be observed at the same occupation, consisting everywhere of a *reversal* and a *return* . . . [H]e looks back towards that feminine chaos, from which the masculine principles have differentiated themselves, as more perfect . . . [and thus] the contemporary man has grown to desire to be a woman.[90]

In Lewis's writings, democracy, hostility to intellect and to abstraction, cultural relativism, (increasingly in the later 1920s and the 1930s) the Jewish conspiracy, and even, ultimately, modernism itself, were all represented as symptoms of cultural decline and as feminine characteristics. Another 'feminine' symptom of cultural degeneration was the so-called 'time-cult' castigated in *Time and Western Man* (1928), which, according to Lewis, privileged (among other things) 'feminine' flow and flux above 'masculine' space and form, and led to the flabby subjectivism of the stream-of-consciousness novel. Among the other aspects of the modern condition which Lewis represented as simultaneously both causes and symptoms of cultural decay and decline were the work of women writers (especially Virginia Woolf) and of feminized male writers (the 'tittering old maids' of Bloomsbury, and the 'girlish' Oscar Wilde) (*MWA* 120–8), and the increasing incidence in contemporary society of sexual inversion, especially among men.

For Lewis, as for so many writers from the late 1880s to the 1930s, feminism itself was one of the key elements in the erosion of the male principle by the female. In *The Art of Being Ruled* (1926), in which he claimed that he was not writing as an 'anti-feminist', Lewis represents feminism (as Lawrence also did in much of his work in the 1920s) as a just cause which has, so to speak, over-achieved its ends, and gone too far. Lewis links feminism to a 'sex war . . . destined to free not only women, but men . . . [which] led off, naturally enough as a war to free the woman': 'When *feminism* first assumed the proportions of a universal movement it was popularly regarded as a movement directed to the righting of a little series of political wrongs . . . The general herd of men smiled with indulgent superiority . . . it was a bloodless revolution' (*ABR* 215–16). But, in a rhetorical move with which we have recently become reacquainted, Lewis asserts that the sex war has moved on to new terrain. It has moved on from 'righting . . . little political wrongs' – which he compares to respecting the 'rights of little nations (like Belgium)' – to 'an attack on *man* and on masculinity' (*ABR* 216). Feminism and the sex war, Lewis argues, have not resulted in 'a stabilization in which the man and the woman exist on *equal* terms', but 'a situation in which feminine values are predominant' (*ABR* 223). In short, feminism is part of 'the world-movement of sex-reversal' (*ABR* 223), a process which is both produced by and induces a crisis in masculinity. The reign of feminism and the feminine is, according to Lewis, ushered in by the facile 'indulgent superiority' of the 'general herd of men'; herd-like behaviour is always associated with the degeneration of mass civilization in Lewis's writings. The feminist ascendancy also produces, and is the product of, male sexual inversion, which Lewis describes as 'the child of feminism' (*ABR* 244). The fashion for male sexual inversion which Lewis discerns in the contemporary world is 'part of the feminist revolution. It is an integral part of feminism proper . . . a gigantic phase of the sex war, the "homo" is the legitimate child of the suffragette' (*ABR* 244). In Lewis's history of gender, or gendered version of history, male inversion is not only the offspring of feminism, and the by-product of the feminization of modern European society, but it is also, more specifically, 'a war-time birth . . . a reply to the implications of *responsibility* of those times; nature's *never again* in the overstrained male organism' (*ABR* 279).

Like the turn-of-the-century sex psychologists and some feminists, Lewis saw both masculinity and femininity as socially constructed categories, not natural givens: 'A man, then, is made, not born' (*ABR* 280), 'the man is not naturally "a man" any more than the woman' (*ABR* 279). 'Masculine' attributes, from an overdeveloped physique to the 'industry, courage and responsibility of the male', have, according to Lewis, 'only been sustained and kept in place by a system of rewards' (*ABR* 282), rewards which are no longer forthcoming in the feminized age about which Lewis writes. Lewis represents the construction of masculinity in the male person as an arduous and burdensome process towards an end which it is difficult to attain and maintain: 'Men were only made into "men" with great difficulty even in primitive society: the man is not naturally "a man" . . . He has to be propped up into that position with some ingenuity, and is always likely to collapse' (*ABR* 279). For most men, it would appear, masculinity is something which is thrust upon them. The man is 'taught in ten years a host of symbols to prepare him for the subsequent feats of independence expected of him: and at every moment of his tutelage he is resentful and rebellious' (*ABR* 280). In Lewis's account, twentieth-century man has either been vanquished by the forces of feminism, or tended to succumb to the seductions of femininity and/or feminization. The modern man has performed a form of self-castration, preferring to be 'a sweet-meat-sucking, joke-cracking, indolently thumb-sucking member of the audience' rather than a 'gladiator' (*ABR* 271). Lewis, the self-proclaimed 'Enemy' and scourge of this feminized democratic 'audience' society, was not the only male writer of the 1920s who sought both to advocate and to perform the role of masculine gladiator.

From the late nineteenth century onwards the manly man and the womanly woman, and feminism (variously defined), were represented as the agents of social and cultural renovation and the regeneration of a race whose future was threatened by the erosion or exaggeration of sexual difference, sexual inversion, and feminism. Like many other writers in the 1920s (including D. H. Lawrence), Ludovici and Lewis reversed the renovationist discourse of the feminists, and advocated the redefined and regenerated manly man, or a return to male/masculine values (although they defined these in rather different ways) as the one thing needful to resolve the crisis of the present, to return woman to womanliness and a restricted feminine sphere, to halt the creeping feminization of culture, and to reverse the degenerationist trend. In later chapters I will show how this contest over the meaning and gender of degeneration and regeneration/renovation was continued in a variety of forms in both the fictional theory and the practice of a range of early twentieth-century novelists.

|3|

Writing and Gender and the Turn of the Century

FICTION AND THE FEMININE

The foundations of the aesthetic of modernism were clearly being laid in the literary debates of the 1880s and 1890s. The journey from symbolism to modernism, from Symonds, Wilde, and Pater, to Yeats, Pound, and Eliot has been well charted. The part played in the making of modernism (and its alternatives) by turn-of-the-century theories and practices of fiction has received less attention, but it is equally important. The beginning of the moment of the modern in fiction can be seen in the debates about fiction and the feminine conducted in the newspaper and periodical press in the 1880s and 1890s, in late nineteenth-century controversies about Realism, Naturalism, and the Fiction of Sex, and in the fictional experiments of the New Woman writers.

From the mid-1880s debates about fiction began to display many of the anxieties which were to be key elements in the production of literary modernism(s), and more generally in the engendering of early twentieth-century English fiction. Prominent among these were anxieties about cultural authority, and about the autonomy of the artist and of the domain of Art in a literary world increasingly dominated by markets in which the masses and women played an important part. The language of degeneration and the issue of gender were at the centre of the turn-of-the-century discourse on fiction. 'Advanced' critics and novelists saw the autonomous authority of the artist and the development of the novel as a bold, experimental 'masculine' art form as threatened by supposedly moralistic and aesthetically conservative women readers, and by the demands of a mass market which was coded 'feminine'. George Moore's strictures in 'Literature at Nurse' (1885) on the tyranny of the taste of the owners of the circulating libraries, and the 'ladies in the country' who use them, provide an interesting example of this strand of the debate.[1] Moore was outraged that a 'mere tradesman', and the ladies whom he served, dared to 'question the sacred right of the artist to obey the impulses of his temperament'. He was particularly incensed that literature, 'Instead of being allowed to fight with and amid the thoughts and aspirations of men ... is now rocked to an ignoble rest in the motherly arms of the librarian ... [and] that from which he turns the breast dies like a vagrant's child.'[2]

As well as women (or feminized) readers, women writers and a 'feminine' fictional practice were also seen as compromising both the novel's claims as a serious art form and its possibilities for aesthetic development. This was partly because women writers have always figured so prominently as producers of popular fiction, a form of literary production that constantly poses a threat to the novel's status as art. The dominant form of what we would now call 'literary' fiction, the three-volume novel in a broadly realist mode, was also perceived to be a 'feminine' form, even if its author was a man. It was coded feminine because it was defined by what Naomi Schor has described as an 'unvalorized' feminine detailism (that is to say by a limiting focus on the surface details of ordinary domestic life), and by an absence (perceived as a failure or lack) of that 'masculine' abstraction, generalization, perspective, and pattern which were considered to be essential components of art.[3]

A concern with the detail also figured prominently in the conservative critique of fiction. Naturalist fiction and the Fiction of Sex were widely perceived as degenerate; their supposed degeneracy was linked to their 'pathological' obsession with the detailed representation of what (according to their critics) would best be left unrepresented. This pathologizing of the detail was often represented by its critics as an invasive feminine and foreign trait, and it was particularly associated with the effeminate or unmanly French. Schor has argued that the gendered aesthetic of the detail – whether the detail be of the domestic, forensic, or ornamental variety – is a general European phenomenon, and she has traced the emergence of a nineteenth-century 'discourse on the detail' in which the arts are represented as being invaded and feminized by 'an anarchic mass of details', an 'unmistakable sign of cultural dissolution'.[4]

In England by the mid-1890s women writers and readers were associated with an entirely different kind of feminization or feminine invasion of fiction in the form of 'the novel of the modern woman' written 'by a woman, about women from the standpoint of Woman'.[5] The novel of the modern woman was, for the most part, produced by the so-called New Woman writers, who not only self-consciously addressed themselves as women to the circumstances of women's lives, but who also developed a new range of fictional forms and techniques for the purpose. Some (Mona Caird, Iota, Menie Murial Dowie) focused on the restrictive social and economic realities of women's lives, mixing forensic or journalistic detail with hortatory feminist (or sometimes anti-feminist) rhetoric. Some (Sarah Grand and Olive Schreiner) developed visionary, allegorical, or utopian forms as a way of representing the present and envisioning a better future for women. Others experimented with new fictional forms. George Egerton and Ella D'Arcy, for example, self-consciously distanced themselves from the traditional plots of the three-volume novel in an effort to find an appropriate form for exploring and articulating the inner lives of women. In so doing they made an important contribution to the relatively new form of the short story which, according to H. G. Wells, 'broke out everywhere' in the 1890s.[6]

In short, many of the New Woman writers of the 1890s were seeking to tell a new story about women, and they sought new forms in which to do it. Laura Marholm Hansson explicitly linked the new view of women to a renovation of fiction: 'Now that woman is conscious of her own individuality as a woman, she needs an artistic mode of expression, she flings aside the old forms and seeks for new.'[7]

Henry James also saw the future development of fiction as closely connected to the future of women. He predicted that the 'revolution . . . in the position and outlook of woman' could lead to a revolution in fiction, and that the plying of the female pen was likely to produce what D. H. Lawrence later described as 'Surgery for the Novel – or a Bomb'.

> As nothing is more salient in English life today, to fresh eyes, than the revolution taking place in the position and outlook of women – and taking place much more deeply in the quiet than even the noise on the surface demonstrates – so we may very well yet see the female elbow itself, kept in increasing activity by the play of the pen, smash with final resonance the window all this time most superstitiously closed . . . It is the opinion of some observers that when woman do obtain a free hand they will not repay their long debt to the precautionary attitude of men by unlimited consideration for the natural delicacy of the latter.[8]

In fact, by the time James gave voice to the prophecy quoted above, women – taking a different outlook on the 'position of women' – had already made a substantial contribution to the shaping of a future direction for fiction. The New Woman writers of the late 1880s and early 1890s not only anticipated many of the developments which have been attributed to twentieth-century modernism, but also, as Ann Ardis has recently argued, suggested another, more socially engaged, direction for modern writing than that taken by the writers (particularly the male writers) of what came to be defined as canonical high modernism.

What points of connection does the New Woman writing have with modernism? First, both the New Woman as fictional subject and the New Woman as writer were represented in terms of what we have come to think of as a modernist discourse of rupture. The New Woman heroine (like the New Woman who was constructed in the newspaper and periodical press) was represented as disruptive, and in terms of a break with the past, with convention, and even with nature. Like the New Woman type, the New Woman writer was seen (and often saw herself) as a revolting daughter, one who, like the modernists, was in revolt against established literary conventions and modes of representation. As I briefly suggested above, the New Woman writing reconceived many aspects of fictional form and structure in ways which the modernists were to claim as their own in the next generation.

Like its modernist successors, much New Woman fiction broke with or modified the representational conventions of realism. Instead of re-presenting a normative view of a prior reality, the New Woman fiction either offered a different view (that of the woman-as-outsider), or constructed a new version of reality shaped to a woman's desires. The New Woman writing also rethought the Victorian concept of the unified character which embodied a fixed and stable identity. In its place we find a problematization and unfixing of identity. The New Woman writing consistently problematized, deconstructed, demystified, or rethought 'womanliness'. Many New Woman novels turn on the conflict in the heroine between a fluid and charging experience of subjectivity and the fixed identity imposed by conventional social gender roles. The New Woman writers also disrupted conventional plotting. They rethought the plots of domestic realism, particularly the marriage plot. Marriage, the destination of the plot of the mainstream Victorian novel, and the resolution of all of its (and supposedly the heroine's) problems, became, in the New Woman novel, both the origin of narrative and the source of the heroine's problems. The New Woman writing also broke with conventions of narration. In place of the wise and witty sayings, and the moral and social guidance of the omniscient narrator, we find a decentred narrative, and (particularly in marriage-problem novels) a polyphonic form in which a multiplicity of voices and views on current issues are juxtaposed.

A brief look at the cases of Mona Caird and George Egerton will serve to suggest the significance of some of the interconnections between the New Woman writing and the critical reaction to it, and later theories and practice of fiction. First, the case of Mona Caird, a campaigning journalist and fictional polemicist, who is perhaps the classic example of the woman-with-a-cause, the socially engaged New Woman writer. From the late 1880s Caird was a prominent contributor to the debates about the 'Marriage Question', and her essays on marriage and the family, collected under the title *The Morality of Marriage* (1897), generated widespread debate. Like her essays, Caird's novels also focus on marriage questions, and propound a very similar critique of marriage as a source of women's oppression. For example, both *The Wing of Azrael* (1889) and *The Daughters of Danaus* (1894) tell the story of the painful consequences of a daughter's sacrifice to a loveless marriage for the convenience of her family. All of Caird's novels, even *Pathway of the Gods* (1898), which tells the story of its female protagonist's escape from her family and her failure to marry, foreground the ideology of female sacrifice and feminine self-sacrifice which the bourgeois family and conventional middle-class marriage produces, and by which it is reproduced.

Contemporary commentators on Caird's novels tended to see them simply as an extension of her journalism: inartistic, clumsy generic hybrids marred by didacticism and by the emotionalism of her commitment to the woman's cause. On the contrary, I would suggest that Caird is a self-consciously innovative writer, who did not merely reproduce a monologic polemicism in fictional form, but who experimented with a range of voices and genres. In novels like *The Wing of Azrael*, *The Daughters of Danaus*, and *Pathway of the Gods* Caird reworked woman's genres, and genres or modes that were coded feminine (such as melodrama, sensationalism, and mysticism) in order to find ways of figuring female interiority and of exploring and dramatizing the effects of prevailing social institutions on individual female lives. Certainly Caird often used her characters as mouthpieces for her own views on marriage and the restrictions of woman's lot. However, unlike the essays, Caird's novels focus minutely on the emotional and psychological effects of the social constraints of women's lives, and especially on the individual woman's *feelings* of frustration, imprisonment, and rebellion. One of the most important achievements of Caird's novels is their sympathetic representation of the tormented and fractured female subject produced by the contradictions inherent in the ideal of the domestic, affective, feminine woman, and also of the tensions between that ideal and the beliefs and practices of middle- and upper-middle-class life: the belief that women must submit to circum-scribed lives for 'the well-being of the race' and the 'good of society',[9] and 'the peculiar claims that are made by common consent, on a woman's time and strength'.[10]

As well as engaging with the feelings of their female characters, Caird's novels also attempt to engage the feelings of the reader. They attempt to make the reader feel the realities of female renunciation and sacrifice, by presenting a succession of complex, feeling women who desire self-expres-sion, and a fuller, wider experience than that offered by conventional familial confinement. The contrast between the constraining actualities of the life of Caird's central female characters and the expansiveness of their desires is often figured in their affinity with the vastness of nature. It is also figured in their aspirations: for knowledge (*The Wing of Azrael*), for artistic expression and achievement (*The Daughters of Danaus*), for an independent social role (*Pathway of the Gods*).

One of Caird's most intriguing novels is the strange and mystical late work *Pathway of the Gods*. This novel addresses the familiar turn-of-the-century issues of transition, the readjustment of male–female relations, and the nature and meaning of history and the historical process. These issues were to be taken up by the novelists whom I shall discuss in later chapters. The central narrative of *Pathway of the Gods* is a typical New Woman plot. It centres on Anna Carrington, a daughter of the vicarage, cast in the mould of Hardy's Sue Bridehead: 'the woman of the feminist movement – the slight, pale, "bachelor" girl – the intellectualized, emancipated bundle of nerves that modern conditions were producing.'[11] Anna has taken the path of the 'revolting daughter' (familiar to readers of the periodical press in the early 1890s), relinquished her 'fervent piety' (*PG* 14) for atheism, and left the vicarage in search of an independent life as a journalist and public speaker. Like many of the female protagonists of early twentieth-century fiction, Anna is represented as a brittle, epigrammatic young woman, whose 'big dreams' (*PG* 96) have been disappointed. As the novel begins, Anna, who like so many New Woman heroines has suffered a nervous collapse, renews her acquaintance with Julian, a man whose attentions she had formerly rejected. The narrative rehearses the history of her abortive relationship with Julian, who is eventually rescued from the 'consuming fire' (*PG* 282) of her love by the actions of a group of womanly women. Anna ends the novel alone and embittered, yet another 1890s' victim of prematurity, like Hardy's Jude and Sue, and countless other New Woman protagonists: 'We luckless beings of the transition period have to suffer the penalty of being out of line with the old conditions, before the new conditions have been formed with which we could have harmonized' (*PG* 316).

Thus summarized, *Pathway of the Gods* might seem like just another *fin de siècle* narrative of defeat (especially in the context of the sex wars), decline, and disillusion. However, this novel has another narrative trajectory: one of victory, regeneration, and ascent. Anna retires from the fray defeated, her defeat engineered in part by a conspiracy of womanly women who are working for the regeneration of humanity by means of a radical and long-term transformation of relations between the sexes. Anna's impatient egotism is contrasted with (and defeated by) the patient spirituality of another kind of New Woman – represented by the ethereal Clutha Lawrenson and the Swedenborgian Mrs Charnley – who put their faith in the evolutionary ascent of man. Mrs Charnley, for example, advises Anna to be patient because 'Man is still a savage and a child' (*PG* 320). Anna, on the other hand, is unwilling to 'wait in captivity and pain, till man had completed his education', and responds to the 'myriads of cages all round me' with a feminist rage and 'able-bodied hatred' (*PG* 320), which, in the event, prove to be self-immolating.

The narrative structure of *Pathway of the Gods* is episodic, its setting is exotic (a strangely timeless version of Italy), and its form is allegorical rather than realist. It is a very self-consciously aesthetic novel. The central narrative is framed by a highly wrought, poeticized Prologue and conclud-ing section. The Prologue has echoes of Browning's 'Two in the Campagna' and also of 'Love among the Ruins', a poem which D. H. Lawrence makes significant use of in *Women in Love*. The concluding section depicts a curious rite of spring, in which Clutha Lawrenson is crowned 'Queen of the Beautiful Past, and Prophetess of the Beautiful Future in a fantastic ceremony of coronation' (*PG* 334–5) which joins together the ancient past and the visionary future in a timeless moment. The rite of spring is celebrated by means of a dance: a dance in which 'it was as if a dead century had turned in its grave' (*PG* 334); a dance very much in the style of the modern dance theatre of the 1890s, and which also anticipates Lawrence's use of dance-like ritual in *The Rainbow*.

The effect of the dream-like and ritualistic frame is to remove the narra-tive from material history into the mystical cycles of time. This move out of history is also signalled in Julian's strange waking dream with which the narrative opens. In this dream (which is repeatedly invoked as a recur-ring narrative motif) the specific struggles of a historical woman, Anna, are subsumed into the long centuries of female sacrifice and martyrdom. The triumphalist pagan ceremony with which the novel concludes also has the effect of moving the narrative out of history. It does so by celebrat-ing an alternative script for feminity to that of female sacrifice: the script of feminine self-sacrifice. Together the Prologue and concluding section of this novel make a move which Anne Ardis has noted in the work of other New Woman writers: the move from culture into nature, as the 'place where culture's most cherished ideas and ideals can be kept safe from history'.[12] It is also a move into a cyclic conception of history. Similar moves are also made by several early twentieth-century writers of fiction as they engage in complex negotiations with the problem of modernity.

In Caird's novel one of 'culture's most cherished ideas and ideals' is feminine self-sacrifice. This ideal is both protected and renewed by the novel's move from culture into nature. It is a familiar move, and it reappears most prominently in the fiction of E. M. Forster and D. H. Lawrence. However, in Caird's case the move is incomplete, since her novel also exposes precisely whose interests are served by the ideal of feminine self-sacrifice, and what the costs of that ideal are. It is an ideal which nurtures men and destroys those women who cannot or will not conform to it: Julian is saved and Anna is painfully sacrificed. *Pathway of the Gods* thus blends formal renovation and innovation with a radical New Woman rhetoric, and what appears to be a kind of feminist conser-vationism, which preserves sexual difference by insisting on the spiritual and moral superiority of the self-sacrificing, womanly woman.

Caird's novels do not simply transpose into fictional form the polemical rhetoric of her essays; rather they develop what I have described elsewhere as a 'rhetoric of feeling',[13] which simultaneously or by turns represents and explores the complex actualities of women's lives, and figures utopian desires. They are self-conscious aesthetic artefacts which situate themselves in relation to the developing aesthetic of the novel of the modern woman, and, hence, I would suggest, constitute an important moment in the shaping of what Henry James saw as the future direction of English fiction. As I will suggest below, it was in opposition to the novel of the modern woman that many aspects of literary modernism were defined. Nevertheless many elements of the novel of the modern woman (as written by Caird and Egerton among others) were to be appropriated in the fictional practice of both the male and the female writers of the early twentieth century, including those who can be considered as modernists.

I will take the work of George Egerton as my second example of the fiction of the modern women: first, because she was a very self-consciously innovatory writer who was committed to the development of a female aesthetic; second, because she provoked such a fierce critical reaction; and third because her fictional subject-matter and techniques are so frequently echoed by later writers. I am not seeking to make a case about influence here, I am rather pointing out convergence. Egerton made something of a sensation in the mid-1890s as the author of two extremely successful collections of short stories, *Keynotes* (1893) and *Discords* (1894). These volumes were very cleverly marketed as daringly modern by John Lane, the publisher of that bible of decadence, *The Yellow Book*, in which some of Egerton's stories also appeared. Egerton subsequently published other, less successful, musically titled collections of stories (*Symphonies*, 1897, and *Fantasias*, 1898) and a strange, fragmentary novel, *The Wheel of God* (1898), the story of a woman 'becoming self-responsible', which in both style and substance anticipates D. H. Lawrence's *The Rainbow*. Egerton's impressionistic narratives, with their self-conscious focus on the female psyche (presented in rather essentialist terms it has to be said), also clearly anticipate the development of a fiction of feminine self-consciousness by Dorothy Richardson and Virginia Woolf.

Egerton put women, the feminine/female condition, and female/feminine subjectivity at the centre of her fictions. I use these awkward obliques because when writing about Egerton it is difficult to know when to use female (which in current terminology usually refers to the biological category woman) and when to use feminine (which usually refers to woman as constructed in and by a particular culture). Egerton seems to believe in the existence of the eternal female: 'some bottom layer of real womanhood that we may not reveal' under current forms of social organization.[14] She conceives of this 'real womanhood' as the 'true womanly' which is 'of God's making' as opposed to the 'untrue feminine' which 'is of man's making'.[15]

Whether writing of the 'true womanly' or the 'untrue feminine', Egerton wrote unapologetically from the woman's point of view. Indeed she claimed that there was little else for the woman writer to do.

I realised that in literature, everything had been better done by man than woman could have hoped to emulate. There was only one small plot to tell: the *terra incognita* of herself, as she knew herself to be, not as man liked to imagine her – in a word to give herself away, as man had given himself in his writing.[16]

In the hands of Dorothy Richardson and Virginia Woolf and countless other woman novelists who came after them, that 'one small plot' seems to have proved capable of almost infinite expansion.

In her 'Keynote' to *Keynotes* Egerton claimed that she wrote from the woman's point of view not only because there was nothing else left for woman to do, but because she was bound to do so.

Unless one is androgynous, one is bound to look at life through the eyes of one's sex, to toe the limitations imposed on one by its individual psychological functions. I came too soon. If I did not know the technical jargon current today of Freud and the psychoanalysts, I did know something of the complexes and inhibitions, repressions and the subconscious impulses that determine actions and reactions. I used them in my stories. I recognised that in the main, woman was the ever-untamed, unchanging, adapting herself as far as it suited her ends to male expectations; even if repression was altering her subtly. I would use situations or conflicts as I saw them with a total disregard to man's opinions. I would unlock a closed door with a key of my own fashioning.[17]

Thus, at around the time that Freud was beginning to develop the techniques of psychoanalysis by probing the secret inner lives of women, and shortly before he began to publish his own short stories or novellas (the case histories in *Studies on Hysteria*) Egerton was developing her own kind of key to what Freud (among others) saw as the riddle of femininity. She was developing a narrative technique in which to 'plot' female desire and to explore, from the woman's point of view, the question of what it is that a woman wants.

The situations in Egerton's stories are often bleak and sometimes shocking, in the manner of Jean Rhys's stories of the 1920s and 1930s. They focus on bored, trapped, dependent, fallen, impoverished, struggling women. Sometimes these are lone women. Often the stories focus on women's relationship with inarticulate, dense, imperceptive, careless, and sometimes drunken, brutal, and exploitative men. Egerton's manner of writing was just as striking as her subject-matter. Her narratives have the characteristics we now think of as distinctively modern: they are impressionistic, compressed, concentrated, allusive, elliptical, episodic, and make much use of dream, reverie, and other forms of interiority. The recording of events and the description of outward circumstances are almost always a means of suggesting inner realities, especially the inner realities of women's experiences and desires.

The paradigmatic Egertonian story, and one much discussed by feminist critics,[18] is 'A Cross Line', the opening story of *Keynotes* (now anthologized in Elaine Showalter's *Daughters of Decadence*). 'A Cross Line' is constructed as a drama in five scenes, or as a musical piece in five movements. Its plot, in so far as it has one, is rudimentary: a woman (called Gypsy by her husband) meets a male stranger (whose name we never learn); she fantasizes about other possible lives she might lead; she contemplates escape (with the stranger) from the companionable tediousness of her marriage, but becomes resigned to her domestic lot when she discovers (or belatedly acknowledges) what the reader has perhaps already guessed, that she is pregnant.

But to tell the story thus is to mistell it, for the main concern of 'A Cross Line' is with the shifting moods of its central female character, with the allusive evocation of the desires and frustrations of this 'creature of moments'. The story is, to adapt the title of another of Egerton's stories, a series of 'psychological moments'. The rhetorical climax of 'A Cross Line' is its penultimate scene, in which the woman is pictured alone amongst the Irish hills in an extended reverie, a sort of interior monologue, in which one fantasy of female power succeeds another as she pictures herself first 'in Arabia on the back of a swift steed', observed by 'flashing eyes set in dark faces', and then 'on the stage of an ancient theatre out in the open air', exulting in her power over the audience before whom she dances, her arms 'clasped by jewelled snakes, and one with quivering diamond fangs coil[ed] round her hips'.[19]

The ending of the story, with its apparent return of the woman to a normative domestic femininity, does not dissipate the power and energy of the fantasy section, nor does it explain or stabilize the 'creature of moments'. Indeed, the elliptical and evasive nature of Egerton's narrative and its refusal to disclose motivation have the effect of disrupting the idea of a stable identity. In 'A Cross Line', as in her other stories, Egerton anticipates Dorothy Richardson, Virginia Woolf, and D. H. Lawrence in getting rid of what Lawrence described as the old stable ego of the character, and presents us with a multiplicity of selves, or a subjectivity in process.

The publication of *Keynotes* created a considerable stir in the literary press, as an example of the erotomania, hysteria, and egotism that some critics felt pervaded the writing of the 1890s, particularly fiction by women. There is much more at stake in this reaction to 'hysterical "yellow" lady novelists'[20] than simple moral outrage or disgust at sexual frankness, as this extract from Hugh Stutfield's 'The Psychology of Feminism' indicates.

The Soul of Woman, its Sphinx-like ambiguities and complexities, its manifold contradictions, its sorrows and joys, its vagrant fancies

and never-to-be-satisfied longings, furnish the literary analyst of
these days with inexhaustible material. Above all do the sex-problem
novelists and the introspective biographer and essayist revel in the
theme. Psychology . . . is their never-ending delight; and modern
woman, who, if we may believe those who claim to know most
about her, is a sort of walking enigma, is their chief subject of investigation. Her ego, that mysterious entity of which she is now only
just becoming conscious, is said to remain a *terra incognita* even to
herself; but they are determined to explore its innermost recesses.
The pioneers of this formidable undertaking must of necessity be
women. Man, great clumsy, comical creature that he is, knows
nothing of the inner springs of the modern Eve's complicated nature.
He sees everything in her, we are told, without comprehending
anything, and the worst of it is that he cannot even express his
ignorance in good English. Man possesses brute force, woman divine
influence, and her nature is in closer relation with the infinite than
the masculine mind. He is an 'utter failure', while her womanhood
'almost guarantees to her a knowledge of the eternal verities', which
he can only hope partially to attain to through woman.[21]

Underlying Stutfield's leaden irony there is a contest about cultural authority in which 'masculine' objectivity vies with 'feminine' interiority, and the
attempt by women writers to reclaim the authority of their own experience is resisted.

The feminization of culture, and the need to protect masculine art from
a process of degenerative (ef)feminization, were constant themes in
discussions of fiction in the 1890s (for a particularly vivid example of
this see the extract from Stutfield's diatribe on the 'pathological novel'
and the literature of degeneration in 'Tommyrotics', reproduced in
Appendix vii). As well as being the year of the New Woman, 1894 was
also the year of several important pronouncements on the threat to 'Art'
posed by the feminization of fiction, most notably Hubert
Crackanthorpe's and Arthur Waugh's essays on 'Reticence in Literature'.
The issues they raised were widely, almost obsessively, taken up throughout the mid- and late 1890s – for example, by William Barry in 'The
Strike of a Sex', Hugh Stutfield in 'Tommyrotics' and 'The Psychology
of Feminism', James Ashcroft Noble in 'The Fiction of Sexuality', and
Janet Hogarth in 'Literary Degenerates'.[22] All of these writers, with
varying degrees of vehemence, humour, or (in Stutfield's case) hysteria,
attacked the New Woman fiction and the Fiction of Sex for its degeneracy and 'effeminacy', and stated or implied a preference for what was to
become the dominant high modernist aesthetic of rigorous impersonality,
classical reticence, and transcendence of the merely local and particular.
Arthur Waugh, for example, called for a 'masculine' rigour and impersonality in art, rather than a sensuous surrendering to detail, and insisted

on the need to separate the man who suffers (or enjoys) from the mind which creates:

> There is all the difference in the world between drawing life as we find it, sternly and relentlessly, surveying it all the while from outside with the calm, unflinching gaze of criticism, and, on the other hand, yielding ourselves to the warmth and colour of its excesses, losing our judgement in the ecstacies of the joy of life, becoming, in a word, effeminate.[23]

Waugh, like many of his contemporaries, appeared to believe that art and femininity were incompatible, indeed that they were contradictory terms:

> The man lives by ideas; the woman by sensations; and while the man remains an artist so long as he holds true to his view of life, the woman becomes one *as soon as she throws off the habits of her sex*, and learns to rely on her judgement, and not on her senses. It is only when we regard life with the *untrammelled view of the impartial spectator*, when we pierce below the substance for its animating idea, that we approximate the artistic temperament. *It is unmanly, it is effeminate, it is inartistic* to gloat over pleasure, to revel in immoderation, to become passion's slave; and literature demands as much calmness of judgement, as much reticence, as life itself.[24]

Not least among Waugh's fears for the future of a feminized fiction was the fear that the novel would cease to be a literary form, that 'art' would be 'lost in photography', and ideas would 'melt into mere report, mere journalistic detail'.[25] Anxieties about the blurring of the boundaries between fiction and mere journalism and polemic in the New Woman writing persisted into early twentieth-century disputes about the future direction of fiction. Henry James's quarrel with H. G. Wells, Lawrence's with Galsworthy, and Virginia Woolf's with Bennett all turned on the issue of the novel as art versus the novel as journalism.

Waugh's anxieties about the contamination of art by a 'feminine' surrendering to the senses, on the one hand, and by journalistic polemic, on the other, were recalled and reproduced by W. L. Courtney in *The Feminine Note in Fiction* in 1904: 'Recently complaints have been heard that the novel as a work of art is disappearing and giving place to monographs on given subjects ... the reason is that more and more in our modern age novels are written by woman for women.'[26] Courtney's equivocations on the subject of the New Woman writing, and indeed women's writing more generally, are based on a masculinist, proto-modernist aesthetic designed to protect English fiction from the destructive incursions of the feminine. Like Waugh, Courtney took the view that the true artist is masculine – even when she is a woman. The test case (as always) is George Eliot, whose genius 'was essentially . . . masculine . . . in no respect characteristically feminine'.[27] On the contrary, 'characteristically feminine' women, with their unruly passions, and their 'passion for detail', lack the 'proper perspective' for true art. The truly artistic mind is neutral, it does not display 'personality' nor 'take sides'.[28] In other words, the true artist, like the male modernist, is aloof, impersonal, paring his finger nails, whereas the New Woman writer is 'self-conscious and didactic', 'she has a particular doctrine or thesis which she desires to expound', and her work is 'strongly tinctured with the elements of her own personality'.[29]

Objectivity versus unruly passions, neutrality versus personality or commitment, perspective versus a passion for the detail. These are some of the oppositions around which theories and practices of fiction in the early twentieth century were defined. As we have seen, these terms enter the debates already gendered.

WRITING MASCULINE

Paradoxically, at the very time when, according to contemporary commentators, fiction was being invaded by women and the feminine, statistics suggest that women were, in fact, being 'edged out' of the high-culture fiction market.[30] Of course there are always at least two ways of interpreting any set of statistics, and I do not wish to become embroiled in the question of the relative numbers of male and female writers actually publishing fiction at the close of the nineteenth and the beginning of the twentieth century. However, in the decades around the turn of the century there were two significant developments in the engendering of modern fiction. The first was the rise, from the late 1880s, of male romance – exotic, adventurous, and/or fantastic stories addressed to a male readership. The second was the attempt to redefine the high-culture novel in terms of what male writers wrote, even when, as in the case of Jamesian aestheticism, it was coded feminine.

KING ROMANCE

[Stevenson's] books are for the most part books without women, and it is not women who fall most in love with them. But Mr. Stevenson does not need, we may say, a petticoat to inflame him.[31]

The benighted regions of the world, occupied by mere natives, offer brilliantly charismatic realms of adventure for white heroes, usually free from the complexities of relations with white women.[32]

The rise of male romance in the 1880s was an attempt by male writers, mainly of a conservative bent, to renovate or reinvigorate fiction. The aim was to provide a solution to the problem posed in H. Rider Haggard's question 'Why do *men* hardly ever read a novel?'[33] The project was to reclaim the middle-brow popular romance from women writers. King Romance was to oust the queens of the circulating library, and both popular and 'serious fiction' was to be rescued from the over-civilized feminization to which it had succumbed. The result was the development by Rider Haggard, G. A. Henty, Robert Louis Stevenson, and Rudyard Kipling (to name only the most well-known exponents) of a masculinist aesthetic of the adventure story, centring on action rather than on reflection and introspection, and on codes of male honour, which were to serve as bulwarks against degenerative feminization. As Rider Haggard's *She* so graphically illustrates, the plots and figures of male romance were also, on occasion, deeply misogynistic, defensive reactions to female power and female sexuality.

The romance project was underwritten by men of letters who acted both as propagandists for the genre and as theorizers of it. George Saintsbury and Andrew Lang, as well as Haggard himself, all produced manifestos for romance in 1887.[34] Indeed, the writers of romance and the defenders of romance seem to have constituted themselves as a distinct literary formation, very much as, later, modernist writers would group together to create the taste by which a particular writer or kind of writing could be read. The group of writers which produced and disseminated male romance is an example of what Eve Segwick has described as a homosocial formation.[35] It was a collaborative and mutually reinforcing network, organized around a desire to confirm masculine values and male bonds, and to resist both feminine values and the sexual and political power of women. It might also be seen as a homoerotic formation in which writers and readers played out their homoerotic desires. Indeed Wayne Koestenbaum has sought to demonstrate that the system of affiliation which produced male romance was precisely such a homoerotic formation in which pairs of male writers working together produced texts which both expressed and concealed their homosexual desire for each other. In *Double Talk* Koestenbaum documents an extensive network of literary collaboration or 'double writing'[36] (full of double homosexual meanings in Koestenbaum's reading) among the practitioners of male romance.

Robert Louis Stevenson, for example, enjoyed the double pleasure of writing both for boys and with a boy in the writing partnership with his stepson Lloyd Osborne which produced *The Wrong Box* (1889), *The Wrecker* (1892), and *The Ebb Tide* (1894). Andrew Lang, after helping Rider Haggard with the planning and revision of several of his romances including *She*, joined with him, in an attempt to flee what Koestenbaum describes as 'an emasculated modernity',[37] as the co-author of *The World's Desire* (1890), a Hellenistic romance about the widowed Odysseus'

wanderings in search of Helen of Troy (a problem in Greek epics to match
J. A. Symonds's suppressed study on homosexuality, 'A Problem in Greek
Ethics'). Whether or not one accepts Koestenbaum's argument that these
collaborations consistently produced a set of 'queer yarns', it is clear that
a concerted process of masculine affiliation was going on in both the
writing and the diffusion of male romance.

The proponents of romance sought to establish its supremacy over
recent feminized fiction by claiming that romance was a primitive
'survival' that had persisted into an over-civilized age. Saintsbury
advocated a 'return to pure romance', and a rejection of 'the more complicated kind of novel . . . [of] minute manners-painting and refined character analysis'.[38] Haggard saw the romance as the repository of fundamental
and enduring human feelings. 'The lover of romance', he wrote, 'is probably coeval with the existence of humanity. So far as we can follow the
history of the world we find traces of and its effects among every people'.[39]
Lang made the case in very similar terms:

> The Coming Man may be bald, toothless, highly 'cultured', and
> addicted to tales of introspective analysis. I don't envy him when he
> has got rid of . . . that survival of barbarism, his delight in the last
> battles of Odysseus . . . I don't envy him the novels he will admire,
> nor the pap on which he will feed . . . Not for nothing did Nature
> leave us all savages under the skin.[40]

Of course, in the novels and tales which Lang and his follows favoured,
white 'savages under the skin' were always superior to the savages whose
skin colour marked them as belonging to the feminized dark races. But
there was always the fear that the white savage would revert to the condition of, or be seduced by, the dark one; 'going native' was a persistent
theme of male romance, from Haggard's *She* to Conrad's *Heart of
Darkness*.

Lang's essay 'Realism and Romance' makes it clear that the rise of
romance was part of a longer-term quarrel with the dominance of realism,
a literary mode which Lang saw as both monotonous and mechanical;
'any clever man or woman may elaborate a realistic novel according to
the rules'.[41] In the 1880s and 1890s male romance was promoted as an
antidote to the degenerative feminization of both the external realism of
the naturalist tradition of Zola, and the interiority of the psychological
realism of George Eliot or Henry James who specialized in 'the microscopic examination of the hearts of young girls'.[42] Both kinds of realism,
Lang argued, tended to foster an unhealthy introspection and unmanli-
ness. Romance, on the other hand, emphasized action, and frankly recognized 'our mixed condition, civilised at the top with the old barbarian
underneath'.[43] Both Lang and Saintsbury employed the rhetoric of degeneration and renovation, and their attendant images of disease and health,

to promote the cause of romance. The degenerative sickness of fiction would only be cured, asserted Saintsbury, when 'we have bathed once more, long and well in the romance of adventure and passion'.[44] Both Saintsbury and Lang thought that, by liberating the imagination from the grip of realism, romance would restore individual and cultural health, and reclaim the novel for art. This quarrel with realism in literature as part of a wider project for the renovation of art was to be continued from two quite different perspectives, and with quite different results, in the contest about the appropriate form for modern writing in the early twentieth century. Realism was rejected as a degenerative mode by masculinist modernists such as Pound, who declared in February 1914 that 'Realism in literature has had its run. For thirty or more years we have had in deluge, the analyses of the fatty degeneration of life . . . we have heard all that the "realists" have to say.'[45] However, perhaps the most famous of the early twentieth-century pronouncements against the realist tradition in fiction is Virginia Woolf's 'Mr Bennett and Mrs Brown', which may be seen in a sense as the manifesto of the new feminine (interior) realism developed by Woolf herself and by Dorothy Richardson in their own attempt to reclaim the novel for art, and also for women.

A final word on collaborating romancers. On the road to modernism Joseph Conrad wrote fictions which closely resembled romances and adventure stories – a resemblance which he was always eager to deny. In 1898 he began collaborating with Ford Madox Ford in the writing of a novel which was titled, unequivocally, *Romance*. John Kemp, the hero of this tale of adventure, leaves his native England in flight from his father, an 'ineffectual' writer, 'powerless and lost in his search for rhymes' who spends his days 'inscribing "ideas" every now and then into a pocket book'.[46] The main part of the narrative relates the young Kemp's violent adventures among the pirates, and ends with his return to England, where he stands trial as a pirate. At the end of the novel the romance hero turns romance narrator as he must tell his story in such a way as to save his life. In the process Kemp's voice is divided into the 'I' who speaks and another 'I' who observes both the speaking 'I', and the judges and court-room audience who listen. The romance hero, the man of action, has become a decentred modernist narrator like the Marlowe of *Heart of Darkness*. The male romancers' project of telling simple manly stories would have seemed to have imploded on its own contradictions.

RECLAIMING THE CULTURAL HIGH GROUND

It has been argued that 'from 1888 through 1917 . . . men were taking over the high-culture novel' in England, and that during this period men 'redefined the nature of a good novel and institutionalized their gains'.[47] Certainly, from the time of George Moore's battles with the circulating libraries (referred to in the first section of this chapter) male novelists and critics were seeking to redefine the nature and status of serious fiction in terms of what they wrote or wished to write. As I have suggested, this process of redefinition was often conducted in terms of sex-wars metaphors, or as a battle about the definition of gender. However, like all cultural changes, this process of the redefinition of fiction was not seamless, and a number of female writers played an important part in it, usually in an oppositional way. I have already discussed the part played by the New Woman writers in challenging existing definitions of fiction. The New Woman fiction was also one of the key sites on which the male redefinition of the high-culture novel was constructed. In the next two chapters I shall consider the part played in the redefinition and remaking of fiction by Virginia Woolf and Dorothy Richardson.

However, in the first two decades of the twentieth century it was largely 'men of letters', and later the professors of the emerging discipline of English (Sir Walter Raleigh and Sir Arthur Quiller-Couch, for example), acting as 'cultural brokers and entrepreneurs',[48] who sought both to set the terms of literary debates and to resolve them according to their standards and values. The male redefinition of the high-culture novel was, like the male romance, at least in part a reaction-formation against the perceived feminine invasion of fiction and the feminization of culture which I have been discussing. The male novelists and critics who sought to define fiction in the late nineteenth and early twentieth centuries entered a field that was perceived either as gendered feminine or as dominated by women and women's issues. So strong was the perceived link between the future of fiction and the future of women that some writers felt obliged to break it. One of the most explicit disavowals of this link is the retrospective one found in E. M. Forster's widely read (and now extraordinarily dated) *Aspects of the Novel* (1927). It comes in the apparently throw-away form of an example. Forster is seeking to develop his own version of Eliot's tradition. Forster's version of the timeless ideal order which Eliot constructs in 'Tradition and the Individual Talent' is a Platonic version of the British Museum Reading Room, a circular room in which all novelists (from whatever period of history) sit together simultaneously writing fiction. It is a timeless world of art in which mere chronology is of no importance. Forster, however, from his own chronological vantage-point in 1927, writes with the enormous condescension of posterity. Like many other men of letters in the universities and elsewhere, he is also concerned to construct a version of 'the tradition' which writes out all but the most exceptional of women.

> If the novel develops, is it not likely to develop along different lines from the British Constitution, or even the Women's Movement? I

say 'even the Women's Movement' because there happened to be a close association between fiction in England and that movement during the nineteenth century – a connexion so close that it has misled some critics into thinking it an organic connexion. As women have bettered their position the novel, they asserted, became better too. Quite wrong.[49]

Whether or not the quality of the novel has improved *pari passu* with improvements in the condition of women, it is certainly the case that, from its inception, the course of fiction has been very closely allied to the condition of women and the cause of woman.

As well as being seen in relation to male writers' responses to the question of woman and to gender issues, the redefinition of fiction in the decades immediately preceding and following the turn of the century also needs to be seen in relation to longer-term changes that were taking place in the organization of the fiction market. The growth of literacy, improved standards of living, and an increase in leisure time led to an exponential expansion of the market for fiction in the late nineteenth century. This was met by a rapid increase in outlets for fiction, and the growth of the syndication of fiction (pioneered by Tillotson's Fiction Bureau in the 1870s) in magazines and an expanding popular press.

There is no more startling phenomenon in the life of today than the enormous increase of journals and newspapers. We have now reached the point where the full effect of national education is being felt. Everyone can read. Books have become cheaper and cheaper. The entire intellectual life of the nation has received an enormous quickening. Hence journals play a part in national life wholly undreamed of in the days when the realm of letters was governed by *The Edinburgh Review* and *Quarterly*.[50]

One result of this expansion was a stratification, fragmentation, and diversification of the fiction market, and of the literary market more generally. This process became even more pronounced in the early decades of the twentieth century. Indeed cultural stratification has come to be regarded as one of the ennabling conditions of modernism, and also one of its defining characteristics.

The little magazine is both a symptom and an agent in this process of cultural stratification. Like Henry Harland's *The Yellow Book* and Arthur Symons's *Savoy* in the 1890s, the little magazine of the early 1900s acted as a forum for experiment and an arbiter of cultural authority. These magazines – Ford Madox Ford's *English Review*, A. R. Orage's *New Age*, Harriet Weaver's and Ezra Pound's the *Egoist*, and later, in the 1920s, T. S. Eliot's *Criterion*, and Middleton Murray's *Adelphi* – each stood for different ideas and had its own distinctive literary agenda (although there was some overlap of interests and personnel), but they were all part of the same cultural formation. On the whole this formation, which was both male dominated and coded masculine, sought to distance itself and the 'literary' from the (feminized) 'debased reading-matter being produced for mass entertainment'.[51] This placing of a *cordon sanitaire* around the domain of literature to keep it free from contamination by the feminized trash of the masses was, of course, an important move in the formation of literary modernism.

The masculine redefinition of fiction in the early twentieth century took many different forms, not all of them in the direction of what we now think of as modernism. Whatever form they took, most of the major developments in writing by men at the turn of the century can be seen as a reaction to (not necessarily against) one or other aspect of the feminization of fiction. For example, the new realism of Wells and Bennett, and (to a lesser extent) Galsworthy, can be seen, in part, as a reaction against the fictional experiments of some of the New Woman writers. As the New Woman writers moved away from realism to experiment with impressionistic, allegorical, and visionary forms in their attempts to represent female interiority, and develop a feminine or feminist aesthetic, some male writers appropriated the discarded feminized form of domestic realism. That composite novelist (and modernist demon) Wells–Bennett–Galsworthy developed a new masculine realism, a forensic, scientific, or sociological realism derived from Zola (particularly in Bennett's case), an 'external realism of accumulated details'.[52] As Virginia Woolf was to argue in her influential rejection of her literary elders, they placed 'enormous stress upon the fabric of things' (*WE* 82), expecting their readers to deduce the nature of its occupants from their descriptions of a house. Bennett's minutely detailed description of the dresser in the Tellwright's kitchen in Chapter Seven of *Anna of the Five Towns* is a case in point, but one which I think gives us cause to question Woolf's dismissal of Bennett. The history of generations of Tellwright women, and the constraining pressure which that history exerts on the life of the current generation, are powerfully suggested by Bennett's description of this 'simple' and 'dignified' piece of furniture whose much-polished surface 'reflected the conscientious labour of generations'.[53] The description of the dresser is not merely a catalogue of details, but is a crucial part of Bennett's evocation of the ordinary tragedy of Anna's life. It is addressed not simply to the reader's eye, but to his or her historical, social, and moral understanding.

Rejecting the move towards interiority in some of the experiments of the 1890s, Wells, Bennett, and Galsworthy returned to the social comprehensiveness and social concern of the Victorian novel, but they also appropriated the journalistic contemporaneity of the more polemical New Woman writers. Wells, in particular (especially after the 1890s), self-consciously resisted experimentation and aestheticism. He claimed that 'the business of a novelist is ... facts',[54] and, in the course of his protracted disagreement about the future of the novel with Henry James, Wells asserted that he would 'rather be called a journalist than an artist'.[55]

Wells, in fact, did not simply react to the New Woman writing; he seems to have been fairly directly influenced by it. His *roman à thèse*, *Ann Veronica* (1909), updates the 1890s' novel of the modern woman and the feminist novel of ideas. Wells's heroine is very much a woman of the first decade of the twentieth century, but his plot is a variant of the 1890s' 'boomerang' plot which retrieves an adventurous or erring heroine and reinserts her into the family. Wells's futuristic science fictions of the 1890s also perhaps owe something to feminist-inspired visionary and utopian fiction (as well as to William Morris and Samuel Butler). *The Island of Dr Moreau* (1896), Wells's own degeneration fantasy, seems to take up several of the concerns of the New Woman novel, not least in its treatment of vivisection and its fascination with the issue of who controls human reproductivity: Dr Moreau dismembers animals in a Frankensteinian attempt to bypass the female rôle in reproduction.

Other experiments of self-consciously feminine and feminist writing, rejected by most 1890s' critics, were nevertheless taken up by male writers. The open ending, which many academic critics see as a distinctively twentieth-century development (notwithstanding the fact that it was used with considerable ingenuity by Thackeray in the nineteenth century), was one of the devices used by New Woman writers to suggest the danger and unknowability of the future that awaits the woman who breaks with the traditional plots of femininity. It also became the standard device for representing the modern hero's break with or alienation from his society, as in the ending of *Sons and Lovers* to take the standard example. Similarly the New Woman writers' fragmentation of the labyrinthine plot of the three-volume novel into a more episodic structure, and their mixing of fictional modes (realism, dream, allegory), provided a model for Lawrence's reworking of the nineteenth-century family saga in *The Rainbow*, and for his development, in *Women in Love*, of a novel form that approximates a nest of short stories (to paraphrase Katherine Mansfield's description of Dorothy Richardson's *Pilgrimage*).

Male short-story writers in particular seem to have taken up the lead provided by some of the New Woman writers. The stories of Lawrence and Joyce, although remarkable, look less startlingly original when read alongside the plotless short fictions and lyrical psychological sketches of Egerton, D'Arcy, Frances E. Huntley (Ethel Colburn Mayne), and Evelyn Sharp. Again I do not seek to make a point about influence, but simply note that the Joycean epiphany and his evocation of the paralysis of Dublin life (in 'Eveline', for example) have their counterparts in the stories of a writer like Egerton. In *Dubliners*, as elsewhere, we are looking at the development and not the beginning of a particular mode of writing.

The *fin de siècle* mysticism and pantheism of some New Woman writers, and their fascination with pagan rituals, also reappear in some of the male short-story writers. The visionary mysticism, Classical settings, and pagan rituals of Mona Caird's *Pathway of the Gods*, for example, are variously echoed in the 'Pan-ridden stories'[56] of numerous other Edwardian writers: writers as different from each other as Henry James, Rudyard Kipling, Maurice Hewlett, G. K. Chesterton, M. R. James, Arthur Machen, and Ford Madox Ford. The mysticism of both the decadents and some of the New Woman writers, and their experiments with the short story and the literary sketch, seem to have made a very strong impression on E. M. Forster. In several of the stories in *The Celestial Omnibus* (published in 1911, but many of the stories date from the early 1900s), restricted, confined, and/or apparently improperly socialized (and hence improperly gendered) young men or boys – such as the 'indescribably repellent' (*CSS* 9) Eustace in 'The Story of a Panic' – are transformed by pagan gods or other supernatural means, and liberated into a new life. Forster's stories repeatedly enact the renovation of, or escape from, a masculinized bourgeois culture, by means of feminine (or at least not conventionally masculine) forces: the god Pan in an Italian setting in 'The Story of a Panic'; the poets of the past in 'The Celestial Omnibus'; the seductive old man with the drink who makes the central character in 'The Other Side of the Hedge' (a parable against Progress) forget 'the destiny of our race' (*CSS* 40), and leave the narrow 'discipline' of the road of ordinary mechanized life to join humanity, or 'all that is left of it' (*CSS* 40).

As the last example might suggest, some of the fiction written by men in the first decades of the twentieth century appropriated the renovatory discourse of both the feminists and the anti-feminists. The idea that women have a sacred mission to mother the race, or to rescue it from decline and/or destruction, is deployed by both Forster and Lawrence. Forster, in his short stories and in his longer fiction, regularly creates female figures or feminized males who act as repositories of threatened human values, and who renew declining or atrophying families or communities. Lawrence, as we shall see in a later chapter, engages with this discourse in an altogether more complex way, and ends by reassigning the renovatory task to the male.

THE NEW FEMININE REALISM

Some people think that women are the cause of modernism, whatever that is.[57]

In the previous section I suggested that male writers at the end of the nineteenth and the beginning of the twentieth centuries sought to redefine fiction in their own terms, and that this process of redefinition was in part a reaction to or against social changes, particularly changes in the roles of women and changing gender relations, and partly a reaction to perceptions about the gender of fiction, or of particular fictional modes. Whether traditionalists of one kind or another, or experimentalists, the writers who were involved in this process of redefinition engaged in complex, often contorted, negotiations with contemporary discourses on gender and also with discourses on and of fiction which were organized in gendered terms. In some cases, I have suggested, this redefinition involved the self-concious rejection of women, the woman's cause, and 'feminine' values, and also of literary forms and modes associated with women or coded feminine. In other cases it involved the (re-)appropriation of forms and modes which had previously been marked as feminine or as effeminately foreign, notably a detailistic realism or forensic naturalism.

The women writers most commonly associated with modernist experimentation in English fiction in the early twentieth century – Dorothy Richardson and Virginia Woolf – were also engaged in their own complex negotiations with the discourses of gender and the gendered discourses of fiction which I have been describing. In their theorizing of fiction and their fictional practice both Richardson and Woolf self-consciously set themselves against established (and for *them* this meant *masculine*) traditions and writing practices, and indeed against specific male writers. Their project, like that of some of the New Woman writers of the 1890s, was to develop a distinctively and self-consciously feminine form of fiction that would enable them, as Richardson put it, to 'think the feminine' and hence rethink the world.

Richardson and Woolf both rejected the external, scientific, objective realism of the mainstream realist novel. They habitually represented this tradition as masculine, although, as I suggested earlier, in the critical discourse of their immediate predecessors its gendering was shifting and unstable. The new feminine realism of Richardson and Woolf was also a rejection of the more specifically masculine 'new realism' of Wells, Galsworthy, and Bennett. Indeed it was Richardson's clearly stated aim to 'produce a feminine equivalent of the current masculine realism' (*P*. i. 9). The new feminine realism of Richardson and Woolf is, then, a new, 'new realism', which continues and develops the impressionistic experiments of some of the New Woman writers of the 1890s. It is a reappropriation of the feminine (or feminized) aesthetic of the detail, but one which reconceives and revalues the detail. It is an interior realism rather than a realism based on the external accumulation of details; an impressionistic realism which was founded on the registering of perceptions rather than on the recording of an inventory. The links between the New Woman and a new realism were emphasized by R. Brimley Johnson in his consideration of *Some Contemporary Novelists (Women)*:

The new woman, the female novelist of the twentieth century has abandoned the old realism. She does not accept *observed* revelation.

She is seeking, with passionate determination, for that Reality which is behind the material, the things that matter, spiritual things, ultimate Truth. And here she finds man an outsider, wilfully blind, purposely indifferent.[58]

In the wake of the feminist intervention in literary studies since the early 1970s many miles of print have been covered in explicating, exploring, and celebrating the new feminine realism of Woolf and Richardson, and latterly of writers like May Sinclair, Sylvia Townsend Warner, and a host of American expatriates in Paris who have been inserted into both the new feminist canon and an expanded (and expanding) canon of modernism. The next two chapters aim to join in that exploration, but to do so by problematizing as well as exploring the project and practice of feminine realism. That the project was bound to be problematic should be evident, I hope, from the foregoing discussion: the new feminine realism was conceived and articulated within a network of intersecting discourses in which the feminine was an extremely problematic and contested term. The attempt to establish a new 'feminine note in fiction' in the first decades of the twentieth century could not be separated from turn-of-the-century histories of fiction and the feminine.

4

Dorothy Richardson: Thinking the Feminine

Most of the prophecies born of the renewed moral visibility of woman, though superficially at war with each other, are united at their base. They meet and sink, in the sands of the assumption that we are, today, confronted with a new species of woman.

Nearly all of the prophets, nearly all of those who are at work constructing, hells or heavens, upon this loose foundation, are men. And their crying up, or down, of the woman of today, as contrasted to the woman of the past, is easily understood when we consider how difficult it is, even for the least prejudiced, to think the feminine past, to escape the images that throng the mind from the centuries of masculine expressiveness on the eternal theme: expressiveness that has so rarely reached beyond the portrayal of woman .... in her moments of relationship to the world as it is known to men.[1]

Virtually everything that Dorothy Richardson wrote was addressed, in one way or another, to the problem of 'thinking the feminine' in the shadow of the 'centuries of masculine expressiveness' in which woman and women had been portrayed solely in relation to 'the world as it is known to men'. Richardson was particularly exercised by the problematic nature of the relationship of the woman artist to dominant, in Richardson's view masculine, traditions of representation. In a *Vanity Fair* article in 1925 she wrote about the stifling effects on women artists of being 'surrounded by masculine traditions'; traditions that were 'based on assumptions that are largely unconscious and whose power of suggestion is unlimited' (GM 422). Recalling her own beginnings as a writer, she emphasized her sense of the irrelevance and inadequacy of masculine traditions and forms as developed by both men and women novelists.

Monstrously, when I began, I felt only that all masculine novels to
date, despite their various fascinations, were somehow irrelevant,
and the feminine ones far too much infl [*sic*] by magic traditions,
and too much set upon exploiting the sex motif as hitherto seen and
depicted by men.[2]

As far as Richardson was concerned there was a more or less total lack
of fit between the female author's vision and desires and the available
forms of fiction.

The material that moved me to write would not fit the framework
of any novel I had experienced. I believed myself to be, even when
most enchanted, intolerant of the romantic and realist novel alike.
Each, so it seemed to me, left out certain essentials and dramatised
life misleadingly. Horizontally. Assembling their characters, the
novelists developed situations, devised events, climax and conclusion.
I could not accept their finalities . . . One was aware of the author
deliberately present telling his tale.[3]

Richardson's essays, and more particularly her massive life-novel in
thirteen chapter-volumes, are an extended argument for what Woolf called
'the difference of view'. 'If women had been the recorders of things from
the beginning,' wrote Richardson, 'it would all have been the other way
round' (*P*. ii. 250). The project of *Pilgrimage* is quite simply to reconfigure the map of fiction. It aims to record the world differently, to show it
the other way round, indeed to turn the dominant system of representation upside-down and inside-out by questioning what had previously been
taken for granted as a given. It also aims to re-evaluate the dominant
system of values. In *Pilgrimage* Richardson has her central character,
Miriam Henderson, repeatedly question the nature and value of the
cultural tradition. But, most importantly, Miriam is used to expose the
cultural tradition as a masculine construct.

'Art,' 'literature,' systems of thought, religions, all the fine products
of masculine leisure that are so lightly called 'immortal.' Who makes
them immortal? A few men in each generation who are in the same
attitude of spirit as the creators, and loudly claim them as humanity's highest spiritual achievement, condoning, in those who produce
them, any failure, any sacrifice of the lives about them, to the
production of these crumbling monuments. (*P*. iv. 93)

Miriam's recognition that 'the Bible is not true; it is a culture (*P*. ii. 99)
is the starting-point for Richardson's elaboration of a series of alternatives
to that culture, in her own book of Miriam. If *Pilgrimage* is the story of
how Miriam becomes a writer, it is also the story of Miriam's becoming

an increasingly resistant reader. It is the history of her learning to read and then to reread the literary and scientific texts of a culture which, as we have seen in earlier sections, habitually represents her – a woman – as a problem to be investigated and as an object of knowledge, rather than as an experiencing subject. Such enlightenment frequently brings despair, especially when Miriam first begins on her journey of learning to read as a woman. 'There was nothing to turn to. Books were poisoned. Art. All the achievements of men were poisoned at the root. The Beauty of nature was tricky femininity' (*P.* ii. 222).

As well as exposing the dominant cultural tradition as a masculine construct, Richardson was equally dismissive of what she saw as masculine modes of perception and representation. She was particularly scathing about the masculine reliance on logic. From her earlier articles in *The Dental Record* (for which she wrote regularly between 1912 and 1922) she articulated a profound hostility to masculine science and to men's 'mental tendency to departmentalize, to analyse, to separate single things from their flowing environment'.[4] Richardson's opposition to science derives from her own tendency towards a turn-of-the century mysticism (one of Nordau's symptoms of degeneration), an Edwardian vitalism, and a belief in the force of 'life' which was also shared by Lawrence and Forster.[5] In Richardson's case 'life' seems to have been the source of consciousness, human identity, and the moral sense. It was also the source of freedom and self-realization. 'Masculine' materialism, science, and logic were, for Richardson, antithetical to life. She put this case forcefully in one of her *Dental Record* 'Comments' on an essay in *Science Progress*, arguing for 'the desirability of substituting "life" direct, first-hand energizing experience, for interest in life, thinking and writing about life'. On the subject of 'life', at least in this essay, Richardson strikes a rather Lawrentian note:

> Every day, every moment is in a new sense a new creation. Only he [*sic*] who lives and reconquers his freedom every day is truly alive and free . . . It is the characteristic vice of the intellect to see the past as a straight line stretching out behind humanity like a sort of indefinite tail. In actual experience it is more like an agglomeration, a vital process of crystallization grouped in and about the human consciousness, confirming and enriching human experience.[6]

The structure and organization of *Pilgrimage*, and the texture of its language, are designed as part of a self-conscious attempt to substitute ' "life" direct, first hand energizing experience', in the form of 'an agglomeration, a vital process of crystallization grouped in and about the human consciousness', for the more ratiocinative or scientific ways of 'thinking and writing about life' which Richardson found in scientific discourse and the current masculine realism. In addition, Richardson's heroine and textual centre of consciousness, Miriam Henderson, repeatedly rejects the masculine imagination, men's categorizing, hierarchizing, materialistic minds, and their 'absence of personality' (P. iii. 280). In Richardson's novel all of these characteristics are presented as givens, which are integral to the masculine condition. They are, it would appear, part of the essential nature of men. They are 'original. Belonging to maleness; to Adam with his spade; lonely in a universe of things' (P. iii. 280). Miriam, like Richardson, attributes this existential masculine loneliness to men's inability to live in the present moment, to their preoccupation with becoming rather than being, and their inability to take in the multiplicity and flux of experience.

> It is man, puzzled, astray, always playing with breakable toys, lonely and terrified in his universe of chaotic forces, who is pitiful. The chaos that torments him is his own rootless self . . . Men . . . never *are*. They only make or do; unconscious of the quality of life as it passes . . . Men have no present; except sensuously. That would explain their *ambition*. (P. iii. 280–1)

Women, on the other hand, are in Richardson's view more concerned with being than becoming. Women can 'hold all opinions at once, or any, or none' (P. iii. 259). They supposedly see 'everything simultaneously'. Women 'see in terms of life', men see 'in terms of things, because their lives are passed among scraps' (P. iii. 393). Women, as conceived by Richardson, are thus not simply different from men, they are superior. They are vital, supra-rational, intuitive, synthesizers. These powers are apparently innate, part of woman's nature, but they are not universally found in women since individual women can be 'warped into seeing only one thing at a time. Scientifically. They are freaks' (P. iii. 393). This conception of the feminine clearly owes a great deal to nineteenth-century discourses on woman, and particularly to the feminist reworking of the Victorian ideal of the spiritually superior maternal womanly woman. I will return to some of the problems this raises shortly.

As well as rejecting generalized masculine traditions and modes of perception, Richardson, like Woolf, also defined her own thinking about fiction in relation to specific male writers. This relationship was usually, although not exclusively, an oppositional one. Richardson thought highly of both Joseph Conrad and Henry James amongst the older generation of novelists, despite what she felt to be their rather restrictive reliance on character. As Michèle Barrett and Jean Radford have pointed out, Richardson inclined to the Jamesian side in the 'debate on saturation versus selection which took place between James and H. G. Wells in 1914–15'.[7] In her Foreword to the 1938 edition of *Pilgrimage* Richardson acknowledged James's claim to be considered as a 'pathfinder', 'a far from inconsiderable technical influence' on the development of the new novel (as practised by herself, James Joyce, and Virginia Woolf). But (in a sentence of Jamesian intricacy) she also criticized the limitations of this 'charmed and charming high priest of nearly all the orthodoxies', who inhabited

> a softly lit enclosure he mistook, until 1914, for the universe, and celebrated by evolving, for the accommodation of his vast tracts of urbane commentary, a prose style demanding, upon the first reading, a perfection of sustained concentration akin to that which brought it forth, and bestowing, again upon the first reading, the recreative delights peculiar to this form of spiritual exercise. (*P*. i. 11)

James is also one of the novelists against whom Miriam defines her sense of the novel's possibilities in *Pilgrimage*. Miriam thinks that she has found in James's *The Ambassadors* 'the first completely satisfying way of writing a novel', but ultimately she is repelled by the intrusiveness of his style and of the point-of-view technique, by the 'monstrous illuminated pride' of the author: 'Pride in discovering the secrets of his technique. Pride in watching it labour with the developments of the story' (*P*. iii. 409).

But perhaps the most important sounding-board on which Richardson defined her own thinking about fiction was H. G. Wells, whom she first met in 1896, and who was for a time her mentor and lover. It was Wells's fictional practice against which Richardson began to define her own conception of the differences between masculine and feminine realism in fiction. Thus, in an early review in *Crank*, Richardson praised Wells's *In The Days of the Comet* as being a marked improvement on his previous fiction. He had, she argued, moved beyond the more facile fiction of criticism and analysis which marked the period of his 'exuberant career among things'.[8]

> He has discovered humanity. There is, in this new book, an emotional deepening, a growth of insight and sympathy . . . there is for the first time that indefinable quality that fine literature always yields, that sense of a vast something behind the delicate fabric of what is articulated – a portentous silent reality. (*GM* 400)

Whether or not Wells deserves the accolade, he is here being credited with at least partial success in achieving the end which Richardson was to set herself: the task of finding a fictional form in which to articulate that numinousness, that immaterial reality that she finds essential to 'fine literature', and which she comes to associate particularly with a feminine fictional practice.

Wells appears in *Pilgrimage* as Hypo Wilson, Miriam's lover, and even more importantly, her intellectual sparring partner on a wide range of subjects, on which they take up almost diametrically opposed positions: science, rationalism, materialism, religion, mysticism, evolution, literature, and so on. Richardson's technique of ventriloquism is particularly effective in this case. Like everything else in the novel sequence, Hypo's words are mediated through Miriam's consciousness, in the form of recollected dialogues. The reader thus has the illusion of experiencing at first hand the full force of Hypo's masculine authority (underlined by his habitual finger-stabbing gesture), and is given direct access to the personal and cultural obstacles that have to be negotiated by the woman whose experience of the world does not fit the world as found in masculine representations. In particular the reader is given a powerful impression of the problems confronted by the woman who wishes to write, and thus make representations of her own.

Pilgrimage is, among other things, a novel about its own genesis. It is a novel about the making of a woman novelist and about her redefinition of the available forms of fiction. All of these things are represented in terms of opposition to and negotiation of dominant traditions and dominant forms of representation which are coded masculine and often represented in the text by particular male figures, particularly Hypo. In the course of Miriam's progress towards her goal of being a writer, Hypo is used by Richardson to demonstrate various manoeuvres in that well-known game 'how to suppress women's writing'. For example, he claims to know the nature and extent of Miriam's powers, and attempts to impose that 'knowledge' on her as the truth: 'You're not creative. You've got a good sound mind, a good style, and a curious critical perception. You'll be a critic' (*P*. iii. 369–70). (In fact, Wells had initially discouraged Richardson from writing fiction and encouraged her instead to write literary sketches for the *Saturday Review*.) Elsewhere Miriam's fiction-writing ambitions, and her search for an alternative to masculine traditions of fiction, are represented, in part, through her grappling with Hypo's views of the relationship of women to fiction, as in the following dialogue.

> 'Perhaps the novel's not your form. Women ought to be good novelists. But they write best about their own experiences. Love-affairs and so forth. They lack imagination.'
>   'Ah, imagination. Lies.'
>   'Try a novel of ideas. Philosophical. There's George Eliot.'
>   'Writes like a man.'
>   'Just so, Lewes. Be a feminine George Eliot. Try your hand.'
> (*P*. iv. 240)

Here Wilson reproduces one of the leading assumptions of the nineteenth-century debates about women and fiction – that women lack imagination – and offers the aspiring woman writer the choice between writing the 'Silly Novels by Lady Novelists' castigated by George Eliot, and being George Eliot, the novelist of ideas in the high realist mode. 'You have in your hands material for a novel,' Hypo advises, 'a dental novel, a human novel and, as to background, a complete period, a period of unprecedented expansion in all sorts of directions ... you ought to document your period' (P. iv. 397). Miriam's response to Hypo's various pieces of advice is to question his notion of imagination ('Lies'), and to place (and reject) George Eliot as merely a ventriloquist of masculine language. Her most important response, however, it to learn to write as a woman, as she herself defines that term, and to become the kind of writer who could write a novel like *Pilgrimage*, which is, among other things, a very thorough documentation of its period, and particularly of what it was like to be a certain kind of woman in that period.

In fact Miriam's progress as a writer is continually impeded by the inadequacy of existing models and unhelpful advice of Hypo and other men. One of Miriam's false starts as a writer of fiction is attributed to another man's advice that women write best about their own experiences. Like the scene with Hypo quoted above, this episode is used to contrast two different versions of 'women's writing' – the conventional view of women's fiction as a restricted form, and the barely articulable view of women's writing as a form which has yet to be discovered.

> It was Bob, driving so long ago a little nail into her mind when he said, 'Write the confessions of a modern woman,' meaning a sensational chronicle with an eye, several eyes, upon the interest of sympathetic readers like himself – 'Woman, life's heroine, the dear exasperating creature – who really likes to see how life looks from the other side, the women's side, who put me on the wrong track and created all those lifeless pages. Following them up, *everything would be left out that is always there*, preceding and accompanying and surviving the drama of human relationships ... (P. iv. 525; emphasis added)

Richardson, of course, seeks to write about how life really looks from the other side, about a woman's and indeed women's 'own experiences', experiences that comprehend far more than simply 'love-affairs and so forth'. *Pilgrimage* is founded on the authority of a specifically feminine experience, and on the authority of feminine (or even female) subjectivity. This authority, too, is defined in opposition to the more insistent authority of Hypo's masculine observing, classifying, analysing, and ordering objectivity. Indeed in *Pilgrimage* the authority of feminine experience is defined and established in terms of a tense contest in which the woman only resists subordination both to and by masculine discourses by giving herself up to inner energies which demand articulation, and which are represented as the authentic form of feminine expression.

> The joy of making statements not drawn from things heard or read but plumbed *directly from the unconscious accumulations of her*

own experience was fermented by the surprise of his [Hypo's] increased attention, and the pride of getting him occasionally to accept an idea or to modify a point of view. It beamed compensation for what she was losing in sacrificing, whenever expression was urgent in her, his unmatchable monologue to *her own shapeless outpourings*. But she laboured, now and then successfully, to hold this emotion in subjection to the urgency of the things she longed to express (*P.* iii. 255; emphasis added)

In this passage, as elsewhere throughout *Pilgrimage* and in many of her essays, Richardson develops a theory of radical sexual difference, a sexual difference grounded not simply in biology but also in language and representation, or what Lacan calls the Symbolic Order. In the world, according to Miriam, 'by every word they use men and women mean different things' (*P.* iv. 93); men and women simply 'speak different languages' (*P.* ii. 210).

An important part of Richardson's project in *Pilgrimage* is to engage with the problems which arise for men and women, but especially for women, in a culture in which the man's meaning is the dominant one. This can be illustrated at a local level by returning the short quotations given above to their contexts. The first quotation occurs in an exchange between Miriam and Michael Guerini which both asserts and is designed to demonstrate or enact the difficulty of unthinking or thinking outside representation (Miriam's is the first voice):

'The thing most needed is for men to *recognise* their illusion . . . They seem incapable of unthinking the centuries of masculine attempts to represent women only in relation to the world as known to men.'
    It was then he was angry.
    'How else shall they be represented?'
    'They *can't* be represented by men. Because by every word they use men and women mean different things. (*P.* iv. 93).

The continuation of the second quotation above adds to the assertion of the fundamental difference between masculine and feminine meanings, the suggestion of the different status of that difference.

In speech with a man a woman is at a disadvantage – because they speak different languages. She may understand his. Hers he will never speak or understand. In pity, or from other motives, she must therefore, stammeringly, speak his. He listens and is flattered and thinks he has her mental measure when he has not even touched the fringes of her consciousness. (*P.* ii. 210)

Richardson's novel makes it quite clear that she is writing about radical sexual difference within a pattern of domination and subordination. The apparently unending flow of *Pilgrimage*, its resistance of closure, is one of the ways in which Richardson attempts to combat this pattern. Miriam's pilgrimage is another; it is, in part, a quest undertaken to find a way of thinking outside this pattern, to find another way of thinking the feminine, of becoming what Hélène Cixous calls a 'newly born woman'. 'There was a woman, not this thinking self who talked with men in their own language, but one whose words could be spoken only from the heart's knowledge, waiting to be born in her' (*P.* iv. 230). As we have already seen, like some more recent attempts to rethink representation and the feminine, Richardson attempts to combat the pattern of dominance and subordination within which she finds herself by reversing it. In doing so Richardson inevitably reproduces the binarism of the dominant discourses on masculinity and femininity. She simply (though perhaps one should not underestimate the importance of this move) transvalues the terms, rather as recent French theorists of the feminine have done. In the newly born world envisaged by Richardson the inclusivity of feminine multiplicity and flow (the 'shapeless outpourings of women') is valued more highly than the consolations of masculine form and order which, ultimately (in Richardson's view), prove unsatisfactory:

> It is because ... men write so well that it is a relief, from looking and enduring the clamour of the way things state themselves from several points of view simultaneously, to read their *large superficial statements*. Light seems to come ... *But the after reflection is gloom, a poisoning gloom over everything.* (*P.* iii. 275; emphasis added)

Richardson's fictional and her non-fictional writings thus work within, but also rework the late nineteenth-century discourses on gender that I examined earlier in this study. In some of her journalistic pieces Richardson intervened directly in the debates on the feminine and femininism, and degeneration and renovation that I discussed earlier. An examination of one of those interventions will serve to suggest the extent to which she began to think beyond late nineteenth-century discourses on gender and sexual difference, and the extent to which she continued to work within them. In her 1924 essay in *Vanity Fair*, 'Women and the Future', she neatly and wittily summed up the current state of discursive play by summarizing a variety of (male) ways of conceptualizing woman. First, there is the Wellsian view which looks forward to 'the emergence of an army of civilized, docile women, following modestly behind the vanguard of males at work upon the business of reducing chaos to order' (*GM* 413). A second group of thinkers 'sees the world in process of feminization, the savage wilderness where men compete and fight, turned into a home'. To a third group, 'feminism is the invariable accompaniment of degeneration'. This last group draws back 'in horror before the oncoming flood of mediocrity ... a democratized world, overrun by hordes of inferior beings, organized by majorities for material ends; with primitive, uncivilizable woman rampant in the midst' (*GM* 413).

Richardson's summary is based on a perceptive analysis of recent and current debates on women and the discourse in which those debates were conducted. But she *reproduces* as well as *analyses* this discourse in her own survey of modern women when she distinguishes between a more or less disparaged 'growing army of *man-trained* women, brisk, positive, rational creatures with no nonsense about them, *living from the bustling surfaces* of the mind; sharing the competitive partisanships of men', and the supremely centred 'womanly woman' who 'lives, all her life, in the *deep current of eternity*, an individual, self-centred' (*GM* 413; emphases added). As we have seen earlier, the turn-of-the-century womanly woman was a concept which meant different, often contradictory, things to different people (or even to the same people). She was the earth mother or the mother of Empire, the pacifist or the (militaristic) patriot, the reformer of the family and purifier of men and/or the feminist/suffragist. In 'Women and the Future' Richardson, too, is ambivalent about the meaning and future role of the womanly woman. This ambivalence is partly a function of Richardson's own discourse. Her essays, like her fiction, are polyvocal. She has a habit of ventriloquizing a series of views on a given subject and setting them in opposition to each other, so that it is difficult to see where she herself stands. Indeed, the taking of sides would seem to be a suspect activity to Richardson. It is an activity which belongs to the limited and partial vision of the masculine order. Although Richardson writes on feminist issues, she nevertheless distances herself and her fictional protagonist from specific feminist campaigns and positions. Miriam, for example, regards female suffrage and the political emancipation of women as irrelevances. The political commitment involved in voting and political activism are seen as antithetical to those distinctive female qualities, the ability to see everything at once, and to synthesize.

Despite her ambivalence, Richardson, I think, does seek to reappropriate the late nineteenth-century belief in the superiority of the womanly woman for her own kind of feminism, and for her own theory of fiction. Richardson's version of the womanly woman in 'Women and the Future' has many of the qualities that are valorized in *Pilgrimage*. She is self-conscious, centred in the self, intuitive, associative, thinks through her feelings, and has a vital connection with the forces of her life.

> Because she is one with life, past, present, and future are together in her, unbroken. Because she thinks flowingly, with her feelings, she is relatively indifferent to the fashions of men ... Only completely self-centred consciousness can attain to unselfishness – the celebrated unselfishness of the womanly woman. (*GM* 413)

In her attempts to rethink 'woman' in her modernist novel sequence Richardson revisits the fictional terrain of the *fin de siècle*, and in particular the ground occupied by the New Woman writers. Egerton is, in many ways, the most obvious point of comparison, although the gargantuan dimensions of Richardson's novel sequence, and its inability to end, might also be compared with both Sarah Grand's massive fictions, and Olive Schreiner's large-scale (if more modest than Richardson's) and apparently unfinishable fictional projects. *Pilgrimage* certainly starts from Egerton's founding assumption, that the woman novelist's concern should be with 'the *terra incognita* of herself, as she knew herself to be, not as men like to imagine her'.[9] Both Richardson and Egerton strive for an inner, psychological realism, and use an associative, impressionistic technique, and both use their central female character as the fictional point of view. However, Richardson's most important point of contact with the New Woman fiction is precisely that she *revisits* its preoccupations and makes them part of her own subject-matter. *Pilgrimage* explores, among other things, the 'shadows' cast by 'Nietzsche, the problem of free love, the challenge of Weiniger [*sic*], the triple tangle of art, sex, and religion' (*P.* iii. 482). As Jean Radford points out, *Pilgrimage* is a historical novel. The New Woman fiction, the discourse within which it was produced, and the debates into which it intervened are part of the history which Richardson's novel sequence both records and interrogates. *Pilgrimage* rereads the last decade of the nineteenth and the first decade of the twentieth century from several different perspectives in the 1920s, 1930s, and later, and does so 'through the new discourses about women and femininity produced after the First World War – discourses which were not available to Miriam, nor to Egerton'.[10]

The effects of these multiple perspectives and the constantly changing historical ground are complex. They certainly play an important part in complicating the novel's perspective on gender. In the course of Richardson's mammoth novel sequence the reader repeatedly encounters, as some of my earlier examples will have indicated, what appears to be essentialist statements about male/masculine traditions, language, or modes of perception and representation, and about the differences in masculine and feminine modes of perception. Moreover, as I have suggested, because *Pilgrimage* depicts its central character in the process of defining herself in opposition to dominant assumptions which she perceives to be male and masculinist, there is a sense in which the novel becomes locked into the conventional male/female binarism. However, partly through its representation of sexual difference as an effect of the symbolic order, partly through its representation of Miriam's interrogation and relativization of masculine culture and modes of perception, and partly through the various means by which it focuses on different and changing ways of conceptualizing and representing woman, *Pilgrimage* puts gender categories into question. If ' "Art", "literature", systems of thought, religions' (*P.* ii. 280) are simply the self-perpetuating tradition of a few like-thinking men, rather than the aesthetic and moral absolutes they claim to be, then so are the available definitions of gender.

Gender categories and gender boundaries are further problematized by the way in which Miriam herself is repeatedly represented as occupying an unconventional gender position. Miriam is portrayed as disrupting or breaking out of conventional feminine boundaries. She crosses that threshold that conventionally contained middle-class women within the household in a world of domestic protection and becomes a city streetwalker. Her marginal class position as a daughter of a feckless middle-class father whose bankruptcy compels her to earn her own living releases her from the domestic interior to the streets, not as a fallen woman, but as a liberated woman. Richardson's female protagonist is also portrayed as occupying a range of masculine identifications. From early childhood she colludes with her family in occupying the masculine identification of the brother/son that her family of daughters and sisters lacked, and she identifies with her father's misogynistic perspective.

> Pater knew how hateful all the world of women were and despised them.
> He never included her with them; or only sometimes when she pretended, or he didn't understand . . . (P. i. 22)

At other times Miriam sees herself as a member of an intermediate sex, 'something between a man and a woman; looking both ways' (P. ii. 187). As in the case of Edward Carpenter's 'Intermediate Sex', Miriam's ambivalent and shifting gender identifications become a route to the rethinking and redefining of gender roles. The position of 'woman' is thus revealed as precisely that, just a position which the individual woman may choose or refuse to occupy. The category of 'woman' is provisional and subject to change. *Pilgrimage* enacts the ways in which the category definition can be changed, and the ways in which different feminine subject positions can be taken up. At the same time, however, its depiction of Miriam's struggles enacts the real, material and ideological constraints on the individual woman's freedom to manœuvre.

In Richardson's case, as in the case of some of the New Woman writers, the project of redefining and remaking woman goes hand in hand with the project of renovating fiction. Richardson's novel sequence and her heroine's life are constructed as a questing journey. Both the life story (Miriam's life) and the story of that life (the narrative of *Pilgrimage*) are stories which cross lines and boundaries of various kinds. The heroine is portrayed as a thought-adventurer, living at the limits of experience, and the narrative which relates her pilgrimage tests the limits of narrative form and of genre. Richardson's experimentation with genre, narrative form, and language were undertaken out of a desire to remake the novel for and from a female perspective, and not simply out of a desire to make it new. It was, as Jean Radford has argued, 'not modernist-for-modernism's sake', but a gender-motivated attempt to 'find alternatives to a masculinist discourse'.[11]

Pilgrimage disrupts genre boundaries and resists classification. Is it fact or fiction? Is it philosophy, psychology, autobiography, poetry, or a novel? Is it one novel or several novels? Is it a *Bildungsroman* or a *Künstlerroman*? Richardson's novel sequence also disrupts existing narrative conventions. It resists linear plot, which Richardson equates with a masculinist hierarchizing and ordering, and which she finds incapable of rendering the 'essential', the 'unexpressed mass' of 'first hand life'. In 1909 Richardson wrote that she felt 'choked by the necessities of narrative. Close narrative too technical, dependent on a whole questionable set of agreements & assumptions between reader and writer.'[12] In the Foreword which she wrote for the first four-volume edition of *Pilgrimage* in 1938 she emphasized the exhilaration of moving beyond the 'necessities of narrative'. *Pointed Roofs* was, she says, 'written to the accompaniment of a sense of being upon a fresh pathway'. The abandonment of linear narrative is part of the process by which Richardson developed a form of writing that would not merely *record* reality, but would *discover* it.

Richardson's disruption of language, and especially her departures from conventional punctuation, are also part of an attempt to free herself and her text from what she perceived to be the choking constriction of the masculine order and the tyranny of the authoritative, always interpreting, male voice. 'A man's reading', she writes in *Pilgrimage*, 'was not a reading; not a looking and a listening', but always 'an assertion of himself'. Men read 'as if they were the authors of the text', and in such a way as to suggest how the text should be read (*P.* ii. 261). Richardson's views on modern punctuation take us back to nineteenth-century theories of linguistic degeneration. She argues that modern punctuation, and hence modern writing, are based on this masculine reading practice, which has 'devitalized the act of reading' and 'tended to make it less organic, more mechanical'. In her essay 'About Punctuation' she recommends, instead, the liberating pleasures of 'the slow, attentive reading demanded by unpunctuated texts'. In such a reading, she argues, 'the faculty of hearing has its chance, is enhanced until the text *speaks* itself'.[13]

Richardson's linguistic theory and her writing practice are based on the vitalism which is espoused and argued for in all of her work. She wishes to restore the vital force of the human voice to a written language which, in her view, has degenerated to the state of a merely efficient and superficial instrument of communication. In short she wishes to restore to the disembodied process of reading the physical exchange of speaking and listening. Participation, listening, exchange, the sharing of the making of meanings – these are Richardson's avowed priorities in the processes of writing and reading. Both Richardson and her heroine regarded these activities as feminine practices and the defining characteristics of a feminine realism.

|5|

Virginia Woolf: Rethinking Realism, Remaking Fiction

The habit of continually measuring women's wants by men's achievements seems out of date, ignominious, and intolerably boring. 'Here we have a world', we say, 'which has been shaped by men to fit their own needs. It is on the whole a poor sort of world ... Now that we have secured possession of the tools of citizenship, we intend to use them not to copy men's models but to produce our own.'[1]

Virginia Woolf's writing life was a prolonged dialogue with herself and others about the nature and possibilities of fiction. Like Henry James, Woolf saw the future of fiction as inextricably connected with the future of women. More particularly she saw it as linked to changing attitudes to sex gender roles, to the changing of women's attitudes to men, to themselves, and to other women. As Woolf told the female audience of the lecture that became *A Room of One's Own*, 'Women are hard on women. Women dislike women.' Most importantly Woolf linked the future of fiction to the changing of men's attitudes to women.

> The future of fiction depends very much upon what extent men can be educated to stand free speech in women ... But whether men can be civilised ... whether given a better environment the results might be such that women too can be artists lies on the lap of the Gods, no not upon the laps of the Gods, but upon your laps, upon the laps of professional women.[2]

Woolf's writing life was also a continual process of development and innovation in fictional practice. This was a process which involved both a series of experiments with new fictional forms and a reworking of the traditional forms of fiction – in the latter case most notably in her reworking of the 'feminine' form of the family chronicle in *The Years*. As in the case of Richardson, the cultural norms and literary forms with which Woolf engaged, and which she sought to interrogate, were perceived as masculine. Woolf, like Richardson, argued that the old masculine forms of fiction were inadequate and outmoded. She even, on occasion, suggested that the English language itself had become an inadequate vehicle for rendering the complex subtleties and nuances of modern experience because it had degenerated from its former richness.

> In the old days . . . when English was a new language, writers could invent new words and use them. Nowadays it is easy enough to invent new words – they spring to the lips whenever we see a new sight or feel a new sensation – but we cannot use them because the language is old . . . In order to use new words properly you would have to invent a new language. ('Craftsmanship', *CDML* 141)

Throughout her writings on fiction Woolf emphasized the importance, even urgency, of the project of remaking or renovating the language and the forms of fiction. She particularly emphasized the importance of opening up new areas to representation, and of representing more truthfully what had hitherto been misrepresented. As she famously asserted in 'Mr Bennett and Mrs Brown' (1924), the 'tools and established conventions' which did the 'business' of fiction for the Edwardians were 'ruin' and 'death' to writers, like herself, who wished to extend the franchise of fiction and increase its range of representation.

In her deliberations of her own writing practice in her diaries, and more especially in her analyses of the current state of fiction and her prognostications on its future in her reviews and essays, Woolf constantly focused on the connections between gender and writing. She discussed writing in gendered terms, and, on occasions (although by no means consistently), asserted a belief in the necessity to engender a new kind of fiction by gendering writing differently. Dorothy Richardson's fictional experiments clearly formed an important part of the context in which Woolf formulated her own renovatory project for fiction. Woolf reviewed both *The Tunnel* and *Revolving Lights* (parts 4 and 7 of *Pilgrimage*) in terms which indicate that she regarded Richardson as a significant, if flawed, contributor to the engendering of modern fiction. Four of the chapter-volumes of *Pilgrimage*, Woolf's own review of *The Tunnel*, and May Sinclair's essay on 'The Novels of Dorothy Richardson'[3] had already appeared by April 1919, when Woolf published her essay on 'Modern Novels' in *The Times Literary Supplement*. Slightly revised in 1925, and retitled as 'Modern Fiction', this essay became one of the key documents in the theorizing of modern and modernist fiction.

'Modern Fiction', like 'Mr Bennett and Mrs Brown', is in part an analysis of the ills of the 'current masculine realism' beyond which Richardson sought to move in *Pilgrimage*. When Woolf surveyed the scene of contemporary fiction in these two essays she found a traditional and an experimental or innovatory fictional practice which were both disappointing in different ways. In these essays Woolf connects the failings of both traditionalists and innovators with their definition and practice of realism, and with their attitude to and use of the detail. In the end, as far as Woolf was concerned, both traditionalists and modernists were in danger of sinking in a sea of detail, clinging to a heap of fragments.

The traditionalists, represented in both essays by Bennett, Galsworthy, and Wells, are found wanting because of their materialism. In 'Modern Fiction' Woolf glosses this as a laborious inventorizing of external details and a failure to select: 'they write of unimportant things . . . they spend immense skill and immense industry making the trivial and the transitory appear the true and the enduring' (*CDML* 7). Enslaved by outmoded conventions, the materialists labour in vain to represent the totality of outer, external details; they fail to 'look within', and meanwhile 'life escapes' (*CDML* 8).

> Whether we call it life or spirit, truth or reality, this, the essential thing has moved off, or on, and refuses to be contained any longer in such ill-fitting vestments as we provide . . . So much of the enormous labour of proving the solidity, the likeness to life, of the story is not merely labour thrown away but labour misplaced to the extent of obscuring and blotting out the light of the conception. (*CDML* 8)

What is this 'life' that evades the documenting eye of the materialists? It is a semi-mystical concept. It is hardly susceptible of definition, but can perhaps be explained by analogy. 'Life' is that Wordsworthian sense of 'something far more deeply interfused' ('Tintern Abbey'). It is 'the relation between man and his circumambient universe, at the living moment' which D. H. Lawrence argued, in 'Morality and the Novel', it was the duty of the novel to capture (*Px* 527). 'Life', as one suffragette slogan put it, 'is feminine'.[4] It would appear that 'life' was also gendered feminine for Dorothy Richardson. 'Life' is that deeper, inner ('true') reality which Richardson was seeking to capture by means of her associative 'feminine realism' in her vast book of life. For Woolf 'life' is that sudden epiphanic glimpse into the heart of things that some of her characters (usually a female or feminized character) attain, and which she attempts to articulate in her experiments with fictional form. In her essay on 'Life and the Novel', 'life' is a seductive, disruptive, and elusive woman, who would appear to be in need of masculine control.

Stridently, clamorously, life is forever pleading that she is the proper end of fiction and that the more he sees of her and catches of her the better his book will be. She does not add, however, that she is grossly impure; and that the side she flaunts uppermost is often, for the novelist, of no value whatever. Appearance and movement are the lures she trails to entice him after her, as if these were her essence, and by catching them he gained his goal. (CE ii. 135)

Like nineteenth-century critiques of realism, Woolf's writings on fiction constantly (sometimes playfully, sometimes anxiously) probe the relationship between depth and surface, and it would appear from this example that they do so in similarly gendered terms.

Despite her strictures on the laborious detailism of the materialists, Woolf's theorizing of fiction is not posited on a hostility to the accumulation of details in itself. She does not appear to think, for example, that a profusion of details inevitably annihilates 'life'. Indeed, she is constantly preoccupied with the problem of developing an aesthetic form that could capture the details of the 'myriad impressions' that the mind receives, and which constitute 'life'. With this end in view Woolf advocates a writing practice that would focus on a different kind of detail, and which would dispose or display the detail in a different manner and a different structure from that of the materialists. She requires less of the representational conventions of realism and more of the texture of modern reality as experienced by her readers, who, in the space of the average day, have had 'thousands of ideas' coursing through their brains, and in whom 'thousands of emotions have met, collided, and disappeared in astonishing disorder' ('Mr Bennett and Mrs Brown', WE 86). More particularly Woolf requires a new or modern form of realism, a realism which would record not merely external details (as the Edwardian materialists did), but which would also record how the individual mind perceives and orders those details. In 'Modern Fiction' Woolf uses her quarrel with the materialists as a means of formulating a new psychological realism which would 'record the atoms as they fall upon the mind in the order in which they fall', and 'trace the pattern, however disconnected and incoherent in appearance, which each sight or incident scores upon the consciousness' (CDML 9).

The passage in 'Modern Fiction' in which Woolf formulated her aesthetic of the detail is one of the most frequently quoted in all of her writings, and has become almost a manifesto of modernism. Despite its (over)familiarity, it is worth quoting again, because it reveals some of the ambivalences and contradictions of Woolf's position. These ambivalences and contradictions are partly (perhaps largely) the product of the critical discourse within which Woolf is seeking to articulate her own position.

Examine for a moment an ordinary mind on an ordinary day. The mind receives a myriad impressions . . . From all sides they come, an

incessant shower of innumerable atoms; and as they fall, as they
shape themselves into the life of Monday or Tuesday, the accent falls
differently from of old; the moment of importance came not here
but there; so that, if a writer were a free man and not a slave, if he
could write what he chose, not what he must, if he could base his
work upon his own feeling and not upon convention, there would
be no plot, no comedy, no tragedy, no love interest or catastrophe
in the accepted style, and perhaps not a single button sewn on as
the Bond Street tailors would have it. Life is not a series of gig-lamps
symmetrically arranged; life is a luminous halo, a semi-transparent
envelope surrounding us from the beginning of consciousness to the
end. Is it not the task of the novelists to convey this varying, this
unknown and uncircumscribed spirit ... (*CDML* 8)

For Woolf the strength (but also, as we shall see, the weakness) of the
break with the conventions of realistic representation, and the development of alternative, 'modern' tools by Joyce and Richardson, lie precisely
in their ability to give the reader the impression of the flux of experience.
It lies in their ability 'to convey this varying ... unknown and uncircumscribed spirit'; 'to register one after another, and one on top of another,
words cries, shouts, notes of a violin, fragments of lectures' (*WE* 16).

It is very easy to read the *locus classicus* of 'Modern Fiction' simply as
an example of the modernist discourse of rupture, as an unequivocal
exhortation to the modern writer to break with the past and to abandon
traditional aesthetic modes and forms. Indeed in the passage in question
Woolf rejects a whole tradition of detailistic, realistic representation,
which, she suggests, is as anachronistic as the lamps of horse-drawn
carriages which they symmetrically arrange. In its place Woolf offers a
blend of scientific modernity (the atoms of particle physics), a modern
Bergsonian sense that it was no longer possible to think in terms of a fixed
identity or a common reality,[5] and a Georgian version of Edwardian vitalism. In her reflections on her own writing practice Woolf sought a fictional
form which would replace the profusion of details found in the materialists (a saturation of details) with a saturation of the detail. A form that
would 'saturate every atom ... eliminate all waste, deadness, superfluity
... give the moment whole ... This appalling narrative business of the
realist: getting on from lunch to dinner ... is false, unreal, merely conventional' (*WD* 139). However, to read 'Modern Fiction' simply in terms of
the modernist discourse of rupture is to misread it, since it is as much a
story of negotiating tradition as it is a narrative of rupture. Woolf's
utopian aspirations for fictional form are mixed with a strong streak of
realism. She fiercely resists the disabling force of the status quo, but she
never underestimates its power: '*if* a writer were a free man and not a
slave, *if* he could base his work upon his own feeling and not upon
convention ... '. In 'Modern Fiction' Woolf articulates her sense of the

need to break with and think outside existing conventions, but she also sees the difficulties of doing so. She addresses the problem of articulating the fragmentary multiplicity of experience, but she also problematizes 'experience', suggesting that it is always mediated by the conventions of representation. Her sense of the coercive power of representational conventions and their ability to enforce a common-sense view of the world is indicated in the example she gives in 'Mr Bennett and Mrs Brown' – interestingly an example which focuses on the perception of sexual difference – of how 'the public' will 'actually learn to see women with tails and men with humps' if told 'with sufficient conviction' and for long enough that this is the way things are (*WE* 83).

Woolf's writing practice is designed to change the way in which we *see* how things are. No one who has read *A Room of One's Own* and *Three Guineas* (to take only the most obviously polemical examples) could be in any doubt that Virginia Woolf also had a commitment to changing the way things actually are. In her essays on fiction in general and in those on individual novelists Woolf constantly emphasized the need for the writers and readers of modern fiction to learn to look differently and to learn to look at different things. In her own fiction she attempted to provide structures in which they might do so. For example, the structure that masks structure in *Jacob's Room* (1922), 'no scaffolding; scarcely a brick to be seen; all crepuscular' (*WD* 23). In the 'tunnelling process' (*WD* 61) which she uses in *Mrs Dalloway* (1925), by means of which she 'dig[s] out beautiful caves behind my characters' (*WD* 60). In the 'great splashes of exaggeration' (*WD* 120) in *Orlando* (1928), the 'play-poem idea' (*WD* 108) of *The Waves* (1931), and in her attempt to 'lyricize the argument' (*WD* 238) and subjectivize history in *The Years* (1937).

Both the old and the new ways of looking which are discussed or enacted in Woolf's writings are crucially linked to issues of gender and sexual difference. The materialism of the Edwardians whose shortcomings Woolf dissects in 'Modern Fiction' and more minutely in 'Mr Bennett and Mrs Brown' is inextricably connected in her analysis with their masculinism. The obviously female 'narrator' of 'Mr Bennett and Mrs Brown' wishes to rescue her central female character from the 'ugly', 'clumsy', 'incongruous' representational tools of the male novelists who (as Woolf tells it) would do violence to her story. 'It is not only that they celebrate male virtues, enforce male values and describe the world of men,' Woolf writes of Galsworthy's novels in *A Room of One's Own*, but also 'that the emotion with which these books are permeated is to a woman incomprehensible' (*RO* 100). A book by a man is, after all, just a man's book.

In short, Woolf's objections to the Edwardian materialists are based as much on what they leave out as on how they represent what they include. For Woolf their most important omission is the 'difference of view' provided by woman as both observer and observed. The 'difference of view' is the key to the 'plot' of 'Mr Bennett and Mrs Brown', which, like many of Woolf's essays, discusses fiction by employing the devices of fiction. In 'Mr Bennett and Mrs Brown' a woman writer expresses her dissatisfaction with the gaze of male writers by telling a story about how that gaze works, and at the same time telling a story about how she, a woman writer, would write it differently. 'Mrs Brown must be rescued' from the external gaze of the male materialists who cannot see *her*. Woolf, the modern novelist, must begin again. However, one of the most important problems with which Woolf's essay narratives engage is that, in beginning again, one can never simply and smoothly begin at the beginning. The new writer, like the narrator of *A Room of One's Own* – who begins her lecture with the words 'But, you may say' – is always interrupting, butting in to a conversation or narrative whose lines are already established. Thus, as Woolf deconstructs her own narrative ('if you will allow me to pull my own anecdote to pieces') in 'Mr Bennett and Mrs Brown', she acknowledges the extent to which she remains locked into the dominant paradigms:

> you ... see how keenly I felt the lack of a convention ... The incident had made a great impression on me. But how was I to transmit it to you? All I could do was to report as accurately as I could what was said, to describe in detail what was worn, to say, despairingly, that all sorts of scenes rushed into my mind, to proceed to tumble them out pell-mell ... to tell you the truth, I was also strongly tempted to manufacture a three-volume novel ...
>
> But if I had done that I should have escaped the appalling effort of saying what I meant. (*WE* 81–2)

As I have been trying to emphasize, for Woolf the 'appalling effort of saying what I meant' is not simply the existential situation of the writer, nor is it merely a function of belatedness – a problem caused by having to work with the outmoded tools inherited from the older generation, or with a language that has degenerated from its former glories. It is also, and importantly, a problem of difference. The woman writer is doubly disadvantaged by the force of the existing conventions, because 'men are the arbiters' of those conventions. Woolf makes the point forcefully in the much-quoted passage from 'Women and Fiction':

> It is probable ... that in both life and art the values of a woman are not the values of a man. Thus, when a woman comes to write a novel, she will find that she is perpetually wishing to alter the established values – to make serious what appears insignificant to a man, and trivial what to him is important. And for that she will be criticized; for the critic of the opposite sex will be genuinely puzzled and surprised by an attempt to alter the current scale of values, and will see in it not merely a difference of view, but a view that is weak, or trivial, or sentimental, because it differs from his own. (*CE* ii. 146)

In other words, there is all the difference in the world in this 'difference of view'. The importance of Woolf's statement is precisely that she emphasizes that the difference of view provided by the woman is not simply another way of looking at the world, but rather that it changes the world: 'And so the smashing and the crashing' of masculine conventions must begin (*WE* 84). The story Woolf tells in her essay narratives from 'Modern Fiction' to *A Room of One's Own* is a story of rupture, and the abandonment of tradition – 'in or about December 1910 human character changed' (*WE* 70); but it is also, as I have suggested, a story about continuity and the force of tradition. It is a story, too, about intervening in and disrupting the dominant tradition; a story about negotiating and reworking the established conventions. In short, it is a story of renovation. Thus, although Woolf wishes to do more or less everything differently from Bennett, Galsworthy, and Wells, she shares their belief that the novel begins with character. She endorses the break with plot and story, and with the conventions of realistic representation made by Joyce and Richardson, but in her own fiction she never quite dispenses with 'plot', 'tragedy', or 'comedy', or with the dynastic narrative or family chronicle of the Victorians. Rather she returns to and interestingly reworks and complicates these apparently outmoded tools. Moreover, when she looks closely at the work of writers who do attempt a radical break with realistic representation, Woolf calls attention to the dangers of narrowness and constriction of the 'cramp and confinement of personality' (*CE* ii. 159), and the 'egotistical self' which 'ruins Joyce and Richardson' (*WD* 23).

Woolf's response to the experimentation of Joyce and Richardson is partly the quibbling of a literary rival. One recalls that Woolf responded to the news of Katherine Mansfield's death with the remark that at least this made for one less competitor. More importantly, the ambivalence of Woolf's attitude to Joyce and Richardson is evidence of the persistence in her own critical discourse of the terms of the late nineteenth-century debates on fiction, particularly the gendered discourse on realism. 'We want to be rid of realism, to penetrate without its help into the regions beneath it,' Woolf writes in her review of *The Tunnel*. However, she also requires 'that Miss Richardson shall fashion this new material into something which has the shapeliness of the old accepted forms' (*WE* 17). She approves Joyce's commitment 'at all costs to reveal the flickerings of that innermost flame which flashes its messages through the brain':

> The scene in the cemetery [in *Ulysses*], for instance, with its brilliancy, its sordidity, its incoherence, its sudden lightening flashes of significance, does undoubtedly come so close to the quick of the mind that, on a first reading at any rate, it is difficult not to acclaim a masterpiece. (*CDML* 9)

Ultimately, however, she finds the Joycean method limiting, enclosing, 'centred in a self which, in spite of its tremor of susceptibility, never embraces or creates what is outside itself' (*CDML* 10). In addition she finds Joyce 'difficult' and 'unpleasant' and she is suspicious of his didactic 'emphasis . . . upon indecency' (*CDML* 10). Thus Woolf, the modern novelist of subjectivity, like the late nineteenth-century conservative critic confronting the experiments of the New Woman writers, is troubled by the problematic relationship between the inner and the outer in modern fiction, by its apparent obsession with the 'unpleasant' details of physical life, and by the dangers of egotism. Woolf, on the contrary, preferred a fictional form that would 'enclose everything, everything . . . enclose the human heart' and have everything 'dancing in unity' (*WD* 23); a form which would enable both writer and reader to inhabit lives, experiences, states of consciousness other than their own and give them 'the illusion that one is not tethered to a single mind' ('Street Haunting', *CDML* 81).

It would be wrong to see Woolf as wishing simply to recuperate the Arnoldian project of seeing things steadily and seeing them whole, but there are a number of occasions on which she seemed to express a preference for a fictional method that would (as it were) see the fragments of experience in all their fragmentary and evanescent detail and yet still see them whole. She retained, too, something of the Victorians' contradictory attitude to the detail and its gendering. She rejected the materialists' forensic external inventorizing of the detail which she codes masculine (in any case, all of Woolf's regularly cited materialist demons are male), but she also retains misgivings about the 'feminine' detail of Richardson.

> That Miss Richardson gets so far as to achieve a sense of reality far greater than that produced by the ordinary means is undoubted. But, then, *which reality* is it, the *superficial or the profound?* . . . we still find ourselves *distressingly near the surface.* Things look much the same as ever. (*WE* 16; emphasis added)

For Woolf, as for some Victorian critics of domestic realism, 'feminine realism' is associated with surfaces, the superficial, an absence of significant pattern, and perspective.

'BUT WHAT ABOUT MY CULTURE?' READING AND WRITING DIFFERENTLY

In women's writing, language seems to be seen from a foreign land . . . Virginia Woolf describes suspended states . . . but she does not dissect language as Joyce does. Estranged from language, women are visionaries, dancers who suffer as they speak.[6]

In all of her writing Woolf was concerned with the question of 'which reality?' The outer or the inner, the superficial or the profound? She was also centrally concerned with the question of whose reality, men's or women's? In fact, 'which reality?' and 'whose reality?' often turn out to be the same question. The centrality of these questions to her work complicates Woolf's relationship to modernism and to early twentieth-century writing more generally. Woolf inherited both questions from the nineteenth-century feminist debates, which she replays in her own terms in her novels and essays. Both questions are central to the project of cultural renovation which informs much of her writing. I will look at two areas of Woolf's work in which these questions are particularly important: her cultural critique, and her ideas on the gender(ing) of writing.

Like Richardson's, Woolf's project of renovating or making fiction anew was grounded in a fundamental critique of the dominant culture. Woolf's cultural critique, like Richardson's, took the form of an exposure of its masculinism, an analysis of the masculine perspectives and values upon which 'culture' was based, and an interrogation of male authority. Woolf describes the social structure of contemporary England as a patriarchy (RO 35), and dissects culture as a system which validates patriarchal rule and keeps it in place. She articulates her cultural critique by constructing a narrative of cultural history which tells the story of how men have made the world in their own image and to serve their own interests.

> Women have served all these centuries as looking glasses possessing the magic and delicious power of reflecting the figure of man at twice its natural size. Without that power probably the earth would still be swamp and jungle. The glories of all our wars would be unknown . . . whatever may be their use in civilized societies, mirrors are essential to all violent and heroic action. That is why Napoleon and Mussolini both insist so emphatically upon the inferiority of women, for if they were not inferior they would cease to enlarge. And it serves to explain how restless they are under her criticism . . . For if she begins to tell the truth, the figure in the looking glass shrinks; his fitness for life is diminished. How is he to go on giving judgement, civilizing natives, making laws, writing books, dressing up and speechifying at banquets, unless he can see himself at breakfast and at dinner at least twice the size he really is? (RO 37–8)

The difference of view offered in this passage is articulated most explicitly in the later polemical works, A Room of One's Own and Three Guineas, but it is present right from the beginning, and is found in all of her work 'creative' and 'critical', 'imaginative' and 'polemical' (I will return shortly to the question of the difficulty of assigning any one of Woolf's works to one or other of these categories). In virtually all of her writings Woolf, like Richardson, revisited the history of turn-of-the-century feminism and appropriated, reworked, and, increasingly, updated its arguments in the light of the new social feminism of the post-war period.[7] She also retold (and revised) that history, most notably in *The Years*, in which she constructed a history of women and the upper-middle-class patriarchal family from the 1880s to 'the present day'. In all her work, as Alex Zwerdling has noted, Woolf was interested in 'the underlying psychological and economic causes', and one might add consequences, of 'masculine dominance and feminine repressed anger or acquiescence'.[8] In this respect she continued the work begun by the New Woman writers of the 1890s, and indeed often did so in rather similar terms, by giving the reader privileged access to the subjectivity of her female characters, and focusing on women's subjective experience of social and familial structures.

In fact Woolf's cultural critique has two main motivating forces, both of which might be described as feminist, and both of which have their origins in the feminist debates and degeneration debates of the turn of the century. The first is a sense of cultural crisis. The second is the need to construct an alternative to the dominant cultural tradition. Like many of her contemporaries and her late nineteenth-century predecessors, Woolf both implicitly and explicitly addresses the question, 'whither civilization?' – is it an illusion and does it have a future? In the course of her writing life, in the aftermath of the First World War and as another major conflict loomed through the low dishonest decade of the 1930s, these questions acquired a greater force and urgency than they had had at the *fin de siècle*. They became particularly pressing for Woolf in her late works, *Three Guineas* and *Between the Acts*, in which she considered the social origins of Fascism and the decline of civilization. However, in all her work these questions were articulated differently for Woolf than they were for her male contemporaries. For her the question of whither civilization was often quite explicitly a gender/ed issue (as it was for D. H. Lawrence). She was faced not simply with the danger of the destruction of civilization, but with the question of whether the ethos of (masculine) civilization was itself destructive.

Woolf's analysis of the crisis of modern culture is inseparable from her sense of its masculinism and of the need to construct a counter-narrative, a counter-tradition to the dominant cultural tradition. 'But what about *my* culture?' she asks in her diary (*DVW* iv. 298), and in her essays and novels Woolf attempts to answer that question by writing a different story. She attempts to introduce a difference of view, an alternative set of values to those of the dominant culture. In her fiction she does this by means of her focus on female characters, by her continuation of the feminist critique of the family made in the New Woman novel, by her focus on the social and subjective circumstances of women's lives, on interiority, and, in particular, on a socially constructed subjectivity. In her essays she does it by rethinking the history of women, which, as she shows in *A Room of One's Own*, has largely been written by men. She also advocates a process of thinking back through our mothers. Many of the feminist critics who

have done so much to revise our readings of Woolf and enhance her critical reputation in the latter part of the twentieth century have seen her
introduction of the difference of view simply in terms of opposing
'feminine' values such as spirituality, interiority, subjectivism, vitalism, and
co-operation to the 'masculine' values of objectivity, materialism, scienti-
cism, rationalism, and confrontation. There is something to be said for
this model, but it has the disadvantage of replicating nineteenth-century
gender ascriptions (masculinity equals objectivity, femininity equals subjectivity). Viewed thus, Woolf's project would appear to be merely a continuation of the renovatory project of those late nineteenth-century feminists
who wished to rescue a diseased, degenerative patriarchal society by an
infusion of womanly, matriarchal values.

Certainly Woolf returns to the questions that preoccupied late
nineteenth-century feminists, and to some extent she thinks within the
terms in which those questions were posed, but she also attempts to think
beyond them, and to complicate gender ascriptions. She does not simply
oppose a fixed and essentialist conception of femininity to an equally fixed
and essentialist conception of masculinity. Instead, she articulates in her
fiction (most dramatically in *Orlando*) a conception of the self and a
gendered identity as fluid, unstable, and in process. Most importantly,
Woolf articulates a conception of a gendered identity which is produced
in particular historical and cultural circumstances, and which is therefore
capable of being changed in changed social circumstances. 'Can one
change sex characteristics?' she asked in a letter written towards the end
of her life. 'How far is the woman's movement a remarkable experiment
in that transformation?' The experience of the Second World War led
Woolf to believe that it would perhaps be possible 'to alter the crest and
spur of the fighting cock': 'It looks as if the sexes can adapt themselves;
and here (that's our work) we can, or the young women can, bring
enormous influence to bear. So many of the young men, could they get
prestige and admiration, would give up glory and develop what's now so
stunted.'[9] When Woolf offers the 'feminine' values of '*my* culture' as an
antidote to the competitive, militaristic values of patriarchal culture, she
is not, unlike some of her nineteenth-century predecessors, offering the
reassuringly stable and natural values of the spiritual mother, but rather
the flexible conciliatory values produced by the distinctive social experience of women.

When Woolf looks at the question of woman she writes, not in terms
of the eternal feminine (as Richardson often does), but rather in terms of
the precise economic, material, familial, and social circumstances which
shape women's lives and values, and in which those values are articulated.
Woolf sees women's lives, feminine values, and women's writing in
relation to specific historical cultures. She sees them in relation to the 'law
and custom' (*CE* ii. 142) of a patriarchal society which generated the
permissions and constraints which determined whether or not women's

voices were heard, and how they were heard – the law and custom, for example, by which 'a woman was liable, as she was in the fifteenth century, to be beaten and flung about the room if she did not marry the man of her parents choice' (CE ii. 142), and by which 'even in the nineteenth century, a woman lived almost solely in her home and her emotions' (CE ii. 143).

Like many more recent feminist historians, Woolf attempted to add women's voices to the conversation of culture and to recover the lost or hidden histories of women. Indeed, in 'Women and Fiction' and *A Room of One's Own* Woolf seems to have set the agenda for much of the Anglo-American feminist literary history of the 1970s and 1980s. In these essays Woolf returned to the question which had been used to taunt nineteenth-century feminists. 'Where are the female Shakespeares?' In answering this question Woolf formulated an alternative to the affiliative model of literary history outlined in T. S. Eliot's 'Tradition and the Individual Talent'. On the contrary, Woolf sees the history of women's literary endeavour (and indeed of women's contributions to the dominant culture in general) in terms of the female talent which is isolated and excluded by and from a male-defined tradition. Woolf does not find the absence of a female Shakespeare at all surprising, for 'masterpieces are not single and solitary births; they are the outcomes of many years of thinking in common, of thinking by the body of the people, so that the experience of the mass is behind the single voice' (RO 66).

Woolf also addressed the question of the missing female Shakespeares by developing a materialist history of gender. Her history of Shakespeare's hypothetical sister Judith in *A Room of One's Own* is perhaps the most vivid example of the practice. The theory and method of Woolf's materialist feminist history is briefly outlined in 'Women and fiction'.

> Thus, if we wish to know why at any particular time women did this or that ... [we] should turn history wrong side out and so construct a faithful picture of the daily life of the ordinary woman ... It is only when we know what were the conditions of the average woman's life – the number of her children, whether she had money of her own, if she had a room to herself, whether she had help in bringing up her family, if she had servants, whether part of the housework was her task – it is only when we can measure the way of life and the experience of life made possible to the ordinary woman that we can account for the success or failure of the extraordinary woman ... (CE ii. 142)

Woolf's critique of culture, based as it is on a sense of the systematic devaluing, omission, and misrepresentation of women's voices and women's social experience in and by the dominant culture, is thus grounded quite differently from the modernist cultural critique of T. S.

Eliot, Ezra Pound, W. B. Yeats, and D. H. Lawrence. Unlike the male modernists and cultural critics, Woolf does not locate the present threat to civilization in the loss of Christianity, or in the erosion of other traditional belief and value systems. Nor does she attribute it to the challenge to social and political structures (ruled by masculine political and cultural élites) posed by the rise of a (feminized) mass society. On the contrary, Woolf offers a critique of the structures and discourses of a hierarchical, capitalist, imperialist, patriarchal culture based on dominance and submission, exploitation and militarism. Very often those values and structures whose disappearance is mourned by the male cultural critics as signs or symptoms of cultural degeneration and disintegration are seen by Woolf as the source of the problem.

Something of the way in which Woolf's cultural critique differs from that of her fellow (male) modernists can be seen in her treatment of popular culture and the city. Unlike the best known of the male modernists, Woolf does not condemn popular culture as merely sentimental and meretricious, but rather develops a theory of usefulness which gives to the novels of Marie Corelli and to the cinema the saving power which is more conventionally attributed to the works of high culture. Similarly she celebrates the 'wild confusion' of the architecture of Oxford Street department stores ('The London Scene', *CDML* 116), and the evanescent 'charm of modern London' (*CDML* 115). Eliot's representation of London as the 'unreal city' has its roots in the late nineteenth-century vision of London as the decaying Heart of Empire, the home of the degenerate masses, the heart of urban darkness and modern neurasthenia. Eliot's cityscape is one of decay and disillusion. His London is the locus of modernist anomie. It is the nightmarish location in which robotic city workers daily perform their death-in-life routines, silently tracing and retracing their route across London Bridge. London is the space from which culture has vanished, or in which it persists only in historic traces.

For Woolf, on the other hand, as for Richardson (as I indicated in the previous chapter) London is a space of vitality and adventure which liberates rather than confines the imagination. Woolf uses the city setting in this way in some of her fiction, most famously in *Mrs Dalloway*, but also in *Night and Day*, and in *The Years* (though in the latter case there is also the undercurrent of sexual danger in the city streets, figured in Rose's meeting with the strange man at the postbox). Woolf's most interesting representation of the city belongs more to the Auden generation than to the moment of *The Waste Land*. In 'Street Haunting: A London Adventure' (first published in 1927 and reissued as a pamphlet in 1930) Woolf represents London as a place of endless possibilities, an imaginative space to be occupied and colonized by the female narrator who glories in the city as a spectacle which she not only observes but also invents. As the narrator journeys across London on the pretext of buying a pencil, the city becomes a narrative space which demands interpretation and completion through the making-up of stories. Woolf, like Richardson, represents the city as particularly liberating for the woman. Street haunting is a means of escaping from the confinement of the interior private spaces of the domestic setting and of occupying a different form of interiority in the public spaces of the streets: 'We are no longer quite ourselves. As we step out of the house . . . we shed the self our friends know us by and become part of that vast republican army of anonymous trampers' (*CDML* 70). On the city street identity and subjectivity are dispersed and reconfigured. 'Am I here, or am I there? Or is the true self neither this nor that, neither here nor there, but something so varied and wandering that it is only when we give the rein to its wishes and let it take its way unimpeded that we are indeed ourselves' (*CDML* 76). When Woolf depicts alienation in the city it is as much the product of gender as it is of modernity. 'If one is a woman one is often surprised by a sudden splitting off of consciousness, say in walking down Whitehall, when from being the natural inheritor of that civilization, she becomes, on the contrary, outside of it, alien and critical' (*RO* 96).

Despite her own social position as a daughter of the upper middle classes, Woolf was suspicious of cultural and political élites, and she became increasingly suspicious of coterie culture. Her feelings about the barbarian hordes pressing at the gates of civilization were, perhaps, almost bound to differ from those of Eliot and Pound, and indeed of her fellow Bloomsburyites, since, as a woman, she too was a cultural outsider. As her fiction graphically demonstrates, and as her essays fiercely assert, Woolf felt that because of her gender she was marginalized and excluded from the privileges of her social class. In *A Room of One's Own* she figures this sense of cultural alienation in the trespasser caught walking on the lawns of an Oxbridge college.

> Instinct rather than reason came to my help; he was a beadle; I was a woman. This was the turf; there was the path. Only the Fellows and Scholars are allowed here; the gravel is the place for me. Such thoughts were the work of a moment . . . The only charge I could bring against the Fellows and Scholars . . . was that in protection of their turf, which had been rolled for 300 years in succession, they had sent my little fish [her train of thought] into hiding. (*RO* 8)

This passage suggests with great force and economy the history and psychology of the processes by which women internalize patriarchal culture's sense of their inferiority. It also demonstrates how women who stray from their socially prescribed territories, and who cross the boundaries put in place by masculine culture, are positioned as transgressors. But Woolf does not simply use the figure of the trespasser to articulate a rather pessimistic psychology of subordination, she also seeks to put it to work in new ways as an instrument of change. The project of *A Room of One's Own* is precisely to incite women to trespass: 'Let us trespass freely and fearlessly and find our own way for ourselves' (*CE* ii. 181). She pursues a similar line in her 1930s' polemic *Three Guineas*, in which she exhorts women to make positive use of the fact that they are positioned outside the political structure. She proposes the creation of an oppositional Society of Outsiders (made up of 'educated men's daughters working in their own class'), a title chosen, despite its lack of resonance, because 'it has the advantage that it squares with facts – the facts of history, of law, of biography; even, it may be, with the still hidden facts of our still unknown psychology'.[10]

Woolf also put her outsider status to new uses in her own writing practice. She began her fiction-writing career as an insider–outsider, that is to say, as a modernist experimenter who, like her fellow modernists, wrote for a fit audience though few: 'I write for half a dozen instead of 1500' (*D*. ii. 107). Although she retained her fear and suspicion of the public in an age 'deafened with boom and blatancy' ('The Humane Art', *CE* i. 105), and although (to my ear at least) her voice retained the mandarin tones of her class, she nevertheless sought to find a voice in which to address 'the common reader', and a polyphonic fictional form (based on giving a voice to, rather than speaking on behalf of, characters) that would include rather than exclude by its difficulty (though it has to be said that 'difficulty' remains a problem for many of Woolf's readers).

In her essays she developed a reflective, conversational voice designed to include her readers in a sharing of knowledge and perceptions, and to empower them. Like Richardson, Woolf developed a sentence structure and a mode of address designed to embody the voice and restore the speaking presence to writing. In those essays which have their origins in lectures, such as *A Room of One's Own*, Woolf deconstructs the form of the lecture. She occupies the authoritative position of the lecturer only to give back that authority to her audience. She does this by constantly undermining her own positions, by presenting the members of her audience with questions which she is unable to answer, but to which she challenges them to find an answer if they can, and by setting up projects which she refuses or is unable to complete: 'I have shirked the duty of coming to a conclusion upon . . . the true nature of women,' she concedes in *A Room of One's Own* (*RO* 6).

Woolf's cultural critique is thus based on the difference of view provided by a self-consciously gendered perspective. Woolf's own writing and her writing about writing suggest that this difference of view is both produced by and requires a different language, a gendered language. Similarly Woolf's project of cultural renovation, based as it is on the addition of women's voices to the cultural narrative, is also a project of linguistic renovation. Again this involves an awareness of the gender of language. Woolf's project of remaking the novel and her own struggles with the language and form of fiction also has to be seen in the context of her

views on the gender(ing) of language. In Woolf's view women's relationship to language and literary form was different from that of men.
Women, she argues, have had to write against the grain of a literary tradition whose dominant forms and genres were

> made by men out of their own needs for their own uses. There is no
> reason to think that the form of the epic or of the poetic play suits
> a woman any more than the [man's] sentence suits her. But all the
> older forms of literature were hardened and set by the time she
> became a writer. (RO 77)

This is one reason, Woolf argues, why women in the eighteenth century
took to the newest form of writing, the novel (there was no 'anxiety of
influence'). It is also perhaps why women writers tend to go in for 'genre
bending'.

Like the New Woman writers of the 1890s, Woolf herself persistently
crossed generic boundaries, turning her essays and reviews into narratives,
mixing fiction and polemic, writing novels which use the techniques of
drama and/or aspire to the lyric intensity of poetry. 'The book has somehow
to be adapted to the body,' Woolf maintained, and it seems clear that she
meant the social body rather than the biological rhythms which characterize the feminine writing more recently advocated by Cixous and others.
Woolf exhorted women to find new forms which they might adapt to their
specific social circumstances: 'women's books should be shorter, more
concentrated, than those of men, and framed so that they do not need long
hours of steady and uninterrupted work. For interruptions there will always
be' (RO 78). In this last sentence Woolf conjures up a host of New Woman
novels which explore the predicament of a woman writer, and which focus
on her search for an appropriate form in which to articulate both an
aesthetic vision and a sense of the lack of fit between a woman's desires
and the social actualities of woman's lives, while at the same time negotiating the constraints imposed by those social circumstances.

Woolf also argued that women have had to write against the grain of
the dominant language. The woman writer had 'no common sentence
ready for her use' (RO 76), because the history of writing is dominated
by 'the man's sentence' which is 'unsuited for a woman's use' (RO 77,
73). In the matter of linguistic renovation, as in so many other matters,
Woolf advocated renewal by means of trespassing and transgression. In
order to express 'the whole of that extremely complex force of femininity', 'whole flights of words would need to wing their way illegitimately
into existence' (RO 87). Thus, although she had reservations about the
tendency to egotistical restriction and fragmentation of Dorothy
Richardson's fictional form, Woolf was unequivocal in her praise for
Richardson's feminine remaking, or feminization, of language. As far as
Woolf was concerned, Richardson's major achievement was that:

She has invented, or, if she has not invented, developed and applied to her own uses, a sentence which we might call the psychological sentence of the feminine gender. It is of a more elastic fibre than the old, capable of stretching to the extreme, of suspending the frailest particles, of enveloping the vaguest shapes. Other writers of the opposite sex have used sentences of this description and stretched them to the extreme. But there is a difference. Miss Richardson has fashioned her sentence consciously, in order that it may descend to the depths and investigate the crannies of Miriam Henderson's consciousness. It is a woman's sentence, but only in the sense that it is used to describe a woman's mind by a writer who is neither proud nor afraid of anything she may discover in the psychology of her sex.[11]

Woolf's views on feminine language are complex. They are also contradictory. In her review of Brimley Johnson's *The Women Novelists* Woolf expresses agreement with his contention that 'a woman's writing is always feminine', but goes on to suggest that 'the only difficulty lies in defining what we mean by feminine' (*WE* 13). This 'difficulty' is present in the above extract, her best-known pronouncement on the subject. The reference to 'other writers of the opposite sex' would suggest that 'the psychological sentence of the feminine gender' is not necessarily tied to the biological sex of its user, nor, despite the reference to 'a woman's mind', to a specifically gendered experience. The distinctive qualities of the psychological sentence of the feminine gender would appear to be its elasticity, its modernity (as opposed to the 'old' sentence), and its ability to 'descend to the depths' of consciousness. It is here that I think we encounter a different sense of the 'femininity' of the Richardsonian sentence. It is a sentence that can chart the 'dark places of psychology' (*CDML* 10) which, Woolf argued in 'Modern Fiction', constituted the chief 'point of interest' of 'the moderns' (*CDML* 10). Woolf's attempts to think the gender of writing thus seem to be caught up in a specific discourse of gender in which the feminized dark places of the world which so preoccupied late nineteenth-century writers join up with the 'dark continent' by which Freudian psychology figured female sexuality.

Ambivalence and contradiction also characterize Woolf's views on difference and androgyny. In her insistence in her cultural critique and in her own writing practice on the importance of difference – the difference of standard, the difference of view, the difference of language of men and women – Woolf seems to be polarizing and possibly reinforcing gender categories. Elsewhere, however, she appears to argue for a transgressing or erosion of traditional gender categories. 'It is fatal for anyone who writes to think of their sex,' she asserts when considering the task of the woman writer in *A Room of One's Own*. 'It is fatal to be a man or a woman pure and simple . . . one must be woman-manly or man-womanly'

(*RO* 156–7). In the figure of Mary Carmichael, Woolf represents the woman writer who masters the art of writing as a woman, by writing 'as a woman who has forgotten that she is a woman, so that her pages were full of that curious sexual quality which comes only when sex is unconscious of itself' (*RO* 92).

Woolf's apparent slipperiness on the question of androgyny and difference to some extent replicates the confusions and contradictions of the late nineteenth-century concepts of sex-gender difference which she was trying to rethink. In her cultural critique and in her attempt to formulate a theory of women's writing Woolf does sometimes polarize gender categories, but she does so in such a way as to challenge the separate-spheres ideology of the nineteenth century. In her novels and in her essays Woolf seeks to interrupt that nineteenth-century explosion of discourse on woman which I discussed in earlier chapters. This move is foregrounded in *A Room of One's Own* in her narrative about her visit to the British Museum to research the topic of 'W.' (woman).

> Have you any notion how many books are written about women in the course of one year? Have you any notion how many are written by men? Are you aware that you are, perhaps, the most discussed animal in the universe? . . . Why are women . . . so much more interesting to men than men are to women? (*RO* 28–9)

In all of her writings Woolf seeks to rescue women from being the objects of the masculine gaze, and make them speaking subjects.

But, the question remains, how can Woolf's insistence on the importance of difference be made to square with her apparent advocacy of androgyny, a concept which seems to move outside or beyond difference? As Rachel Bowlby points out, among all the 'models of what constitutes the relation between "women" and "writing" ' in Woolf's work, it is androgyny which 'has provoked some of the wildest outbursts of indignation and celebration'.[12] The indignation has come from those feminists who, believing that women's writing should articulate a specifically feminine subjectivity, disapprove of Woolf's insistence on the need for the woman writer to forget her sex. On the other hand, Woolf's concept of androgyny has been celebrated by those who see it as a utopian, post-gendered state. The crux of the problem seems to be that Woolf wants to think beyond sex-gender difference, but that she remains locked in a discourse of difference in which the masculine is the privileged term. It is worth quoting at length from the passage in *A Room of One's Own* in which Woolf formulates her 'vision' of androgyny. It is also worth emphasizing that it is a vision – it is a scene in which the female lecturer/narrator watches herself watching a man and a woman meet together and enter a taxi. As she meditates on the scene she has 'witnessed' (conjured into being), Woolf implicitly thinks back through the turn-of-the-century concepts of bisexuality and the bisexuality or the intermediate sex found in Weininger, Ellis, and Carpenter.

> When I saw the couple get into the taxi-cab the mind felt as if, after being divided, it had come together again in a natural fusion. The obvious reason would be that it is natural for the sexes to cooperate . . . But the sight of the two people getting into the taxi and the satisfaction it gave me made me also ask whether there are two sexes in the mind as in the body, and whether they also require to be united in order to get complete satisfaction and happiness? And I went on amateurishly to sketch a plan of the soul so that in each of us two powers preside, one male, one female; and in the man's brain the man predominates over the woman, and in the woman's brain the woman predominates over the man . . . If one is a man still the *woman part of the brain must have effect*; and a *woman also must have intercourse with the man in her* (RO 96–7; emphasis added)

Not only does this passage reproduce, as Rachel Bowlby argues, 'the dualism according to which the difference between the two sexes is known in advance',[13] but it also (unconsciously?) reproduces the hierarchizing of gender categories in which the masculine is the privileged term. In a man 'the woman part of the brain must *have effect*,' but the woman (in an interestingly sexual metaphor) must '*have intercourse with the man in her*'; the man contains an element of the woman, but the woman is suffused by the man. In any case, the concept of androgyny that Woolf invokes is that of a male writer, Samuel Taylor Coleridge. In this case Woolf does not think back through her mothers as she has previously suggested, but tentatively attempts to interpret the male poet to her audience of women. 'Coleridge *perhaps* meant this when he said that a great mind is androgynous . . . *Perhaps* a mind that is purely masculine cannot create, any more than a mind that is purely feminine, I thought' (RO 97; emphasis added). Woolf is considerably less tentative in suggesting what 'Coleridge certainly did not mean, when he said that a great mind is androgynous'. He did not mean 'that it is a mind that has any special sympathy with women; a mind that takes up their cause or devotes itself to their interpretation. Perhaps the androgynous mind is less apt to make these distinctions than the single-sexed mind' (RO 97). The androgynous mind, it would appear, has an Arnoldian disinterestedness. Here is another contradiction in Woolf's theory of fiction, and a tension between her theorizing and her practice of gendered writing. Although she herself was so forceful an advocate of the woman's cause, Woolf repeatedly protested against the introduction into women's writing of that sex consciousness that took the form of arguing the cause of women: 'It introduces a distortion and is frequently the cause of weakness' (CE 144). Like W. L. Courtney, Woolf – at least in theory – saw the 'truly artistic mind [as] neutral, it does not . . . take sides'.[14]

Woolf's protests against feminist protestation are perhaps inadvertent or unconscious examples of the persistence in her own writing of that nineteenth-century figure 'the Angel in the House' whose death sentence Woolf issues in 'Professions for Women'. Like the heroine of May Sinclair's *Life and Death of Harriett Frean* (1922), the 'Angel in the House' is obsessed with 'behaving beautifully'. She is the internal censor, the still small voice who whispers her insidious message into the ear of the woman writer: ' "My dear, you are a young woman. You are writing about a book that has been written by a man. Be sympathetic; be tender; flatter; deceive . . . Never let anybody guess that you have a mind of your own. Above all, be pure" ' (*CDML* 102). Similarly, Woolf's strictures against sex-consciousness and her advocacy of androgyny can perhaps be explained (if not explained away) by placing them in their historical context, in the context of a culture in which the discourse on sexual difference had become extremely polarized.

> No age can ever have been as stridently sex-conscious as our own; those innumerable books by men about women in the British Museum are a proof of it. The Suffrage campaign was no doubt to blame. It must have roused in men an extraordinary desire for self-assertion; it must have made them lay an emphasis upon their own sex and its characteristics which they would not have troubled to think about had they not been challenged. (*RO* 97–8)

Like Havelock Ellis and Edward Carpenter had done before her, Woolf attempted to dance through this particular minefield by developing a conciliatory model of the post-gendered mind, a concept of gender that lay both between and beyond traditional sex-gender categories.

A final word on Woolf and the gender of writing. Woolf's fiction, like Dorothy Richardson's, developed and refined the 'super-subtlety and microscopic self-examination'[15] that was said to characterize the New Woman writing of the 1890s. Woolf's own critical reputation has always been mediated through the complex of ideas about gender that I sketched in earlier in this book, and by means of a critical discourse whose descriptive and evaluative terms are themselves gendered. Whether it is praised or disparaged, her writing is described as being feminine or as having characteristics which are coded feminine in a critical discourse which increasingly associated the fictional forms and processes of interiority and subjectivity with the feminine. The operations of this gendered critical discourse produce some surprising critical meeting points. So, for example, we find a pioneering feminist critic of the 1970s and an anti-feminist and aggressively masculinist writer of the 1930s discussing Woolf's work in much the same terms. The feminist critic, Elaine Showalter, represents Woolf as taking 'flight into androgyny' and (like other women writers of her time) withdrawing into a 'female aesthetic' that was a 'retreat from the material world, retreat into separate rooms'[16] – in other words a retreat into a privatized space of femininity which was a perpetuation of the nineteenth-century separate sphere. Woolf's contemporary (and sometimes critical tormentor), the masculinist misogynist Wyndham Lewis, also identified Woolf as a distinctively, even iconically, feminine writer. As such, she is a writer of restricted scope and importance, if not significance:

> while I am ready to agree that the intrinsic literary importance of Mrs Woolf may be exaggerated by her friends, I cannot agree that as a symbolic landmark – a sort of party-lighthouse – she has not a very real significance. And she has crystallized for us, in her critical essays, what is in fact *the feminine* – as distinguished from the feminist standpoint. (*MWA* 159–60)

Lewis located Woolf in the feminine private sphere. He represented Woolf's subjective writing as symptomatic of the feminization of culture that threatened to annihilate the masculine:

> we have been invited, all of us, to instal ourselves in a very dim Venusberg indeed: but Venus has become an inverted matriarch, brooding over a subterranean 'stream of consciousness – a feminine phenomenon after all – and we are a pretty sorry set of knights too . . . at least in Mrs Woolf's particular version of the affair. (*MWA* 168)

In *Men Without Art*, as elsewhere in his writings, Lewis traced this feminization of culture (and Woolf's aesthetic) back to the 1890s:

> there is, of course, a very much closer connection than people suppose between the aesthetic movement presided over by Oscar Wilde, and that presided over in the first post-war decade by Mrs Woolf . . . It has been with a considerable shaking in my shoes, and a feeling of treading upon a carpet of eggs, that I have taken the cow by the horns in this chapter, and broached the subject of the part that the feminine mind has played – and minds as well, deeply feminized, not technically on the distaff side – in the erection of our present criteria. For fifteen years I have subsisted in this to me suffocating atmosphere. (*MWA* 170)

In the next two chapters I shall examine some of the ways in which early twentieth-century male writers subsisted in, or resisted, the 'suffocating atmosphere' of a feminized fiction.

|6|

Male Novelists and the Engendering of Modern Fiction

We have to hate our immediate predecessors, to get free from their authority. (LL i. 509)

Like the new 'feminine realism' of Richardson and Woolf, the modern realism, mystical realism, or impressionist or abstract modernism of their male contemporaries, such as D. H. Lawrence, E. M. Forster, James Joyce, Ford Madox Ford, and Wyndham Lewis, was based in a variety of ways on a repudiation of the cultural authority of their immediate predecessors. It also involved a (sometimes tortuous) negotiation of the contradictory discourse on gender and of the gendered discourse of degeneration and renovation which I discussed in Chapter 2, and a reworking of the gendered critical discourse explored in Chapter 3.

In some cases the male novelists of the early twentieth century attempted to establish their literary credentials and situate their own fictional practice by means of a critique of the old external 'masculine' realism or materialism of the Edwardians. In others this process involved a critique and repudiation of the new 'feminine' realism, and of the 'interiorised novel of psychology' (from Henry James through to Richardson and Woolf), which 'romanticized consciousness'.[1] The former process can be seen variously in the attacks of Forster and, more particularly, Lawrence on the Galsworthy–Bennett–Wells tradition, and in Ford Madox Ford's avowed repudiation of the entire English tradition in favour of a Jamesian impressionism and a Flaubertian commitment to formal perfection. Lawrence's irritation with Bennett's grubby English 'resignation' (*LL* i. 459) just as he had begun work on *The Rainbow* is well known, as is his critique of Galsworthy's focusing on the 'social being' rather than on the

'alive human being', and of his failure to carry through the satirical potential of the Forsyte novels (*Px* 541). Lawrence had a higher opinion of
Wells, as a writer of 'brilliant' and 'genuine' novels (*Px* 350), but thought
he was a 'suburbian' and a class traitor (*Px* II 596). Forster, on the other
hand, viewed Wells, as Woolf did, as a writer 'tethered . . . to observation', a 'visualizer' who catalogues details and scratches surfaces, and to
whom the 'world of beauty . . . is entirely closed'.[2] As far as Ford Madox
Ford was concerned, the world of art and beauty was closed to virtually
'the whole of the fiction of England from the days of Beowulf to those of
Meredith'; it 'is – as art – almost entirely negligible'.[3]

The repudiation of the 'feminine note' in fiction, on the other hand, can
be seen in Lawrence's diatribes in the 1920s against the narcissistic self-
absorption of the 'serious novel', and in Wyndham Lewis's aggressively
'dogmatic' adoption, from *Tarr* onwards, of 'The *external approach* to
things (relying on the evidence of the *eye* rather than the more emotional
organs of sense)', and his commitment to 'the Great Without', an art of
'polished and resistant surfaces' (*MWA*, 127, 120). It can be seen too in
Lewis's later attacks (in *Men without Art*, 1934) on what he saw as the
'idealism' of both James and Lawrence; on Jamesian psychologizing and
his preoccupation with interiority; on Virginia Woolf's preoccupation with
feminine consciousness (rather than the great masculine world that lay
beyond its boundaries); on Lawrence's 'romantic' (and hence feminized)
attitudes to primitive consciousness and 'blood knowledge', and on his
'sentimental and backward looking' fascination with 'aztec blood-sacri-
fices, mystical and savage abandonments of the self, abstract sex-rage etc.'[4]

Some of the emotional force of the Georgians' critique and repudiation
of their Edwardian predecessors is indicated in the declaration by D. H.
Lawrence quoted at the head of this chapter. Indeed, a forceful freeing of
fiction from the dead hand of the past seems to have been an integral part
of Lawrence's own modernist project of making the novel anew, a process
which he figures variously – as did several of his male contemporaries –
as bombing and smashing one's way into the future, and spitting out the
dregs of outmoded feelings and forms. The future of the novel, he declared
in 'Surgery for the Novel – or a Bomb' in 1923, depended upon its liberating itself from its past and growing up: 'Poor old novel, it's in a rather
dirty, messy tight corner. And its either got to get over the wall or knock
a hole through it' (*Px* 519). Or again: 'It is time somebody began to spit
out the jam of sentimentalism . . . [and] turned a straight line on the horde
of rats, these younger Forsyte sentimentalists whose name is legion' (*Px*
550). Lawrence's diagnosis of the ills of the early twentieth-century
English novel, and the language in which he offered his prescription for
the restoration of its health, echo some of those pre-war manifestos of
(masculine) modernism which called for a violent rupture with the decayed
past and a (feminized) degenerate present – for example, Wyndham
Lewis's exhortation to readers of the second issue of *Blast*, to ' "Blast

years 1837 to 1900" ' and the 'triumph of the commercial mind in England', and the ascendancy of 'the "eunuchs and stylists" [i.e] the Paterists and Wildeites' over which they presided (*B&B* 38). Writing on the Futurists in 1914, Ford Madox Ford anticipated both the tone and the preoccupations of Lawrence's 1920s critique of the English novel: 'what we want most of all in the literature of today is religion . . . intolerance . . . persecution, and not the mawkish flap-doodle of culture, Fabianism, peace and good will. Real good religion, a violent thing, full of hatreds and exclusions.'[5]

Ford and Lewis are both, in rather different ways, interesting cases in the context of the complex and convoluted process of the engendering of modern fiction. Ford is in many ways the archetypal 'transitional' figure who formed a link between the social and literary debates of the 1890s and those of the first three decades of the twentieth century. He was an energetic literary journalist, and the editor of an influential periodical (the *English Review*). He was a propagandist for both the 'feminized' interiority of the Jamesian novel and for Conrad's modernist reworking of the *fin de siècle* male romance. An occasional pamphleteer for the woman's cause, he also helped nurture the careers of such women writers as Rebecca West and Jean Rhys. His own fiction combines the interiority and indirection of the new feminine realism with the art of 'polished and resistant surfaces' which we associate with the masculinist tradition of modernism – the 'attempt at objectivity' that was the renovatory project of Lewis's 'men of 1914' (Pound, Eliot, and Joyce), those 'first men of a Future that has not materialised' (*B&B* 249, 216). Published in 1915, the same year as *The Voyage Out, Pointed Roofs*, and *The Rainbow*, Ford's novel *The Good Soldier*, with its subjective narration and its Jamesian 'hesitancies and indirection, its air of fracture and tension',[6] is, in terms of the gendered discourse of criticism that I discussed earlier, a 'feminine' novel: introspective, subjective, and impressionistic. (It also, incidentally, reworks a number of preoccupations and plot situations commonly found in the New Woman novel: the sexual double standard, the problems caused by sexual ignorance, the arranged marriage which is unconsummated.) However, Ford combines his 'feminine' indirection and introspection with the 'hard' ('masculine') technique of the Vorticists, polishing his narrative 'like a steel helmet'.[7]

Lewis, whose work has recently been the object of renewed critical interest, has been thought of 'as an abstract artist who revolted against Modernism after the First World War and rejected most of his original principles'.[8] It would perhaps be more accurate to argue that, on the contrary, it was precisely Lewis's adherence to his 'principles' and more particularly to the gendered discourse in which they were grounded that led to his post-war rejection of modernism. Lewis's initial affiliation to 'the men of 1914' and his later rejection of them and their modernist successors were both grounded in that championing of a masculine classicism in art against a feminized romanticism which can be found throughout his writings. The persistence of at least this 'principle' can be seen in Lewis's later recommendation of 'coarseness' in fiction in *Men without Art* (1934), in which he offers (*inter alia*) a programme for the novel in a mass society – 'a world without art' (*MWA* 225). The following quotation from *Men without Art*, with its privileging of the 'masculine' qualities of impersonality, universality, and rationality, both shows the consistency of Lewis's own critical discourse, and suggests its continuity with the late nineteenth-century discourse on fiction. It also indicates the extent to which Lewis feels that the 'masculine' has been eclipsed. 'To be impersonal rather than personal; universal rather than provincial; rational rather than a mere creature of feeling – these . . . are very fine things indeed: but who possesses more than a tincture of them today?' (*MWA* 193–4). Like D. H. Lawrence, Lewis was a modernist against modernism, and in his later writings repudiated literary modernism as a kind of *trahison des clercs* – a masculine movement for literary renewal and a break with the past which had, in its preoccupation with style, declined into a 'femininized' decadent aestheticism.

Although he adopted a different aesthetic from both Ford and the men of 1914, Lawrence's negotiations with the genders of fiction and the discourses on fiction were similarly complex and contradictory. His repudiation and critique of the Wells–Bennett–Galsworthy tradition has been seen (with some justice), like Joyce's fleeing the nets of the novelistic tradition, as an Oedipal drama, a filial revolt in which the son strikes the father dead in order to assert his own literary virility. For Lawrence, as for Joyce, it can also be seen as a turn to the mother and the feminine. It is important to emphasize from the outset, however, that this turn to the feminine takes quite different trajectories in each of these two writers. In Lawrence's case in particular its trajectory is both tortuous and tortured, veering between thinking back through the mothers (in *Sons and Lovers*, and in the matrilineal narrative of *The Rainbow*, for example), to a repudiation of the feminine and the female, and a search for the lost (male) leader in the novels of the 1920s – *Aaron's Rod* (1922), *Kangaroo* (1923), and *The Plumed Serpent* (1926). I shall return to the question of gender in Lawrence's writing in my final chapter, in order to underline one of the general points that emerges from this study: that one of the most interesting and important aspects of the engendering of the 'modern' writing that comes out of the turn-of-the-century literary experiments and contests that I have been exploring is not the question of the gender of modernism (feminine writing or masculine writing?), but rather the complex ways in which that writing is produced by and within contradictory and contesting discourses of and on gender.

The 'femininity' of Joyce's writing has been much discussed of late by feminist and post-structuralist critics who have championed his development of a 'feminine' modernism. I do not propose to go over that particular ground again except to note that Joyce's writing has been celebrated as a form of *écriture féminine*, an example of that liquid, flowing, pre-symbolic language that French theorizers of the feminine, following the psychoanalytic theories of Jacques Lacan, associate with the mother. Lawrence's writing has often been seen as 'babble', and his critics have disparaged the seemingly endless 'flow' of his repetitive style, but they have not (on the whole) tended to analyse these aspects of Lawrence's writing in terms of the semiotic chora or of *écriture féminine*. Lawrence himself would, of course, have resisted any comparison of his own fiction with that of Joyce. Lawrence in fact anticipated F. R. Leavis's posing of what the latter saw as the fundamental question of twentieth-century culture – 'Lawrence or Joyce?' – by outlining the case against Joyce, and implicitly offering himself as the writer who would remake fiction and provide 'Surgery for the Novel – or a Bomb'. Lawrence, like Woolf, was a modernist against modernism; he defined his project of remaking the novel as much in opposition to modernist experimentation (whether it be the 'purely male . . . scientific line' of the Futurists or Vorticists, or the 'vague emotion' of the 'pale-faced, highbrowed earnest novel' of Proust, Joyce, or Richardson) as to the Edwardian materialists. For Lawrence, Joyce's fiction was a cultural dead-end. It marked the end of a feminized, over-civilized phase of culture: 'this democratic-industrial-lovey-dovey-darling-take-me-to-mamma-state-of-things' (*Px* 520). Interestingly, Lawrence's critique of Joyce (whom he pairs for this purpose with Dorothy Richardson) reproduces the discourse in which the conservative critics dismissed the 'super-subtlety and microscopic self-examination'[9] of the New Woman writing of the 1890s.

It is self-consciousness picked into such fine bits that the bits are most of them invisible . . . Through thousands and thousands of pages Mr. Joyce and Miss Richardson tear themselves to pieces, strip their smallest emotions to the finest threads . . .
    And there's the serious novel: senile-precocious. Absorbedly, childishly concerned with *what I am*. 'I am this, I am that . . . My reactions are such, and such . . . And, oh, Lord, if I liked to watch myself closely enough, if I liked to analyse my feelings minutely, as I unbutton my gloves, instead of saying crudely I unbuttoned them, then I could go on to a million pages instead of a thousand. In fact, the more I come to think of it, it is gross, it is uncivilised bluntly to say: I unbuttoned my gloves. After all the absorbing adventure of it! Which button did I begin with?' etc. (*Px* 518)

Lawrence not only shared the 1890s critics' distaste for the egotism, self-consciousness, and self-absorption of feminized 'modern' writing, but he also shared their objections to its detailism. In his review of Dos Passos's *Manhattan Transfer* ('the best modern book about New York that I have read'), Lawrence dismissed the modernist work of art as merely mechanical reproduction, a failure, 'from the point of view of life':

> If you set a blank record revolving to receive all the sounds, and a film-camera going to photograph all the motions of a scattered group of individuals at the points where they meet and touch in New York, you would more or less get . . . [the] method. It is a rush of disconnected scenes and scraps, a breathless confusion of isolated moments. (Px 363–4)

Lawrence's fiction is not without its own forms of egotistical self-absorption and microscopic self-examination, nor does it lack its own particular kind of automatism (his tendency towards repetition of particular words, phrases, and images, for example). However, I am not concerned at the moment to argue that Lawrence was in fact a practitioner of the 'feminine' self-consciousness and modernist detailism which he castigates in the above extracts. Rather, I want to pursue another line of connection between the novels of some early twentieth-century male writers and 'feminine fiction' by suggesting that the critique of modern imperialist urban-industrial or commercial society in writers such as Lawrence, E. M. Forster, and Ford Madox Ford is grounded in the critique of scientific, imperialist masculine culture which, like Richardson and Woolf, they took over from late nineteenth-century fiction, particularly New Woman and feminist fiction, and from feminist writing more generally, as well as from socialist or liberal-reformist writing.

Literary history has tended to see Lawrence and Forster as representing two quite different directions taken by English fiction in the twentieth century. However, as John Beer has noted, their careers have 'a common curve',[10] which is shaped by their 'radical dissatisfaction with modern civilization'.[11] Both novelists, like the Edwardians from whom they sought to distance themselves, wrote 'condition-of-England' novels which represented and analysed a society poised on the brink of crisis. In both cases this social critique was articulated within the gendered discourse of degeneration and renovation which I outlined in the first part of this study. Anne Wright has described both *Howard's End* and *Women in Love* as examples of a 'literature of crisis', which she characterizes in terms which could be applied just as aptly to much *fin de siècle* writing: a preoccupation with 'social fission, and the split between material power and humane values; sexuality and sterility; madness and hysteria; violence, death, murder and suicide'.[12]

In *Howards End* (1910), the novel which is most commonly compared with Lawrence's 'English' fiction, Forster presents a picture of the strange degenerative disease of modern English life. Forster, among other things, anatomizes the psychopathological succumbing to introspection, sensation, and emotion which is the chief symptom of degeneration 'discovered' by Nordau, but equally importantly he focuses on the degenerative effects of the denial of the inner life of the emotions and the holiness of the heart's affections. The novel portrays a divided society whose problems are represented, as is so often the case in turn-of-the-century writing, in terms of gender imbalance and a polarization and/or confusion of conventional gender roles. These divisions and polarities, and the potentialities for confusion associated with them, are represented by two families – the Schlegels and the Wilcoxes – and are articulated in the following reflection by Margaret Schlegel, to whom Forster assigns the task of mediating between polarities and resolving the confusion:

> Ours is a female house ... I don't mean that this house is full of women. I mean that it was irrevocably feminine, even in father's time ... it must be feminine, and all we can do is to see that it isn't effeminate. Just as another house that I can mention [the Wilcoxes] ... sounded irrevocably masculine, and all its inmates can do is to see that it isn't brutal. (*HE* 42–3)

The feminine versus the masculine, effeminacy versus brutalization: Margaret Schlegel's reflections on the Scylla and Charybdis of modern society, and indeed the narrative structure which traces the paths that might be steered between them, repeat the gendered terms of the late nineteenth-century debates about culture and civilization, progress and regression/reversion, and degeneration and renovation which I explored in Chapter 2.

The femaleness of the Schlegels' house is not, as Margaret asserts, the consequence of the gender of its inhabitants; rather it is the result and expression of – and also a way of representing – the Schlegels' values and a complex network of cultural and social forces. The Schlegel household is not merely female; it is a 'feminine' or feminized domain of culture: it is European (the Schlegels are half German), socially unconventional, and hospitable to (or, from the Wilcox perspective, seduced or invaded by) progressive even socialistic ideas, especially ideas on the role of women, and on relations between the classes. Margaret and her sister Helen are both, in their different ways, sisters of the New Woman of the 1890s: Margaret is the rational New Woman, Helen, the New Woman as a creature of moments, or as hysteric. They devote themselves to art, the imagination, and ideas. They take up causes and belong to all-women discussion groups. Unlike most of the earlier New Woman protagonists, however, they pursue their interests protected by their private incomes and untrammelled by the demands of a mother and father, or by the structure of the patriarchal family. The senior family member is an ineffectual aunt who resides comfortably in Swanage, and their closest male relative is their invalid brother Tibby, an extremely unpromising patriarch whose preferred position is that favoured by the *fin de siècle* decadent – reclining on a sofa in a drawing-room – and whose spiritual home is an Oxford college.

Modern, urban, mercantile, Imperial England, on the other hand, is represented as masculine. The modern, masculine imperial 'civilization' of the Wilcoxes is a public world of hurry and change, telegrams and anger, energy and power. It is a world in which power derives from energy, and in which power is reinforced by and reinforces the certain certainties of which its inhabitants appear to be assured. Indeed, not the least of Forster's achievements in *Howard's End* is the way in which his narrative both dramatizes and anatomizes (and, in its resolution, neutralizes) the operations of masculine power – its effective mixture of tyranny, seduction, and co-option. The impulsive Helen's rapid succumbing to the masculine 'romance' of the 'robust ideal' (*HE* 24) at the beginning of the narrative is a satirical example:

> She had liked giving in to Mr Wilcox, or Evie, or Charles; she had liked being told that her notions of life were sheltered or academic; that Equality was nonsense, Votes for Women nonsense, Socialism nonsense, Art and literature, except when conducive to strengthening the character, nonsense. (*HE* 24)

However, if the masculine world of 'civilization' is characterized by power and energy, it also conceals (is, perhaps, built on) the 'panic and emptiness' which Helen Schegel discovers in Paul Wilcox in particular and the Wilcox men in general. The Wilcox world is violent and defensive, and verges on the barbaric; it is all it can do (as Margaret has it) 'to see that it isn't brutal' (and in the actions of Charles Wilcox the plot contrives to demonstrate the difficulties it has in doing this). In its representation of their brutality, and in the way in which it juxtaposes the Wilcoxes with the Schlegels, Forster's novel is, in a sense, continuing the Arnoldian debate about culture and anarchy. In the process, it gives to Arnold's terms a local habitation and a gender, and modifies the Arnoldian model of class. The feminized, European Schlegels are in touch with Arnold's 'best that has been thought and said in the world', but the Schlegel sisters (unlike their brother) have an unArnoldian grasp of the economic base of their 'sweetness and light'. The Wilcoxes, representatives of the new aristocracy of power which has not inherited land (as Arnold's barbarian aristocrats had) but which seeks to inherit the land (England), are Forster's barbarians. Theirs is an outward, masculine civilization, dedicated to sport and relying on physical force, and on machines (from motor cars to the machinery of the Imperial company). Wilcox barbarianism subjugates women: Mrs Wilcox is marginalized by her family and betrayed by her husband, Evie is a good chap, and Charles's wife Dolly is silenced and confined to the home by motherhood. Wilcox barbarianism also represses the 'feminine' sphere of culture, and the feminized realm of the emotions.

Although Forster was a self-professed remnant of the fag-end of Victorian liberalism, Arnold is, ultimately, not the most important point of reference for the reworking of the debates about culture and anarchy, barbarianism and civilization undertaken in *Howard's End*. As I suggested earlier, *Howard's End* is a 'condition-of-England' novel, and, like other pre-war (and some post-war) novels of this kind, it represents the condition of England in terms of the turn-of-the-century discourse of degeneration. Both the Wilcoxes and the Schlegels are represented in degenerationist terms. The Wilcox men are examples of the savages beneath the skin who were a recurrent *fin de siècle* fantasy. The Wilcoxes – in whose patriarch Margaret sees the 'real man' (*HE* 162), the engine of material progress who keeps 'us literary people' from 'savagery' (*HE* 164) – are represented in their excessive masculinity and dedication to machinery and materialism as one step away from reverting to the barbarism and savagery which haunted the degenerationists. On the other hand, cultured literary people like the Schlegels are but one step away from the feminized (or, in Tibby's case, effeminate) morbidity which, as my discussion of Nordau demonstrated, was another important figure in the rhetoric of degeneration. Forster's novel engages with and, to some extent, reinscribes some of those complexities and contradictions of the discourse of degeneration which are evident in the following quotation from *Civilisation: Its Cause and Cure*, written on the eve of the 1890s by Edward Carpenter, who, as is well known, had a profound effect on Forster's thinking. Like his fellow New Life socialists, Carpenter figures the degenerative state of modern civilization by means of an ironic reversal of the civilization/barbarism couple, and by embracing a pre-cultural primitivism as the route to regeneration. In this example, 'civilization' is figured not as the antithesis of the barbaric and the savage, but as their equivalent, a state of reversion to barbarity. At the same time, civilization is also figured as (ef)feminizing. Modern urban man, writes Carpenter, 'deliberately turns his back upon the light of the sun, and hides himself away in boxes with breathing holes (which he calls houses) . . . And . . . with [this] denial of Nature comes every form of disease; first delicateness, daintiness, luxury, then unbalance and enervation'.[13] If the first half of the quotation summons up the masculine civilization of luggage, telegrams, and anger of the Wilcoxes, its second half directs us to the morbid, introspective, and enervated Tibby and the unbalanced Helen.

The spectre of degeneration lurks everywhere in *Howard's End*. It appears in the conversation initiated by Leonard Bast's neighbour about the declining birth-rate in Manchester: 'If this kind of thing goes on the population of England will be stationary in 1960,' Mr Cunningham opines (*HE* 46). More importantly, the rhetoric of degeneration is a central component of Forster's construction of the character of Leonard Bast. Bast is one of the New Town types invoked by Masterman (see Chapter 2):

a young man, colourless, toneless, who had already the mournful eyes above a drooping moustache that are so common in London, and that haunt some streets of the city like an accusing presence. One guessed him as the third generation, grandson to the shepherd or ploughboy whom civilization had sucked into the town; as one of the thousands who have lost the life of the body and failed to reach the life of the spirit. Hints of robustness survived in him . . . and Margaret . . . wondered whether it paid to give up the glory of the animal for a tail coat and a couple of ideas. (*HE* 109)

Bast is a figure familiar to readers of the sociological narratives of Booth, Rowntree, Masterman, Jack London, and others: the creature of the abyss. If the Wilcoxes acquaint Helen with the chaos, panic, and emptiness upon which the edifice of Imperial society is constructed, Bast, wherever he goes, carries with him 'odours from the abyss' (*HE* 111), the abyss that lies at the heart of empire, and into which he is in constant fear of falling. Bast is, in fact, an intriguingly liminal figure, occupying the borderlands of each of the social locations represented in this novel. He is perched on the brink of the abyss which lies beyond the pale of civilized society, but which, at the same time, constitutes a continuing threat to it. An all too dispensable cog in the wheel of the brutalized business world, he also hovers on the margins of the morbid effeminized world of culture – 'Borrow, Thoreau and sorrow' (*HE* 114). Bast's eventual expulsion from the novel is, perhaps, symptomatic of its recognition of the impossibility of the Arnoldian dream of holding society together and of seeing things steadily and whole, except in the quasi-utopian terms of the novel's closure.

In place of the Arnoldian dream, and as an antidote to the modern disease of degeneration, Forster's novel invokes the myth of a virile rural England and a feminized version of tradition. The 'real England', rural England, is the last repository of that vigorous yeoman stock of which Leonard Bast is a degenerate descendant. The real England is represented by Howard's End itself, presided over by the earth-mother goddess, Mrs Wilcox, and her feminized spirit of place. Forster's novel, like some of the New Woman fiction at the turn of the century (for example, Mona Caird's *Pathway of the Gods*), charts the operations of a sort of female priest-hood, by means of which the womanly woman Mrs Wilcox passes on her role of mothering and saving the race to the motherless (and childless) Margaret. Margaret herself acts out Forster's motto of 'only connect'. She connects the passion and the prose, the masculine and the feminine, high culture and the world of business, and in so doing she may, perhaps, save the country and tradition (an idealized view of south-east England) from the city and modernity (the creeping 'red rust' of London, Forster's version of the 'dry brittle corruption' of Lawrence's mining town of Wiggiston in *The Rainbow*).

The process of renovation-by-connection which Forster's novel enacts also involves disruption as well as continuity, again in a manner which owes something to the New Woman fiction. The patriarchal Wilcox family is disrupted and fragmented: Charles is imprisoned for manslaughter and will not inherit Howard's End; Mr Wilcox is broken by the series of catastrophes at the end of the novel, and more particularly by Margaret's forcing him to confront the implications of the double standards (particularly in the area of sexual morality) by which he has lived his life. The Wilcox 'fortress' gives way, and is replaced by an unconventional family formation based on the Schlegel sisters and including Leonard Bast's bastard son – a child of nature rather than a son of Empire – who will inherit Howard's End. Bucolic, rural England is reinvigorated by the Schlegel sisters' European culture. However, the most important element of disruption lies in the way in which, ultimately, Forster's emphasis on connection undoes itself. His novel is replete with nostalgia for the rural past, but it also contains a recognition of both the pastness and the passing of that past. The resolution of *Howard's End* is provisional. The inhabitants of the house are represented, like Birkin and Ursula at the end of *Women in Love*, as occupying an island in a sea of change, shoring fragments against their ruin. Margaret Schlegel's affirmation of continuity, her belief that 'our house is the future as well as the past' (*HE* 316), is held in unresolved tension with her sister's modernist sense of dissolution, her sense that 'London is only part of something else . . . Life's going to be melted down, all over the world' (*HE* 316)

Ford Madox Hueffer's [Ford's] *The Good Soldier* is similarly preoccupied with, and, indeed enacts, this sense of life melting down. Published some five years after Forster's critique of 'the Imperialist . . . destroyer . . . [who] prepares the way for cosmopolitanism' (*HE* 301), Ford's novel also addresses the imperial crisis of the pre-war period. Although it is set mainly in a German spa town, *The Good Soldier* is, like *Howard's End* and *The Rainbow*, a 'condition-of-England' or, at least, a 'condition-of-the-English' novel which, to paraphrase its narrator, sounds the depths of the English heart. Like Forster and Lawrence, Ford too is concerned with the decline of the English, and with social and sexual corruption and degeneration.

Howard's End can be read either as a novel which vindicates feminine values, or as a recommendation of a process of accommodation between men and women, and a delicate balancing of the masculine and the feminine. On the other hand, like Lawrence's, several of Forster's other fictions (including *The Longest Journey*, 1907, and *A Passage to India*, 1924) present a search for comradeship between men as a possible resolution of the problems of modern life. Whether recommending male comradeship or the accommodation of masculine and feminine, Forster's fiction rejects the dominant English model of manliness represented by the Wilcox males. In fact, both Forster and Lawrence interestingly rework turn-of-the-century representations of both Englishness and manliness. While many commentators on late nineteenth- and early twentieth-century culture see foreignness, feminized men, and degeneracy as interchangeable terms, Lawrence and Forster reverse this discourse and often use foreign men, and on occasions feminized, foreign (especially southern European or Mediterranean) men, as agents of social and psychological renovation.

Lawrence's view of the degeneration of social disintegration which constitute the condition of modern England is much bleaker than Forster's is in *Howard's End*, but like Forster's it is represented in terms of gender polarization, and gender imbalance or inversion. In Lawrence's earlier fiction in particular, social regeneration is also represented in terms of the gendered discourse of renovation inherited from the late nineteenth century, especially the New Woman fiction. Thus the main critic of modern civilization in *The White Peacock* (1911) – a novel of 'fashionable cultural pessimism'[14] – is the aggressively masculine Annable, a clergyman turned gamekeeper. Annable is 'a man of one idea: – that all civilisation was the painted fungus of rottenness'. He has been made into the enemy of culture by marriage to a spiritualized New Woman (Lady Crystabel) who refused to have children, and humiliated 'the pride of [his] body'.[15] *The Trespasser* (1912) and *Sons and Lovers* (1913) also, in part, represent cultural degeneration by means of the actually or potentially emasculating effects of spiritualized *fin de siècle* dreaming women, or intellectual New Women – Helena, Miriam, Mrs Morel, Clara Dawes. In *The Rainbow* (1915) the degenerative impulse of modern society is figured by a masculinized female character (the 'invert' New Woman Winifred Inger), and a perverse degenerate male (the second Tom Brangwen), who is also portrayed as a member of a negatively defined intermediate sex. Tom combines both masculine and feminine characteristics: his sensuality is represented as a form of feminization – 'the real voluptuary is a man who is female as well as male, and who lives according to the female side of his nature' (*Px* 459) – but his commitment to the machine culture of Wiggiston is represented as a depraved, brutalized masculinity.

It is worth pursuing Lawrence's links to the New Woman novel a little further, since Lawrence's work looks very different when it is removed from its place in the 'great tradition', or in a telescoped history of a modernism which starts with the change in human character in 1910, and is reinserted into a slightly longer historical perspective. Lawrence's 'condition-of-England' novel, *The Rainbow*, is certainly in its latter stages also Lawrence's New Woman novel *par excellence*. More accurately, it is a novel in which George Eliot's *The Mill on the Floss* and *Middlemarch* meet (for example) George Egerton's *The Wheel of God*. It is a blend of English regional realism in chronicle form, and the allegorical, episodic, lyricism of the New Woman novel. Certainly during the earlier part of his writing life Lawrence was sympathetic to the woman's cause, and during the period in which he began work on *The Rainbow* he espoused a non-suffragist form of feminism. Indeed he claimed in 1912 that his fiction would 'do my work for women, better than the suffrage' (*LL* i. 490), a claim, incidentally, that echoes George Moore's contention in the 1880s that his attempts to extend the franchise of fiction were more important to women (and men) than any franchise bill.

The emergent narrative of *The Rainbow*, the story of Ursula, is the familiar New Woman story of a 'woman becoming individual, self responsible, taking her own initiative' (*LL* ii. 165). Ursula's story, like Mary Desmond's in Egerton's *The Wheel of God*, and like that of numerous other heroines of 1890s' fiction (by men and women), is the story of the questing modern woman who seeks to demonstrate (like another, unnamed, Egerton female protagonist) that there 'are no dragons in the world nowadays that one cannot overcome, if one is not afraid of them, and sets up no false gods'.[16] Like many New Woman novels, *The Rainbow* ends with a renovatory vision which portends an alliance (in this case a fragile and tenuous one) between the New Woman and the working class. It is a vision of rebirth which is articulated by means of a transcendent, salvationary rhetoric like that of turn-of-the-century feminism, or Edward Carpenter's socialism. Out of corruption and disintegration will come new life:

> She knew that the sordid people who crept hard-scaled and separate on the face of the world's corruption were living still, that the rainbow was arched in their blood and would quiver to life in their spirit, that they would cast off their horny covering of disintegration, that new, clean, naked bodies would issue to a new germination, to a new growth . . . (R. 495–6)

Lawrence's New Woman novel thus ends with a social vision. The questing New Woman heroine is to be reintegrated into society, unlike the questing hero of *Sons and Lovers*, who takes his lonely, individualistic road towards the anonymity of the city. This important difference should perhaps alert us to the fact that *The Rainbow* also reworks another typical New Woman plot, the 'boomerang' plot, by means of which the experiments in life of the unconventional heroine blow up in her face, and/or she is boomeranged back into social and gender-role conformity. Ursula, like many New Woman heroines, is a 'revolting daughter' who rejects the model of woman's life represented by her hyper-reproductive *magna mater* mother. Like that of many of her fictional predecessors, Ursula's attempt to break free of conventional gender and familial roles ends in chaos and confusion. Ursula's sexual liberation results in pregnancy and a miscarriage which boomerang her into illness and finally into the social readjustment which such female illnesses in fiction have served to prefigure since before Jane Austen's Marianne Dashwood emerged from her sickbed to marry Colonel Brandon in *Sense and Sensibility*.

In *The Rainbow* Lawrence also reworks the boomerang plot as social critique. He constructs a plot that allows his female protagonist to win her battles and make her way in 'The Man's World' (Chapter 13), but he does so in order to make her, and his readers, acknowledge that the battle is not worth winning. Like some nineteenth-century feminists (for

example, those I described earlier as social-purity feminists), Lawrence saw
no point in women striving to gain equal access to 'The Man's World',
which he described as fighting 'an old system of self-preservation to obtain
a more advanced system of preservation' (*Px* 404). Rather they should
strive to change it by finding an alternative to the 'mechanism' (*R.* 377)
of 'this unclean system of authority' (*R.* 380). 'Why should she give her
allegiance to this world, and let it so dominate her life, that her own world
of warm sun and growing, sap-filled life was turning to nothing? . . . She
was not going to be a prisoner in the dry, tyrannical man-world' (*R.* 410).

In *The Rainbow* the 'terrible corruption' (*R.* 495) of the 'man-world' is
replaced by the 'sap-filled life' of Ursula and, potentially, the miners. The
ballot box and social feminism are rejected in favour of books, beauty,
and an inner freedom. One consequence of Lawrence's mixing of his
gendered social critique (the critique of the 'man-world') with his story of
the New Woman is to put the New Woman back into the domestic, spiritual, feminine sphere. Ursula has her vision of the birth of the new world
as she sits at the window of her sick room, following a prolonged period
of domestic incarceration. Moreover, as Lawrence develops Ursula's story
of a modern woman in the more self-consciously modernist form of
Women in Love, he returns to the even older story of 'the daughters of
men coming back to the sons of God, the strange inhuman sons of God
who are in the beginning'.[17]

Lawrence's readers have long learned to see the Ursula of *The Rainbow*
and the Ursula of *Women in Love* as different characters, each part of a
distinctive and discontinuous fictional project. It has also become
commonplace to see *The Rainbow* as marking the end of Lawrence's
development or modernizing of the English realist novel, and to see
Women in Love as marking a significant movement in the direction of a
modernist fictional practice. *The Rainbow* might also be seen as marking
the end of Lawrence's early attempts to renovate fiction by means of a
turn to the feminine. Something of the nature of the gender politics of
both this project and its broader cultural context can be seen in a letter
on the renovation of art, which Lawrence wrote while working on *The
Rainbow*. The letter, stimulated by Lawrence's reading of Marinetti and
the Italian Futurists, is worth quoting at length.

> I like them [the Futurists]. Only I don't believe in them. I agree with
> them about the weary sickness of pedantry and tradition and inert-
> ness, but I don't agree with them as to the cure . . . They will
> progress down the purely male or intellectual or scientific line . . .
> I think the only re-sourcing of art, re-vivifying it, is to make it
> more the joint work of man and woman. I think *the* one thing to
> do, is for men to have courage to draw nearer women, expose
> themselves to them, and be altered by them: and for women to accept
> and admit men . . . That is the start . . . which it will take a big

further lapse of civilisation to exploit and work out. Because the source of all life and knowledge is in man and woman, and the source of all living is in the interchange and the meeting and mingling of these two: man-life and woman-life, man-knowledge and woman-knowledge, man-being and woman-being. (*LL* ii. 181)

After *The Rainbow* Lawrence's fiction seems to take a distinct turn, some would say lurch, to the 'male line', first with the search for comradeship between men which is central to *Women in Love*, and then with an increasingly strident valorization of masculinity and phallicism, and a hostility to the female and feminine in *Aaron's Rod*, *Kangaroo*, and *The Plumed Serpent*, as well as some of the shorter fictions. At first glance this bifurcated view of Lawrence's career – with *The Rainbow* as the watershed – is very persuasive, and it can be supported by reference to Lawrence's discursive writings. Thus the supposedly gender-balancing *Study of Thomas Hardy* is usually seen as providing the theoretical framework for the earlier, quasi-feminist phase of Lawrence's fiction, up to and including *The Rainbow*, and the gender-polarizing *Fantasia of the Unconscious* as the theoretical foundation of the later, masculinist phase.

How does one explain the changes in Lawrence's thinking on gender, his use of a gendered discourse, and his representation of the relations between men and women between *The Rainbow* and *Woman in Love* and its successors? The most obvious way in which to account for the differences is by reference to the war, that defining moment in both modern history and the history of literary modernism. The First World War separated the completion and publication of *The Rainbow* in September 1915, and the successive rewritings and revisions of the material that was to become *Women in Love*. According to Lawrence himself, *The Rainbow* is 'destructive-consummating', while *Women in Love* (1921), the novel which 'contain[s] the results of one's soul of the war', is 'purely destructive' (*LL* iii. 142–3).

Lawrence's thinking about gender also seems to be inextricably connected with his thinking on degeneration, which, as for so many of his contemporaries, took an apocalyptic turn as a result of the war. Among the discarded working titles for *Women in Love* were the more doom-laden *Love among the Ruins* (the title of Robert Browning's poem from which Birkin quotes in Chapter 5), *The Last Days*, and *Dies Irae*. The episodic, fragmentary narrative structure of this novel conveys that sense of the ending of an era, even of a civilization, which Lawrence repeatedly articulated in letters at this time: 'I think there is no future for England: only a decline and fall. That is the dreadful and unbearable part of it: to have been born into a decadent era, a decline of life, a collapsing civilisation' (*LL* ii. 441). If Lawrence's pre-war fiction represents the familiar turn-of-the-century picture of a degenerating civilization, in the post-war fiction the war marks the death of civilization; post-war northern Europe, and England in particular, are its putrefying corpse.

It was in 1915 the old world ended. In the winter 1915–1916 the spirit of the old London collapsed; the city, in some way, perished . . . from being a heart of the world, and became a vortex of broken passions . . . The genuine debasement began, the unspeakable baseness of the press and the public voice, the reign of that bloated ignominy, *John Bull*.[18]

For Lawrence, as for the other early twentieth-century novelists discussed in this book, the war was undoubtedly a significant determinant of his thinking about art, civilization, and gender. However, although a necessary explanation, it is not a sufficient explanation of the changes in their thinking or in their fictional practice. Certainly, the war was an important dividing line for Lawrence, particularly as far as his thinking about, and representation of, gender was concerned. Lawrence's post-war engagement with gender issues, his representations of men and women and of the relations between them, were, as I indicated in the concluding section of Chapter 2, symptomatic of a general polarization of thinking on gender and a hardening of attitudes to women and feminism in the post-war period. However, it is not the case that Lawrence presented a single view of women, men, feminism, and gender issues in the pre-war work, and a diametrically opposed, but equally monolithic view in the post-war writing. Rather, he deployed an inherently contradictory discourse on and of gender throughout his writings, and he used those discourses in contradictory ways. In fact, Lawrence is a writer whose work displays in microcosm most of the issues I have been discussing in this book. In his work the turn-of-the-century debates about gender, and the gendered debates on art, culture, and civilization, and all the manifold contradictions of the representation of gender and gendered representations are replayed and redisplayed. For these reasons I will, in my concluding chapter, explore some of the twists and turns in the engendering of Lawrence's writing as a way of revisiting and summarizing some of those issues.

|7|

D. H. Lawrence: Gender-bending and Sex Wars

*They tell us of all the things that are going to happen in the future –
babies bred in bottle [sic], all the love-nonsense cut out, women
indistinguishable from men. But it seems to me bosh ... People ... are
merely people ... Humanity seems to have an infinite capacity for
remaining the same – that is, human ...*

*And women are just part of the human show. They aren't something
apart ... They say the modern woman is a new type. But is she? ...
Women are women ...*

*Certain phases of history are 'modern'. As the wheel of history goes
round women become 'modern', then they become unmodern again ...*

*Modernity or modernism isn't something we've just invented. It's
something that comes at the end of civilizations. Just as leaves in
autumn are yellow,* so the women at the end of every known
civilization ... *have been modern. They were smart, they were chic,
they said cut-it-out, and they did as they jolly well pleased.* (Px II
539–40; emphasis added)

It is a truth universally acknowledged that Lawrence was a writer who
was obsessed with questions of gender. He persistently conceptualized and
represented the world in gendered terms, and in terms of sexual difference; persistently, but not consistently. 'Women Don't Change' Lawrence
asserted in the title of an article in the *Sunday Dispatch* in 1929, from
which I quote above. However, Lawrence's views of women, and consequently of men, most certainly did change, not only over time and from
text to text, but almost from moment to moment and within a single text.

'Women Don't Change', written near the end of his life (and reprinted, more interrogatively, as 'Do Women Change?' in *Phoenix II*), is a good example of both the persistence and inconsistency of Lawrence's representation of the female and the feminine: first, in the way in which it invokes the eternal feminine as a means of affirming a belief in a common and universal humanity; second, in its association of women and the feminine with modernity, and third in its association of women with the end of civilization. These pairings persist throughout Lawrence's writing, but the nature and the significance of the relationship between the two halves of each pair change. As I have attempted to show throughout this study, neither the pairings, nor the shifting relations within and between them, were peculiar to Lawrence. They were an integral part of social and cultural analysis and critique from the 1890s onwards (if not earlier).

Lawrence's first systematic theorization of gender, or perhaps more accurately his gendered theorizing of human existence, is found in the *Study of Thomas Hardy*, begun '[o]ut of sheer rage' at the 'colossal idiocy' of 'this war' (*LL* ii. 212). The Hardy study remained unpublished during Lawrence's lifetime, but ever since its publication in *Phoenix* in 1936 it has been eagerly quarried by those seeking to unravel the complexities and confusions of Lawrence's thinking on the man-and-woman question. Many commentators have stressed Lawrence's emphasis in this early work (as in his early fiction) on the fusion and complementarity of the sexes, and on the balance and relatedness of male and female, which are 'as one, as axle and wheel are one' (*Px* 442). In an alternative figuration, the male and female meet and flow together, 'the pure male stream' and 'the pure female stream in a heave and an overflowing'.

In its emphasis on sexual harmony and on gender balance and relatedness, the Hardy study has much in common with the thinking of progressive sex psychologists such as Ellis and Carpenter. Hilary Simpson makes precisely this connection when she focuses on what she sees as the *Study*'s advocacy of 'a sensitive openness and receptiveness between men and women', and its urging of its putative readers to 'accept the challenge of sexual difference and use sexuality as a means of plunging into the unknown'.[1] Certainly the Hardy study assigns prime importance to sexuality and sexual difference both in the life of individuals and in Life itself, whose fundamental organizing principles are, according to Lawrence, 'the great male and female duality and unity' (*Px* 443). The Hardy study represents a binary model of a universe organized by opposing but complementary sex-gender categories. Maleness (as Hilary Simpson notes) is the Will-to-Motion, the hub, mobility, change, knowledge, spirit, love, the mind, consciousness, abstraction, doing, purpose achieved. Femaleness is the Will-to-Inertia, the axle, stability, conservation, nature, flesh, law, the soul, the senses, the feelings, being, purpose contained.

Like the progressive sex psychologists, Lawrence did not, at least in 1914, see these sex-gender characteristics as biological givens, tied to the biological male or the biological female. Like Carpenter and Ellis, and also like Otto Weininger, he espoused a theory of bisexuality in which men and women each have a combination of male and female, masculine and feminine characteristics: 'We start from one side or the other, the female side or the male, but what we want is always the perfect union of the two' (*Px* 515). Or again, 'a man who is well balanced between male and female, in his own nature, is as a rule, happy, easy to mate' (*Px* 460). However, as the last sentence quoted suggests, for Lawrence, as for Weininger, maleness, and indeed the man, are always the starting-point. Although 'no new thing [in life] has ever arisen, or can arise, save out of the impulse of the male upon the female, the female upon the male' (*Px* 444), the real importance of the female lies in the completion of the male. The woman roots and stabilizes the man for his leap into the unknown (see *Px* 447): 'Man must seek the female to possess his soul, to fertilise him . . . And the finding of it for himself gives a man his vision, his God' (*Px* 445). Lawrence's view, at least in the *Study*, is marginally less masculinist than Weininger's, in so far as Lawrence assigns to the female the crucial role of completing the male. Weininger sees the function of completion as being the other way around: 'The male lives consciously, the female lives unconsciously . . . The woman receives her consciousness from the man; the function to bring into consciousness what was outside it is a sexual function of the typical man with regard to the typical woman' (*S&C* 102).

In the *Study of Thomas Hardy* Lawrence also develops a gendered model of history, and plots the history of Western culture as a succession of male and female (his terms) cycles. These cycles periodically return to their point of origin in a process which is represented as a kind of dance, rather like the sheaf-gathering ritual between Will and Anna in *The Rainbow*, 'a double cycle, of men and women, facing opposite ways . . . revolving upon each other . . . neither able to move till their hands have grasped each other' (*Px* 449). At other historical moments, however, one or other sex principle is dominant. Thus Judaism is female (as it was for the anti-Semites Weininger and Wyndham Lewis), early Christianity, male. Similarly, the whole history of Western art is plotted as a contest between the male and female principles, between abstraction and the body. As Weininger had done before him, Lawrence maps his gendered theory of history on to a gendered theory of race, and with rather similar results. Like Weininger, Lawrence sees the Jews as excessively female. They are passive, secret, voluptuous, resistant 'to the male or active principle', recognizing only 'male sins' or sins of commission (*Px* 51). On the other hand, since the Renaissance, 'northern humanity', and especially the 'neutral' English race, 'has sought for consummation in the spirit, it has sought for the female apart from woman' (*Px* 469), has denied the body and become excessively male, like the northern, Aryan Gerald Crich in *Women in Love*.

The convolutions of Lawrence's male and female cycles are not easy to follow, partly because he traces the course of those cycles from a masculine perspective; both the 'male' and the 'female' cycles are represented exclusively through male examples. However, it would appear that in the *Study* Lawrence conceives of the modern age as one in which the male is in the ascendant, and that he sees the moment of the war as a moment ripe for feminization, rather than as a crisis induced by feminization. In this respect Lawrence's position in the Hardy study seems to have been nearer to that of the pacificist feminists than to degenerationists such as Nordau or Weininger, who saw 'Our age' as 'not only the most Jewish but the most feminine' (*S&C* 329).

In the Hardy study, as elsewhere, Lawrence's thinking about gender is integrally connected, as is most turn-of-the-century thinking on gender, to a complex of contesting ideas about generation, regeneration, and degeneration. Lawrence shares the sex psychologists' view of the importance of the non-generative, or non-reproductive, function of sex. The parable of the poppy with which the *Study* opens is designed to demonstrate that the purpose of existence is the flower and not the fruit. This is a point that Lawrence underlines later in the Hardy study, and which he develops into a central theme in *The Rainbow*: 'That she bear children is not a woman's significance. But that she bear herself, that is her supreme and risky fate' (*Px* 441). Lawrence's valorizing of non-reproductive sexuality and his diminution of the significance of biological reproduction links him not only to the feminist advocates of birth control and to sex reformers like Havelock Ellis, and radical homosexuals such as Edward Carpenter, but also to Wilde and the decadents. A similar link to the decadents can be seen in Lawrence's modernist rejection of mechanical reproduction and mass society in Chapter IV of the *Study*. Here Lawrence outlines a critique of work, the 'money appetite' (*Px* 427), mass society, and the State, and urges a rejection of mechanical production in favour of self-production.

> Those State educations with their ideals, their armaments of aggression and defence, what are they to me? . . . As for me, I would say to every decent man whose heart is straining at the enclosure, 'Come away from the crowd and the community, come away and be separate in your own soul, and live. Your business is to produce your own real life, no matter what the nations do. (*Px* 429)

As this passage suggests, the seeds of Lawrence's later turn against democracy and the masses, and his valorization of the proud, free, (male) individual, are already evident in the Hardy study. On the whole, however, the rhetoric which Lawrence employs in developing his social critique in the *Study* has much in common with the rhetoric of turn-of-the-century feminism and also with the pacifist feminism of the war years. The introductory chapters of the *Study* paint a *fin de siècle* picture of an exhausted civilization, and a sickness in the body politic. These, like the war, are linked to man's homelessness on the earth and the 'anxiety' which has led him to evolve 'nations and tremendous governments'. It is this 'strenuous purpose, unremitting, [that] has brought to pass the whole frantic turmoil of modern industry' (*Px* 398). In 1914–15 Lawrence saw the war as one of the problems caused by an exhausted, masculinized, routinized, mechanized, and anti-individualistic society. In this situation Lawrence sympathizes with feminists and suffragists who seek to improve things, as he does to an extent in *The Rainbow*. Ultimately, however, the *Study* – like the novel – represents the suffragist feminists as misguided and failing to engage with the real problem. Chapter II of the *Study* ('About Women's Suffrage, and Laws, and the War . . . '), rather like Dora Marsden's *Egoist*, rejects the suffragists' cause on the grounds that they want the vote only to make more laws to prop up an ailing society, rather than to discard 'this clumsy machinery' (*Px* 405) of laws and thereby purge the sick body politic. By late 1914 Lawrence, like the modernist *Egoist*, was looking to individualist and transcendent or metaphysical, rather than social and political solutions to the problems of modernity – the visionary, integrative ending of *The Rainbow* notwithstanding.

In the fiction and in the essays which followed *The Rainbow* and the *Study of Thomas Hardy* (even in his experiment in the Bennett–Galsworthy line of fiction, the woman-question novel, *The Lost Girl*, 1920) Lawrence's degenerationist stance became increasingly pronounced: 'the book frightens me its [*sic*] so very end of the world,' Lawrence wrote of *Women in Love* in 1916 (*LL* iii. 25). Again the war is usually offered as the explanation for Lawrence's end-of-the-worldism. Frank Kermode has accounted for it differently, in terms of what he sees as Lawrence's propensity towards apocalytpic thinking.

> Lawrence was obsessed with apocalypse from early youth . . . He considered the world to be undergoing a rapid decline which should issue in a renovation . . . Lawrence . . . dwelt more on the decadence, and seemed to think the English were rotting with especial rapidity in order to be ready first. He spoke of the coming resurrection – 'Except a seed die, it bringeth not forth,' he advises Bertrand Russell in May 1915.[2]

In the essay from which I have just quoted, Kermode offers a very persuasive reading of *Women in Love* as an apocalyptic novel. It is undeniable that the language of the Bible and biblical typology are important elements of Lawrence's writings throughout his career. Even at the time of his death Lawrence was working on the essay that was to be posthumously published as 'Apocalypse'. But what is particularly interesting, I think, is the way in which Lawrence's biblical apocalypticism becomes entangled with turn-of-the-century degenerationist and renovationist discourse. Even if he had not been so thoroughly imbued with biblical apocalyptic types, Lawrence would have been immersed in the apocalyptic thinking of his degenerationist contemporaries or near-contemporaries. For example, although it may be difficult to prove beyond doubt that Lawrence read Weininger, it is clear that they share a similar conceptual and rhetorical framework, namely that modern civilization has reached the end of a line.

> Mankind waits for the new founder of religion, and . . . the new age presses for a decision. The decision must be made between Judaism and Christianity, between business and culture, between male and female, – the race and the individual . . . between negation and the God-like. Mankind has the choice to make. There are only two poles, and there is no middle way. (S&C 30)

Like Weininger, Nordau, Ludovici, and others, Lawrence does not passively and despairingly await the last days which will bring destruction and possibly renewal. Rather, in increasingly strident tones (especially in the writings of the 1920s), he presents his readers not only with gendered images of degeneration and decline, but also with crucial choices which might issue in a regeneration. For Lawrence regeneration increasingly meant 'regenderation', through a turn to the male or the masculine. The 'old order is done for, toppling on top of us', Lawrence wrote to Cynthia Asquith in 1916; 'it's no use the men looking to the women for salvation, nor the woman looking to sensuous satisfaction for fulfilment. There must be a new Word' (LL ii. 526).

Lawrence's advocacy of a turn to the male, rather than to the female or feminine, as a way out of 'a rotten, idealistic machine-civilisation' (Px 661) begins in earnest following his discarding of the homosexual Prologue to Women in Love, and his exploration in the final version of the novel of Birkin's failed attempt at male comradeship with Gerald. In 'Education of the People', written in 1918, Lawrence began the attacks on democracy and the masses and the feminization of society which he was to develop in his male romances, Aaron's Rod, Kangaroo, and The Plumed Serpent. In this diatribe against what he saw as the misguidedness of idealistic conceptions of elementary education for the masses, Lawrence adopts a rhetorical strategy similar to those employed by the nineteenth-century social critics Matthew Arnold, and (more especially) Thomas Carlyle, and latterly by pre-war avant-gardeists (such as Wyndham Lewis), and post-war degenerationists like A. M. Ludovici (see Chapter 2). He situates himself as the privileged wise-seer of a crisis scenario which is created by his own images of disease and decline. In this case, society is figured as suffering from a 'nasty disease of self-consciousness' (Px 627). As is so often the case in such crisis scenarios, it is difficult to distinguish between the symptoms and the causes of decline, and there is much confusion about causes. Thus, 'Mankind has degenerated into a conglomerate mass' (*Px* 650), but (paradoxically?) a 'disintegration of all society' is threatened by 'the over-development of the individualistic qualities' of the masses (*Px* 613). Lawrence represents an England in which (it should be obvious) 'democracy is gone beyond itself' (*Px* 609), and in which it 'is obvious that the old ideal of Equality won't do' (*Px* 600). In this essay Lawrence figures cultural degeneration as feminization. Both democracy and the idealistic conception of the education of the masses are represented as a 'sort of womanliness' (*Px* 596), or, what Lawrence refers to in 'Surgery for the Novel – or a Bomb', as the 'democratic-industrial-lovey-dovey-take-me-to-mama state of things' (*Px* 520).

In 'Education of the People' Lawrence appears to believe, like Weininger, that 'there is no middle way', and that the one thing needful to avert total disintegration is a stark choice between the male and the female. Lawrence advocates a simultaneous rejection of the feminine, particularly the maternal, and a turn to the masculine. 'Education of the People' takes Birkin's rejection of the *magna mater* a stage further in a fierce denunciation of motherhood and mothers, as Lawrence incites his readers to march under the slogan, '*down with mothers! A bas les mères!*' (*Px* 621). Of course many turn-of-the-century feminists (like many of our own contemporaries) would have sympathized with Lawrence's critique of the sanctification of maternity – 'the grovelling degeneracy of Mariolatry', 'the exaltation of motherhood', which 'threatens the sanity of our race' (*Px* 621–2). However, it would be difficult to argue that Lawrence's repetitive, hysterical attack on mothers constitutes a feminist critique of maternity. Like the eighteenth-century satirist Jonathan Swift (but without the cool edge of Swift's satirical voice), Lawrence makes his own modest proposal about the solution of a social problem by disposing of babies: 'babies should invariably be taken away from their modern mothers and given . . . to rather stupid fat women who can't be bothered with them. There should be a league for the prevention of maternal love, as there is a society for the prevention of cruelty to animals' (*Px* 621). In place of the rejected icon of the mother, Lawrence erects the icon of the questing male: 'scouting, fighting, gathering provision, running on the brink of death and at the tip of the life advance . . . the men, the leaders, the outriders' (*Px* 665). Lawrence's iconic masculinity owes something to the male romance of the *fin de siècle*, and something to Baden Powell's *Scouting For Boys* (1908), and something to Ludovici's (or the Futurists') regenerative male (again I am making a point about convergence rather than – necessarily – about influence). In place of the idealization of mother-love, Lawrence, the critic of Walt Whitman's ideas on democracy, offers a positively Whitmanesque idealization of male comradeship. This idealization is central to the fiction of the 1920s so it is worth quoting at length.

> And between men let there be new, spontaneous relationship, a new fidelity. Let men realize that their life lies ahead, in the dangerous

wilds of advance and increase. Let them realize that they must go beyond their women, projected into a region of greater abstraction, more inhuman activity.

There, in these womanless regions of fight, and pure thought and abstracted instrumentality, let men have a new attitude to one another, a new reverence for their heroes, a new regard for their comrades: deep, deep as life and death ... And the extreme bond of friendship supports them over the edge of the known and into the unknown. (*Px* 665)

By 1918 Lawrence would seem to have substituted a masculine vitalism for the feminized vitalism of the Edwardians. It would also seem that he has begun to adopt the Futurists' cure as well as their diagnosis of the 'weary sickness' of art and society. The 'womanless regions of pure thought and abstracted instrumentality' envisaged in the above passage look remarkably like the 'pure male or intellectual line' which Lawrence had earlier disparaged in the Futurists (*LL* ii. 181).

THE BREACH BETWEEN US

You are yourself, a woman, and I am myself, a man: and that makes a breach between us. So let's leave the breach and walk across occasionally on some suspension-bridge. But you live on one side, and I live on the other ... You look after the immediate personal life, and I'll look after the further, abstracted, and mechanical life ... We're neither better nor worse than each other; we're an equipoise in difference – but in difference, mind, not in sameness. (Px 664)

This statement from near the end of 'Education of the People' signals Lawrence's reversion to the theory of radical sexual difference which underlies *Fantasia of the Unconscious* and the so-called novels of male power. The theory of sex-gender complementarity, developed (although, as I have suggested, by no means consistently and seamlessly) in the *Study of Thomas Hardy*, and figured as two converging streams, is replaced by a metaphor of the male and female as two banks of the river, always separate. *Fantasia* represents men and women as inhabiting radically different spheres, divided by mutual incomprehension: 'Woman will *never* understand the depth of the spirit of purpose in man ... And man will never understand the sacredness of feeling to woman' (*F*. 103).

Lawrence's *Fantasia* re-enacts the manœuvres performed by those scientists, social commentators, and literary critics of the 1890s who responded to actual changes in the social and sexual roles of men and women, and the consequent erosion or blurring of conventional sex-gender distinctions, by reaffirming a rigidly polarized view of sex-gender difference.

A child is born sexed. A child is either male or female; the whole of
its psyche and physique is either male or female. Every single living
cell is either male or female, and will remain either male or female
as long as life lasts ... The talk about a third sex, or about the
indeterminate sex, is just to pervert the issue. (F. 96)

In *Fantasia* Lawrence thus rejects the version of the theory of bisexuality or sexual intermediacy which he appeared to espouse in his gender-
convergence theory in the *Study*. He now relabels sexual intermediacy as
sexual indeterminacy, and dismisses it as 'the hermaphrodite fallacy' (*F*.
100). The apparent 'reversal of the old poles' (*F*. 99) of gender which
Lawrence and his contemporaries were experiencing all around them is
similarly dismissed as merely an illusion, a thing of surfaces: 'Man in the
midst of all his effeminacy, is still male and nothing but male. And
woman, though she harangue in Parliament ... is still completely female.
They are only playing each other's roles, because the poles have swung
into reversion' (*F*. 100). Lawrence himself does some 'reversion' of his
own in *Fantasia*, by transvaluing the sex-gender categories he had elaborated in the *Study of Thomas Hardy*. He relabels as male those categories
which in the *Study* he had labelled as female, and vice versa. Thus love
and spirit, previously valued positively as male categories, become instead
feminine diseases.

However, *Fantasia* does not simply represent a swing 'into reversion'.
Although it appears to reverse many of the key ideas of the Hardy study,
it also develops others. Thus the apparent replacement of the earlier
commitment to the idea of the primacy of the male–female sex relation
by a new privileging of 'the desire of the human male to build a world:
"not to build a world for you dear" ' (*F*. 18), is in fact a development of
Lawrence's thinking on non-generative sexuality. The valorization of non-
reproductive sexuality in the Hardy study is extended, in *Fantasia*, into
an emphasis on non-reproductive and also non-productive (in the material
sense) creativity, and an affirmation of the self-generation and self-fashion-
ing of male creativity. Lawrence's apparently new emphasis on 'the pure
disinterested craving of the human male to make something wonderful,
out of his own head and his own self, and his own soul's faith', a craving
to which 'the motivity of sex is subsidiary' (*F*. 18), is, thus, a development of his valorization of non-reproductive sexuality in the Hardy study.
It is also, of course, a way of privileging male forms of creativity over
female reproductivity.

Like most of Lawrence's work from this period, *Fantasia* situates itself
as a cry from the wilderness of a disintegrating social order: 'We have
almost poisoned the mass of humanity to death with *understanding*. The
period of actual death and race-extermination is not far off' (*F*. 115). In
Fantasia Lawrence adopts a self-consciously oppositional stance, defining
his own theories of sexual difference against both the 'lovey-dovey' and

the scientific explanations of sex offered by the English sex reformers, the English and continental European sex psychologists, and Freud. The 'child is born sexed' passage quoted earlier is a clear example of this. Lawrence writes in the manner of one who has seen the truth and will brook no argument. Indeed in *Fantasia*, as in the fiction of the early 1920s, Lawrence persistently addresses his readers in a rather contemptuous tone, rewriting modernist impersonality as a prophetic, élitist distance: 'I don't intend my books for the generality of readers. I count it a mistake of our mistaken democracy that every man who can read print is allowed to believe that he can read all that is printed' (*F.* 11).

SEX WARS: MANLY WOMEN AND WOMANLY MEN

All fights for freedom that succeed, go too far, and become in turn the infliction of a tyranny ... like the freedom of women. Perhaps the greatest revolution of modern times is the emancipation of women ... The fight [for woman's independence] was deep and bitter, and, it seems to me, it is won. It is even going beyond and becoming a tyranny of woman, of the individual woman in the house, and of the feminine ideas and ideals in the world ... [T]he world is swayed by feminine emotion today, and the triumph of the productive and domestic activities of man over all his previous military or adventurous or flaunting activities is a triumph of woman in the home. ('The Real Thing' (1930), Px 196)

In *Fantasia* Lawrence attributes the imminence of 'death and race extermination' not simply (as he had earlier) to a general feminization of society, but rather – like many turn-of-the-century and also post-war social commentators and cultural critics – to feminism. The disintegrative effects of a generalized feminized self-consciousness noted in 'Education of the People' is now explicitly linked to women and to feminism in a *parti pris* summary of turn-of-the-century women's history, which recirculates the discourse on the New Woman.

First she is the noble spouse of a not-quite-so-noble male: then a *Mater Dolorosa*, then a ministering angel: then a competent social unit, a member of Parliament or a Lady Doctor or a platform speaker ... She can't stop having an idea of herself. She can't get herself out of her own head. And there she is, functioning away from her own head ... till the whole man and woman game has become just a hell, and men with any backbone would rather kill themselves than go on with it – or kill somebody else ...

There will *have* to come an end [to all this], every race which has
become self-conscious and idea-bound in the past has perished. (*F.*
86)

This passage is a good example of the way in which the Lawrence of
Fantasia reverts to the turn-of-the-century anti-feminist discourse which
enjoyed something of a renaissance in the 1920s (see the concluding
section of Chapter 2). At this time, as in the 1890s (and in the 1990s, for
that matter), anti-feminists responded to changes in gender roles and
relations between the sexes by representing feminism as both the cause
and the symptom of degeneration. More especially, in *Fantasia*, as in his
fiction of the same period, Lawrence (like many other writers on the
woman question in the 1920s),[3] represents feminism as both caused by
and the cause of male degeneration and the erosion of 'natural' gender
boundaries. As I indicated in an earlier chapter, it is a circular argument
which has no single point of entry. Society has become self-conscous and
hence feminized and degenerate. If men were really men, then women
would not be feminists ('wherever woman bosses the show, it is because
man doesn't want to' (*Px II* 547). Feminism emasculates men and
feminizes society. Feminists are not really women. Feminists and/or
modern women want to be men, and so on. The argument is circular, and
it seems clear that, in Lawrence's *Fantasia* and his fiction of the 1920s,
the circle always returns to the trouble with women; to the perversion of
nature in women and the perversion of both the natural and social order
by a misdirection and superfluity of the female. To put it crudely, as
Lawrence sometimes does, there are 'Women, women, everywhere and all
of them on the warpath' (*Px II* 547).

In both his fiction and his discursive writings in the 1920s Lawrence
replotted the gendered and cyclical model of history developed in the
Hardy study. The story of successive male and female cycles of history is
retold as a story of warfare, a struggle for dominance between the male
and the female, and, more importantly, between men and women.
Lawrence, as the teller of this story of struggle, places himself firmly on
the side of the male, if not always of men, and affirms the need to reassert
male principles and masculine values: 'instead of this gnawing, gnawing
disease of mental consciousness and awful, unhealthy craving for stimu-
lus . . . we must substitute genuine action' (*F.* 87). The idiocy of the war,
hitherto represented by Lawrence as a symptom of the degeneration of an
over-masculinized society, is now re-presented as a noble episode in the
sex war. 'The war was not a bad beginning. But we went out under the
banners of idealism, and now the men are home again, the virus is more
active than ever, rotting their very souls' (*F.* 87). In *Fantasia*, and in the
fiction of this period, Lawrence frequently invokes the rhetoric of sex war,
urging men and women to 'fight their way out of their self-consciousness
. . . each must fight the other out of self-consciousness . . . Instead of this

leprous [mutual] forbearance . . . there should be the most intense open antagonism' (*F.* 189). Although, in other contexts, he is against the masses, Lawrence, nevertheless, mobilizes the male masses against women, urging them to join battle against women and the feminization of culture:

> And so, men, drive your wives, beat them out of their self-consciousness and their soft smarminess and good, lovely idea of themselves . . . Wives do the same to your husbands.
>
> But fight for your lives, men. Fight your wife out of her own self-conscious preoccupation with herself. Batter her out of it till she's stunned. Drive her back into her own true mode. Rip all her nice superimposed modern-woman and wonderful creature garb off her. Reduce her once more to a naked Eve . . .
>
> Combat her in her cock-sure belief that she 'knows' and that she is 'right' . . . Make her yield once more to the male leadership: if you've got anywhere to lead to. If you haven't, best leave the woman alone . . . You've got to know that you're a man, and being a man means you go on alone, ahead of the woman, to break a way through the old world into the new. (*F.* 191–2)

The concluding sentences of this extract provide a key to the tone of Lawrence's novels of male power. They also throw some light on the nature of his masculinist appropriation of the feminist project of renovation. Some turn-of-the-century feminists envisaged a situation in which women would renovate society and save the race from degeneration by being womanly, deploying their womanliness in new ways, and by making womanly values prevail. Lawrence's renovatory project, on the other hand, depends on the rediscovery of masculinity and male values before they can be made to prevail. Thus, in *Fantasia*, in the novels of male power, and in many of the essays of the 1920s, Lawrence projects a masculine renaissance, based on the rediscovery and reassertion of male values, a process of male affiliation, and also on the enforced submission of women and the subjugation of the feminine. The essay on Hawthorne in *Studies in Classic American Literature* contains a powerful summary of all of these aspects of Lawrence's case: 'you've got to believe in yourself and your gods . . . Sir man; and then you've got to fight [woman] and never give in. She's a devil. But in the long run she's conquerable.'[4] In arguing the case for a masculinist renovation Lawrence, as always, presents himself as a lone voice crying in the wilderness. In fact (as I suggested in Chapter 2) a number of male writers in the 1920s made a similar case for a masculine renaissance as the one thing needful to save humanity. 'Only in this masculine renaissance is there any hope of a revival for humanity as a whole. And as soon as the men appear who will constitute this rebirth of desirable male material, everything will be bound to fall naturally into its proper place'.[5]

If Lawrence's theory of renovation through a masculine renaissance is based on a reversal of turn-of-the-century feminist renovationist discourse, his novels of male power are a reworking of those New Woman novels which projected renovation through feminization and/or feminism. Like the New Woman novels of the 1890s, Lawrence's male-power novels of the 1920s have a contemporary setting and engage directly and polemically with the contentious issues of their day. Both combine the journalistic and the visionary, realism, allegory, and myth. Both are overtly didactic, and employ a rhetoric of excess. Moreover, just as the critics of the 1890s linked the New Woman fiction (usually adversely) to the fiction of sex and to popular romance, Lawrence's novels were similarly linked to the sensationalist romances of the 1920s and to the contemporary sex novel. Both sets of novels are marriage and/or social-problem novels, and both offer a profound critique of family and gender roles which they seek to redefine. Lawrence, however, reverses the perspective of the New Woman critique. His critique of marriage and the family is made from a self-consciously masculine point of view. Like many feminists, Lawrence sees the family as an oppressive institution, but for him it is an instrument for the oppression of men: 'Of late years . . . the family has got hold of a man, and begun to destroy him' (Px II 552). In short, it might be argued that, in seeking to articulate his vision of post-war degeneration-through-feminization, Lawrence appropriated both the forms and the rhetoric of the New Woman fiction as a form of reverse discourse.

In fact, as several critics have pointed out, the novels of male power are, in many ways, more successful in exposing the contradictions in Lawrence's thinking about gender and his gendered thinking than they are in articulating a vision of a masculine renaissance and affirming the process of male affiliation. For this reason, as G. M. Hyde has suggested, the novels of male power might more properly be called the novels of male impotence. The contradictions and ambiguities of Lawrence's turn to the masculine are also evident in his phallicism. Lawrence's doctrine or religion of the phallus, or phallic consciousness, is also a kind of reverse discourse. In Lawrence's fiction the phallus is both instinct with and represents the idea of spontaneous life. Life – especially spontaneous life – as we have seen elsewhere in this study, was usually represented as gendered feminine at this time. In effect Lawrence feminizes the phallus, especially in Lady Chatterley's Lover, which Lawrence himself described as 'a nice and tender phallic novel', in which 'the phallic consciousness . . . is the source of all real beauty, and all real gentleness' (LL vi. 328). By means of this particular conceptualization of phallicism, Lawrence thus redefines masculinity in terms of qualities which have conventionally been gendered feminine in the recent history of English (and possibly Western) culture. Lawrence's feminization of the phallus in and beyond the novels of male power is part of a return, albeit by a circuitous route, to the feminine values which he espoused in the pre-war period. The major difference is that he now calls those values masculine.

By the late 1920s Lawrence's writings represent a world still riven by gender conflict, and articulated by means of gendered oppositions, but Lawrence himself seems to take a more relaxed, even on occasions humorous, attitude to the struggle. For example, in an essay written in 1928 he sees the current matriarchal society as both product and a symptom of gender-role confusion and unnatural female dominance, but he also advises his male readers to turn the situation to their advantage. He advocates a 'drift back to matriarchy' in order to 'let men get free again' (*Px II* 552). With an uncharacteristic irony Lawrence appropriates the feminist critique of the family and argues the case for matriarchy on the grounds that 'a man must be able to get away from his family, and from woman altogether, and foregather in the communion of men' (*Px II* 552).

By the late 1920s Lawrence also appears to have abandoned his commitment to the leader theory. 'The hero is obsolete,' he declared in a letter in 1928, 'and the leader of men is a back number . . . the leader-cum-fellowship relationship is a bore . . . the new relationship will be of the same sort of tenderness, sensitive, between men and men and men and women, and not the one up one down, lead on I follow . . . sort of business' (*LL* vi. 321). He announces a similar turn from the hero in 'We Need One Another' (1930).

> For centuries, man has been the conquering hero, and woman has been merely the string to his bow . . . Then Woman was allowed to have a soul of her own, a separate soul. So the separating business started. Now the freedom and independence have been rather overdone, they lead to an empty nowhere . . . The conquering hero business is as obsolete as Marshal Hindenburg. (*Px* 191)

Indeed in 'We Need One Another' Lawrence returns to the figuration of the male–female relation that he had employed in the Hardy study: 'Man or woman, each is a flow, a flowing life . . . A woman is one bank of the river of my life, and the world is the other' (*Px* 192). Man and woman, male and female, thus flow side by side as river and bank, rather than being the separate banks permanently divided by the river. It would be misleading, however, to end by giving the impression that Lawrence's thinking completed a revolution and closed a circle, unless one also emphasizes that his end, as his beginning, was marked by contradiction and confusion. By the end of his life Lawrence was no longer, perhaps, a militant warrior in the sex war, but he was still wrestling with a language which operates through gendered oppositions. He was still negotiating, too, the gendered discourse of degeneration which was, as I hope this study has shown, one of the central 'fictions' of the turn-of-the-century period, and one within which, and out of which, English modernist fiction was produced.

> I am so tired of being told that I want mankind to go back to the
> condition of savages. As if modern city people weren't about the
> crudest, rawest, most crassly savage monkeys that ever existed, when
> it comes to the relation of man and woman. All I see in our vaunted
> civilization is men and women smashing each other emotionally and
> psychically to bits . . . (*Px* 194)

Two strands of Lawrence's reworking of turn-of-the-century gender(ed)
thinking provide us with equivalents of the metaphors that have governed
two recent influential accounts of the engendering (in the sense of the
begetting and/or the gendering) of canonical modernism – Michael
Levenson's *A Genealogy of Modernism* (1984) and Sandra Gilbert's and
Susan Gubar's *The War of the Words* (1988). These are his version of
non-reproductive male creativity, and his construction of cultural history,
and particularly the history of modernity, around sex-wars metaphors.
Lawrence's emphasis on 'the desire of the human male to build a world',
on 'the pure disinterested craving of the human male to make something
wonderful, out of his own head' (*F*. 18), is replicated in Levenson's
Poundian account of modernism as something made by a self-consciously
affiliated group of male writers. In *The War of the Words*, on the other
hand, Gilbert and Gubar reproduce (and sometimes transvalue)
Lawrence's sex-wars model of cultural history in their own account of
turn-of-the-century literary history which represents the struggle of the
modern, not as a generational conflict, but rather as 'a more profound
sexual-literary struggle'.[6]

Levenson's genealogy is a history of the fathering of modernism by a
group of questing male heroes who, like Lawrence and his fictional male
heroes, 'retreat from mass culture, widening democracy, and . . . an
encroaching scientific materialism'.[7] Gilbert and Gubar, on the other hand,
seek to rescue the lost history of modernism from the hegemony of a male-
defined modernism which they see as a retreat from the feminine, from
woman, and especially from women's perceived invasion of the literary
market-place. Like Lawrence's, Gilbert's and Gubar's cultural history is 'a
story of stories about gender strife'.[8] The story that they tell is summarized in this passage from 'Tradition and the Female Talent'.

> The rise of the female imagination was a central problem for the
> twentieth-century male imagination. Thus when we focus not only
> on women's increasingly successful struggle for autonomy in the
> years from, say, 1880 to 1920, but also on their increasingly success-
> ful production of literary texts throughout the nineteenth and twenti-
> eth centuries, we find ourselves confronting an entirely different
> modernism. And it is a modernism constructed not just against the
> grain of Victorian male precursors . . . but as an integral part of a
> complex response to *female* precursors and contemporaries. Indeed

it is possible to hypothesize that a reaction-formation against the rise of literary women became not just a theme in modernist writing but a motive for modernism.[9]

This hypothesis is, I would suggest, both too linear and too much driven by the rhetoric of sex wars (that old, old story) that drives Gilbert's and Gubar's own attempt to reconfigure the map of literary modernism. In this study I have tried to tell a slightly different story, and to argue that the English fiction produced in the (extended) moment of modernism was not simply a reaction-formation against literary women. Rather it was produced out of a complex of gendered cultural discourses and discourses on gender at the turn of the century. I have tried to show that English fiction in the early twentieth century, whether or not it defined itself (or we now wish to define it) as modernist, was paradoxically both a reaction-formation against the feminization of culture, and, in crucial respects – whether as a self-conscious attempt by women writers to displace or overthrow the masculine tradition, or as an abandonment of politics and a movement towards private and subjective forms – a 'feminized' cultural formation.

NOTES

Introduction

1 Henry James, letter, 1876, quoted by Malcolm Bradbury in *The Modern British Novel* (Secker & Warburg, 1993), p. 11.
2 Tony Pinkney, 'Raymond Williams and the "Two Faces of Modernism" ', in Terry Eagleton (ed.), *Raymond Williams: Critical Perspectives* (Oxford: Polity, 1989), p. 13.
3 Walter Benjamin, *Charles Baudelaire: A Lyric Poet in the Era of High Capitalism* (New Left Books, 1973).
4 Raymond Williams, *The Long Revolution* (1961; Harmondsworth: Penguin, 1965), p. 67.
5 Peter Widdowson (ed.). *D. H. Lawrence* (Longman, 1992), p. 11.
6 T. S. Eliot, 'Tradition and the Individual Talent', in *Selected Essays* (Faber & Faber, 1934), p. 14.
7 Michel Foucault, *The Archaeology of Knowledge*, trans. Alan Sheridan (Tavistock, 1977), p. 191.
8 Raymond Williams, *Culture* (Fontana, 1981), pp. 12–13.
9 Jacques Derrida, *Of Grammatology*, trans. Gayatry Chakravorty Spivack (Baltimore: Johns Hopkins University Press, 1976), p. 158.
10 Valentine Cunningham, *In the Reading Gaol: Postmodernity, Texts and History* (Oxford: Blackwell, 1994), p. 47.

Chapter 1

1 Janet Wolff, *Feminine Sentences: Essays on Women and Culture* (Oxford: Polity, 1990), p. 57.
2 Richard Poirier, *The Renewal of Literature* (Faber, 1988), p. 95.
3 See Graham Hough, *Image and Experience: Studies in a Literary Revolution* (Duckworth, 1960); R. Ellman and C. Feidelson (eds.), *The Modern Tradition: Backgrounds of Modern Literature* (Oxford: Oxford University Press, 1965); Malcolm Bradbury, *The Social Context of Modern English Literature* (Oxford: Blackwell, 1971); Bernard Bergonzi, *The Myth of Modernism and Twentieth-Century Literature* (Brighton: Harvester, 1986).
4 David Trotter, *The English Novel in History, 1895–1920* (Routledge, 1993), p. 4 (emphasis added).
5 George Dangerfield, *The Strange Death of Liberal England* (McGibbon & Kee, 1935, 1966), pp. 13–14.
6 *The Letters of Henry James*, ed. Percy Lubbock (2 vols.; Macmillan, 1920), ii. 384.
7 D. H. Lawrence, *Kangaroo* (Harmondsworth: Penguin, 1950), p. 240.
8 Ezra Pound, 'We have had No Battles but we have all Joined in and Made Roads', in *Polite Essays* (Faber & Faber, 1937), p. 45.

9   J. F. Kermode, *Continuities* (Routledge & Kegan Paul, 1968), pp. 2–3.

10 Frederic Jameson, *Modernism and Imperialism* (Derry: Field Day, 1988), p. 5.

11 Marianne DeKoven, *Rich and Strange: Gender, History, Modernism* (Oxford: Princeton University Press, 1991), p. 5.

12 Peter Keating, *The Haunted Study: A Social History of the Engish Novel, 1875–1914* (1989; Fontana, 1991, p. 2.

13 Trotter, op. cit., p. 4.

14 Eugene Lunn, *Marxism and Modernism: An Historical Study of Lukacs, Brecht, Benjamin and Adorno* (Verso, 1985), p. 34.

15 Raymond Williams, *The Politics of Modernism*, ed. Tony Pinkney (Verso, 1989), p. 37.

16 Bradbury, *Social Context*, p. xxix.

17 Poirier, op. cit., p. 97.

18 Edward Said, 'Criticism', *Boundary 2*: 8 (1979), p. 17.

19 Alice Jardine, 'Opaque Texts and Transparent Contexts: The Political Difference of Julia Kristeva', in Nancy K. Miller (ed.), *The Poetics of Gender* (Oxford: Columbia University Press, 1986), p. 105.

20 Stephen Heath, *The Sexual Fix* (Macmillan, 1982), p. 135.

21 M. Bradbury and J. McFarlane (eds.), *Modernism 1890–1930* (Harmondsworth: Penguin, 1986), pp. 24–5.

22 Sandra Gilbert and Susan Gubar, *No Man's Land: The Place of the Woman Writer in the Twentieth Century*, i. *The War of the Words* (New Haven, Conn.: Yale University Press, 1988), p. 156.

23 DeKoven, op. cit., p. 8.

24 See Alice Jardine, *Gynesis: Configurations of Woman and Modernity* (Ithaca, NY: Cornell University Press, 1985), and Rachel Blau DuPlessis, *Writing Beyond the Ending: Narrative Strategies of Twentieth-Century Women Writers* (Bloomington, Ind.: Indiana University Press, 1985).

25 Heath, op. cit., p. 135.

Chapter 2

1   Terry Lovell, *Consuming Fiction* (Verso, 1987), p. 119.

2   Havelock Ellis, *The Psychology of Sex* (Heinemann, 1933), p. 194.

3   Karl Miller, *Doubles: Studies in Literary History* (Oxford: Oxford University Press, 1985), p. 209.

4   Malcolm Bradbury, *The Modern British Novel* (Secker & Warburg, 1993), p. 22.

5   Michel Foucault, *The History of Sexuality: Volume One: An Introduction*, trans. Robert Hurley (Allen Lane, 1979), p. 104.

6   See, *inter alia*, Mona Caird, 'A Defence of the So-called "Wild Women" ', *Nineteenth Century*, 31 (1892), pp. 811–29; Eliza Lynn Linton, 'The Wild Women as Social Insurgents', *Nineteenth Century*, 30 (1891), pp. 596–605, and also her 'Partisans of the Wild Women', *Nineteenth Century*, 31 (1892), pp. 455–64; Blanche Crackanthorpe, 'The Revolt of the Daughters', *Nineteenth Century*, 34 (1894), pp. 23–31, and 35 (1894), pp. 424–9.

7   Sarah Grand and 'Ouida' [Marie Louise de la Ramée], 'The New Aspect of the Woman Question', *North American Review*, 158 (1894), pp. 271–6, and 610–19 respectively.

8 Eliza Lynn Linton, 'Wild Women as Politicians', *Nineteenth Century*, 30 (1891), pp. 78–88, at p. 79.

9 See Havelock Ellis, *Studies in the Psychology of Sex*, ii. *Sexual Inversion* (Philadelphia: F. A. Davis, 1937). The first edition of *Sexual Inversion* to be published in England originally appeared under the names of both Ellis and John Addington Symonds. A second edition, published in 1897, cited Ellis as the sole author. It was banned, following a court case in 1898.

10 Linton, 'Wild Women as Politicians', p. 83.

11 Laura Marholm Hansson, *Modern Women*, trans. Hermione Ramsden (John Lane, 1896), p. 79.

12 See H. M. Stutfield, 'Tommyrotics', *Blackwood's*, 157 (1895), pp. 833–45, and 'The Psychology of Feminism', *Blackwood's*, 161 (1897), pp. 104–17.

13 Ellis Ethelmer [Elizabeth Wolstenholme Elmy], *The Phases of Love* (Congleton: Women's Emancipation Union, 1897), p..9.

14 See Ellis, *Sexual Inversion*, and IS.

15 In particular, see Ellis, *Sexual Inversion*.

16 Regenia Gagnier, *Idylls of the Marketplace: Oscar Wilde and the Victorian Public* (Stanford: Stanford University Press, 1986), and Ed Cohen, *Talk on the Wilde Side: Towards a Genealogy of a Discourse on Male Sexualities* (Routledge, 1993).

17 Gagnier, op. cit., p. 139.

18 Fraser Harrison (ed.), *The Yellow Book: An Anthology* (Woodbridge: Boydell Press, 1982), p. 25.

19 See e.g. Henry James, 'The Death of the Lion', in *The Figure in the Carpet and Other Stories*, ed. Frank Kermode (Harmondsworth: Penguin, 1986), and Aldous Huxley, 'The Farcical History of Richard Greenow', in *Limbo* (Chatto & Windus, 1920).

20 Linda Dowling, 'The Decadent and the New Woman in the 1890s', *Nineteenth Century Fiction*, 33 (1979), pp. 434–53, at p. 435.

21 Luce Irigaray, 'Ce sexe qui n'en est pas un', in E. Marks and I. de Courtviron (eds.), *New French Feminisms* (Brighton: Harvester, 1981), pp. 99–106.

22 Florence Farr, *Modern Woman: Her Intentions* (Frank Palmer, 1910), p. 81.

23 Edwin Lankester, *Degeneration: A Chapter in Darwinism* (Macmillan, 1880), pp. 28–9.

24 Ibid., pp. 59–60.

25 Quoted in Patrick Brantlinger, *Rule of Darkness: British Literature and Imperialism, 1830–1914* (Ithaca, NY: Cornell University Press, 1988), p. 186.

26 For a history of the development of anthropology, see George W. Stocking, Jnr., *Victorian Anthropology* (Collier Macmillan, 1987).

27 Edward Said, *Orientalism* (1978; Harmondsworth: Penguin, 1985).

28 Edward Carpenter, *Civilisation: Its Cause and Cure* (Swan Sonnenschein, 1889), pp. 1, 6.

29 See especially R. C. Trench, *On the Study of Words* (J. W. Parker, 1851).

30 J. Edward Chamberlin, 'Images of Degeneration', in J. E. Chamberlin and S. L. Gilman (eds), *Degeneration: The Dark Side of Progress* (New York: Columbia University Press, 1985), p. 283. The present chapter owes much to this essay and to the book in which it occurs.

31 Havelock Ellis, 'A Note on Paul Bourget' (1889), repr. in Ellis, *Views and Reviews* (2 vols., Desmond Harmsworth, 1932), i. 52.

32 F. Nietzsche, 'The Case of Wagner: A Musician's Problem', in *Complete Works*, ed. Oscar Levy (18 vols.; T. N. Foulis, 1909–10), viii. 19–20.

33 William Greenslade, *Degeneration, Culture and the Novel, 1880–1940* (Cambridge: Cambridge University Press, 1994), p. 121.

34 'Post-Impressionists', *Morning Post* (16 Nov. 1910), cited by J. B. Bullen, *The Post-Impressionists in England* (Routledge, 1988), p. 116.

35 A. M. Ludovici, 'An Open Letter to My Friends', *New Age*, 14 (8 Jan. 1914), p. 281.

36 Northrop Frye, *T. S. Eliot: An Introduction* (Chicago: University of Chicago Press, 1963), p. 7.

37 See Gustave Le Bon, *The Crowd: A Study of the Popular Mind* (T. Fisher Unwin, 1896), and Graham Wallas, *Human Nature in Politics* (Archibald Constable, 1908) and *The Great Society: A Psychological Analysis* (Macmillan, 1914).

38 Ortega Y. Gasset, *The Revolt of the Masses* (1930; Allen & Unwin, 1932), p. 90.

39 Le Bon, quoted by Andreas Huyssen, *After the Great Divide: Modernism, Mass Culture, Postmodernism* (Macmillan, 1986), p. 52.

40 Lyn Pykett, *The Improper Feminine: The Women's Sensation Novel and the New Woman Writing* (Routledge, 1992).

41 Huyssen, op. cit., p. 47.

42 Peter Keating, *The Haunted Study: A Social History of the English Novel, 1875–1914* (1989; Fontana, 1991), pp. 77–8.

43 See Sandra Gilbert and Susan Gubar, *No Man's Land: The Place of the Woman Writer in the Twentieth Century*, i. *The War of the Words* (New Haven, Conn.: Yale University Press, 1988); Huyssen, op. cit.; David Trotter, *The English Novel in History, 1895–1920* (Routledge, 1993), p. 4.

44 Huyssen, op. cit., p. 52.

45 B. S. Rowntree, *Reports from Commissioners* (1904), xxxii, app. I, 'Report on the Inter-Departmental Committee on Physical Deterioration', p. 103.

46 G. F. G. Masterman (ed.), *The Heart of the Empire: Discussions of Problems of Modern City Life in England* (1901; Brighton: Harvester, 1973), p. 8.

47 R. Baden Powell, *Scouting for Boys: A Handbook for Instruction in Good Citizenship* (rev. edn., C. A. Pearson, 1909), p. 3.

48 Karl Pearson, 'Woman and Labour', *Fortnightly Review*, 55 (1894), pp. 567–70, p. 568.

49 Linton, 'Wild Women as Politicians', p. 80.

50 Arabella Kenealy, *Feminism and Sex Extinction* (T. Fisher Unwin, 1920), p. 74.

51 Ellis Ethelmer [Elizabeth Wolstenholme Elmy], *Woman and the Law* (Congleton: Women's Emancipation Union, 1894), p. 10.

52 Sarah Grand, *Lady's Realm* (1898), quoted in Gillian Kersley, *Darling Madam: Sarah Grand and Devoted Friend* (Virago, 1983), p. 10.

53 Lucy Re-Bartlett, *Towards Liberty* (Longmans, 1913), p. 69.

54 Frances Swiney, quoted in Lucy Bland, 'The Married Woman, the "New Woman" and the Feminist Sexual Politics of the 1890s', in Jane Rendall (ed.), *Equal or Different: Women's Politics, 1800–1914* (Oxford: Blackwell), p. 157.

55 Quoted in Les Garner, *A Brave and Beautiful Spirit: Dora Marsden, 1882–1960* (Avebury: Gower, 1990), p. 50.

56 Olive Schreiner, *Woman and Labour* (1911; Virago, 1978), p. 12.
57 Havelock Ellis, *The New Spirit* (G. Bell & Sons, 1890), p. 9.
58 Jeffrey Weeks, *Sex, Politics and Society: The Regulation of Sexuality since 1800* (Routledge, 1981), p. 174.
59 Ellis, *The Psychology of Sex* (Heinemann, 1933), p. 24.
60 Ibid.
61 Edward Carpenter, *Towards Democracy* (1883; T. Fisher Unwin, 1892), p. 18.
62 Edward Carpenter, *The Drama of Life and Death* (George Allen, 1912), p. 59.
63 Edward Carpenter, *Woman and her Place in a Free Society* (Manchester: Labour Press Society, 1894), p. 40.
64 Quoted in Sheila Rowbotham and Jeffrey Weeks, *Socialism and the New Life: The Personal and Sexual Politics of Edward Carpenter and Havelock Ellis* (Pluto, 1979), p. 34.
65 Ibid.
66 Edward Carpenter, *Some Friends of Walt Whitman: A Study in Sex Psychology* (British Society for the Study of Sex Psychology Papers, 1924), p. 14.
67 Rebecca West, 'The "Freewoman" ', *Time and Tide*, 16 July 1916, pp. 648–9, repr. in *GM* 573–77, at p. 574.
68 Dora Marsden, 'Bondwomen', *Freewoman*, 23 Nov. 1911, p. 3.
69 Ibid.
70 Jonathon Rose, *The Edwardian Temperament, 1895–1919* (Columbus: Ohio University Press, 1986), p. 74.
71 Quoted in Garner, op. cit., p. 115.
72 Quoted in Andrew Thacker, 'Dora Marsden and *The Egoist*: "Our War is with Words" ', *English Literature in Transition*, 36 (1993), pp. 178–96, at p. 184.
73 Dora Marsden, *New Freewoman*, 15 June 1913, p. 4.
74 Ibid.
75 Dora Marsden, *New Freewoman*, 15 Aug. 1913, p. 81.
76 *New Freewoman*, 15 Dec. 1913, p. 244.
77 Dora Marsden, *Egoist*, Dec. 1913, quoted in Gillian Hanscombe and Virginia Smyers, *Writing for their Lives: The Modernist Woman, 1910–1940* (Women's Press, 1987), p. 170.
78 Ibid.
79 Ezra Pound, 'The Hard and the Soft in French Poetry', *Poetry*, 9 (1918), p. 264.
80 T. S. Eliot, 'Reflections on Contemporary Poetry', *Egoist*, 5 (June–July 1918), p. 84.
81 Dora Marsden, 'Women's Rights', *Egoist*, 1 Oct. 1914, p. 361.
82 *Suffragette*, 7 Aug. 1914, p. 301.
83 Elaine Showalter, *The Female Malady: Women, Madness and English Culture, 1830–1980* (Virago, 1987), p. 173.
84 Ibid., p. 168.
85 Greenslade, op. cit., p. 234.
86 A. M. Ludovici, *Lysistrata: Woman's Future and Future Woman* (Kegan, Paul, Trench, Trubner, 1924), pp. 76–7.

87 From a review in the *Referee*, quoted alongside several similar comments on the dust-jacket of Ludovici, *Man: An Indictment* (Constable, 1927).

88 Lucovici, *Lysistrata*, pp. xv–xvi.

89 Ibid., pp. 108, 106.

90 Wyndham Lewis, *Paleface: The Philosophy of the Melting Pot* (Chatto & Windus, 1929), p. 241.

Chapter 3

1 George Moore, 'A New Censorship of Literature', *Pall Mall Gazette* (1884), repr. in *Literature at Nurse, or Circulating Morals: A Polemic on Victorian Censorship*, ed. Pierre Coustillas (Brighton: Harvester, 1976), p. 31.

2 Moore, *Literature at Nurse*, pp. 17–18.

3 See Naomi Schor, *Reading in Detail: Aesthetics and the Feminine* (Methuen, 1987).

4 Ibid., p. 43.

5 W. T. Stead, 'The Novel of the Modern Woman', *Review of Reviews*, 10 (1894), pp. 64–73, at p. 64.

6 Quoted in Derek Stanford, *Stories of the Nineties* (John Baker, 1968), p. 13.

7 Laura Marholm Hansson, *Modern Women*, trans. Hermione Ramsden (John Lane, 1896), pp. 78–9.

8 Henry James, 'The Future of the Novel' (1899), repr. in R. Gard (ed.), *The Critical Muse: Selected Literary Criticism* (Harmondsworth: Penguin, 1987), pp. 343–4.

9 Mona Caird, 'A Defence of the So-called "Wild Women"', *Nineteenth Century*, 31 (1892), pp. 811–29, at p. 815.

10 Mona Caird, *The Daughters of Danaus* (Bliss, Sands & Foster, 1894), p. 322.

11 Thomas Hardy, *Jude the Obscure* (1895; Oxford: Oxford University Press, 1985), p. xxxviii.

12 Ann Ardis, *New Woman, New Novels: Feminism and Early Modernism* (New Brunswick, N.J.: Rutgers University Press, 1990), p. 100.

13 Lyn Pykett, *The Improper Feminine: The Women's Sensation Novel and the New Woman Writing* (Routledge, 1992), p. 145.

14 George Egerton, *Discords* (John Lane, 1894), p. 198.

15 George Egerton, *Keynotes* (John Lane, 1893), p. 42.

16 George Egerton, 'A Keynote to *Keynotes*', in J. Gawsworth [Terence Armstrong] (ed.), *Ten Contemporaries* (Ernest Benn, 1932), p. 58.

17 Ibid.

18 See Ardis, op. cit., and Gerd Bjorhovde, *Rebellious Structures: Women Writers and the Crisis of the Novel, 1880–1900* (Oxford: Oxford University Press, 1987).

19 Egerton, *Keynotes*, pp. 17, 19–20.

20 H. M. Stutfield, 'Tommyrotics', *Blackwood's*, 157 (1895), pp. 833–45, at p. 833.

21 H. M. Stutfield, 'The Psychology of Feminism', *Blackwood's*, 161 (1897), pp. 104–17, at pp. 104–6 *passim*.

22 A. C. Waugh, 'Reticence in Literature', *The Yellow Book*, i (1894), pp. 210–19; Hubert Crackanthorpe, 'Reticence in Literature', *The Yellow Book*,

   ii (1894), pp. 269–73; James Ashcroft Noble, 'The Fiction of Sexuality',
   Contemporary Review, 67 (1895), pp. 490–8; Janet Hogarth, 'Literary
   Degenerates', *Fortnightly Review*, 57 (1895), pp. 586–92.
23 Waugh, op. cit., p. 14.
24 Ibid., p. 210; emphasis added.
25 Ibid., p. 204.
26 W. L. Courtney, *The Feminine Note in Fiction* (Chapman & Hall, 1904), p. xii.
27 Ibid., p. xii.
28 Ibid.
29 Ibid., p. xiii.
30 Gaye Tuchman, *Edging Women Out: Victorian Novelists, Publishers and
   Social Change* (Routledge, 1989).
31 Henry James, *Partial Portraits* (Macmillan, 1888), p. 141.
32 Patrick Brantlinger, *Rule of Darkness: British Literature and Imperialism,
   1830–1914* (Ithaca, NY: Cornell University Press), p. 11.
33 Rider Haggard 'About Fiction', *Contemporary Review*, 52 (1887), pp.
   172–180, p. 177.
34 In addition to Rider Haggard's essay (in the above note), see also George
   Saintsbury, 'The Present State of the Novel', *Fortnightly Review*, 42 (1887),
   pp. 410–17, and Andrew Lang, 'From Realism to Romance', *Contemporary
   Review*, 52 (1887), pp. 683–93.
35 See Eve Kosofksy Segwick, *Between Men: English Literature and Male
   Homosocial Desire* (New York, Columbia University Press, 1985).
36 Wayne Koestenbaum, *Double Talk: The Erotics of Male Literary
   Collaboration* (Routledge, 1989), p. 144.
37 Ibid., p. 157.
38 Saintsbury, op. cit., p. 411.
39 Haggard, op. cit., p. 172.
40 Lang, op. cit., p. 689.
41 Ibid., p. 691.
42 Ibid., p. 690.
43 Ibid., p. 691.
44 Saintsbury, op. cit., p. 417.
45 Ezra Pound, 'The New Sculpture', *Egoist*, 1 (16 Feb. 1914), p. 68.
46 Quoted in Koestenbaum, op. cit., p. 168.
47 Tuchman, op. cit., p. 216.
48 Ibid., p. 203.
49 E. M. Forster, *Aspects of the Novel* (1927; Harmondsworth: Penguin, 1964),
   p. 27.
50 *The Young Woman* (1892), quoted in Cynthia White, *Women's Magazines,
   1693–1968* (Michael Joseph, 1970), p. 59.
51 Peter Keating, *The Haunted Study: A Social History of the English Novel,
   1875–1914* (1889; Fontana, 1991), p. 77.
52 Elaine Showalter, *A Literature of their Own* (Virago, 1978), p. 253.
53 Arnold Bennett, *Anna of The Five Towns* (Harmondsworth: Penguin, 1936),
   p. 136.
54 H. G. Wells, *Kipps* (Macmillan, 1905), p. 116.
55 Leon Edel and G. N. Ray (eds.), *Henry James and H. G. Wells: A Record of
   their Friendship* (Hart-Davis, 1959), p. 264.

56 Samuel Hynes, *The Edwardian Turn of Mind* (Oxford: Oxford University Press, 1968), p. 146.

57 *New York Evening Sun*, 13 Feb. 1917.

58 R. Brimley Johnson, *Some Contemporary Novelists (Women)* (Leonard Parsons, 1920), pp. xiv–xv.

Chapter 4

1 Dorothy Richardson, 'Women and the Future', *Vanity Fair*, 22 Apr. 1924, pp. 39–40. References are to the version repr. in GM 411–14, this epigraph is at p. 411.

2 Dorothy Richardson, letter to Henry Savage, 1950, quoted in Gillian Hanscombe and Virginia Smyers, *Writing for their Lives: The Modernist Woman, 1910–1940* (Women's Press, 1987), p. 62.

3 'Data for Spanish Publisher', ed. Joseph Prescott, *London Magazine*, 6:1 (1959), pp. 14–19, at p. 19.

4 Dorothy Richardson, 'Comments', *Dental Record*, 2 Oct. 1916, pp. 541–4, at p. 542.

5 Jonathon Rose, *The Edwardian Temperament, 1895–1919* (Columbus: Ohio University Press, 1986), pp. 4 ff.

6 Dorothy Richardson, 'Comments', *Dental Record*, 1 Jan. 1918, pp. 350–2, at p. 350.

7 Michele Barrett and Jean Radford, 'Modernism in the 1930s: Dorothy Richardson and Virginia Woolf', in F. Barker *et al.* (eds.), *The Politics of Modernism* (Colchester: Essex University Press, 1979), pp. 252–72, at p. 265.

8 Dorothy Richardson, 'In the Crank's Library', *Crank*, 4 (1906), pp. 372–6. References are to the version repr. in GM 399–400; this quotation is at p. 399.

9 J. Gawsworth [Terence Armstrong] (ed.), *Ten Contemporaries* (Ernest Benn, 1932), p. 58.

10 Jean Radford, *Dorothy Richardson* (Brighton: Harvester, 1991), p. 68.

11 Ibid, p. 107.

12 'Literary Essays', manuscript quoted in Gillian Hanscombe, *The Art of Life: Dorothy Richardson and the Development of Feminist Consciousness* (Peter Owen, 1982), p. 42.

13 Dorothy Richardson, 'About Punctuation', *Adelphi*, 1 (1924), pp. 990–6, repr. in GM 414–18, at p. 415.

Chapter 5

1 Eleanor Rathbone, 'Changes in Public Life', in Ray Strachey (ed.), *Our Freedom and its Results* (Hogarth Press, 1936), pp. 57–8.

2 Virginia Woolf, *The Pargiters*, ed. Mitchell Leaska (Hogarth Press, 1978), p. x1.

3 May Sinclair, 'The Novels of Dorothy Richardson', *Egoist*, 5 (1918), pp. 57–9, repr. in GM 442–8.

4 Quoted in Samuel Hynes, *The Edwardian Turn of Mind* (Oxford: Oxford University Press, 1968), p. 205.

5 See Hermione Lee, *The Novels of Virginia Woolf* (Methuen, 1977), pp. 15, 111.

6 Julia Kristeva, 'Oscillation between Power and Denial', in E. Marks and I. de Courtivron (eds), *New French Feminisms* (Brighton: Harvester, 1980), p. 166.

7 See Naomi Black, 'Virginia Woolf and the Women's Movement', in J. Marcus (ed.), *Virginia Woolf: A Feminist Slant* (Lincoln, Neb.: Nebraska University Press, 1983), pp. 180–97.

8 Alex Zwerdling, *Virginia Woolf and the Real World* (Berkley and Los Angeles: University of California Press, 1986), p. 216.

9 *The Letters of Virginia Woolf*, ed. Nigel Nicholson and Joanne Trautmann (6 vols., Hogarth Press, 1975–80), vi. 379–80.

10 Virginia Woolf, *Three Guineas* (Oxford: Oxford University Press, 1992), p. 309.

11 Virginia Woolf, 'Review of *The Grand Tour* by Romer. Wilson, and *Revolving Lights* by Dorothy Richardson', *TLS*, 19 May 1923, repr. in Deborah Cameron, *The Feminist Critique of Language* (Routledge, 1990), pp. 72–3, at p. 72.

12 Rachel Bowlby, *Virginia Woolf: Feminist Destinations* (Oxford: Blackwell, 1986), p. 41.

13 Ibid., p. 43.

14 W. L. Courtney, *The Feminine Note in Fiction* (Chapman & Hall, 1904), p. xii.

15 H. Stutfield, 'The Psychology of Feminism', *Blackwood's*, 161 (1897), pp. 104–17, at p. 112.

16 Elaine Showalter, *A Literature of their Own* (Virago, 1978), pp. 263, 240.

Chapter 6

1 M. Bradbury, *The Modern British Novel* (Secker & Warburg, 1993), p. 194.

2 E. M. Forster, *Aspects of the Novel* (1927; Harmondsworth: Penguin, 1964), pp. 79, 24.

3 Ford Madox Ford, 'Professor Saintsbury and the English "Nuvvle"', *Outlook*, 32 (1 Nov. 1913), p. 605.

4 Wyndham Lewis, *Paleface: The Philosophy of the Melting Pot* (Chatto & Windus, 1929), p. 247.

5 Ford Madox Ford, 'Literary Portraits, xvii: Nineteen-Thirteen and the Futurists', *Outlook*, 33 (3 Jan. 1914), p. 15.

6 Bradbury, *The Modern British Novel*, p. 89.

7 Quoted in ibid., p. 89.

8 David Ayers, *Wyndham Lewis and Western Man* (Macmillan, 1992), p. 25. Ayers argues against this view of Lewis's career.

9 H. M. Stutfield, 'The Psychology of Feminism', *Blackwood's*, 161 (1897), pp. 104–17, at p. 112.

10 John Beer, ' "The Last Englishman": Lawrence's appreciation of Forster', in G. K. Das and John Beer (eds.), *E. M. Forster: A Human Exploration* (Macmillan, 1979), p. 246.

11 F. R. Leavis, *The Common Pursuit* (Chatto & Windus, 1952), p. 262.

12 Anne Wright, *Literature of Crisis, 1910–22* (Macmillan, 1984), p. 200.
13 Edward Carpenter, *Civilisation: Its Cause and Cure* (Swan Sonnenschein, 1889), p. 29.
14 G. M. Hyde, *D. H. Lawrence* (Macmillan, 1990), p. 21.
15 D. H. Lawrence, *The White Peacock* (Harmondsworth: Penguin, 1950), p. 177.
16 George Egerton, *Discords* (John Lane, 1894), p. 66.
17 D. H. Lawrence, *Women in Love* (Harmondsworth: Penguin, 1960), p. 353.
18 D. H. Lawrence, *Kangaroo* (Harmondsworth: Penguin, 1950), p. 240.

Chapter 7

1 Hilary Simpson, *D. H. Lawrence and Feminism* (Croom Helm, 1982), p. 91.
2 J. F. Kermode, *Continuities* (Routledge & Kegan Paul, 1968), p. 125.
3 See Simpson, op. cit., pp. 103–4.
4 D. H. Lawrence, *Selected Literary Criticism*, ed. Anthony Beal (Heinemann, 1967), p. 358.
5 A. M. Ludovici, *Man: An Indictment* (Constable, 1927), p. 358.
6 Sandra Gilbert and Susan Gubar, *No Man's Land: The Place of the Woman Writer in the Twentieth Century*, i. *The War of the Words* (New Haven, Conn.: Yale University Press, 1988), p. 126.
7 Michael Levenson, *A Genealogy of Modernism: A Study of English Literary Doctrine 1908–22* (Cambridge: Cambridge University Press, 1986), p. 61.
8 Gilbert and Gubar, op. cit., p. xiv.
9 Ibid., p. 156.

♈

Appendix

(i) *FIN DE SIÈCLE* (A DEGENERATIONIST'S VIEW)

The word fin de siècle ... means a practical emancipation from traditional discipline, which theoretically is still in force. To the voluptuary this means unbridled lewdness, the unchaining of the beast in man; to the withered heart of the egoist, disdain of all consideration for his fellowmen, the trampling under foot of all barriers which enclose brutal greed or lucre and lust of pleasure; to the contemner of the world it means the shameless ascendancy of base impulses and motives, which were, if not virtuously suppressed, at least hypocritically hidden; to the believer it means the repudiation of dogma, the negation of a super-sensuous world, the descent into flat phenomenalism; to the sensitive nature yearning for aesthetic thrills, it means the vanishing of ideals in art, and no more power in its accepted forms to arouse emotions. And to all, it means the end of an established order, which for thousands of years has satisfied logic, fettered depravity, and in every art matured something of beauty.

One epoch of history is unmistakably in its decline, and another is announcing its approach. There is a sound of rending in every tradition, and it is as though the morrow would not link itself with to-day. Things as they are totter and plunge, and they are suffered to reel and fall, because man is weary, and there is no faith that it is worth an effort to uphold them ... Meanwhile interregnum in all its terrors prevails; there is confusion among the powers that be; the million, robbed of its leaders, knows not where to turn; the strong work their will; false prophets arise, and dominion is divided amongst those whose rod is the heavier because their time is short. Men look with longing for whatever new things are at hand

... They have hope that in the chaos of thought, art may yield revelations of the order that is to follow on this tangled web. The poet, the musician, is to announce, or divine, or at least suggest in what forms civilization will further be evolved.

Max Nordau, *Degeneration*
(New York: D. Appleton, 1895 – 1993 reprint), pp. 5–6

(ii) *FIN DE SIÈCLE* LITERATURE

The filth of Zola's art and of his disciples in literary canal-dredging has been got over, and nothing remains for it but to turn to submerged peoples and social strata. The vanguard of civilization holds its nose at the pit of undiluted naturalism, and can only be brought to bend over it with sympathy and curiosity when, by cunning engineering, a drain from the boudoir and the sacristy has been turned into it ... Elegant titillation only begins where normal sexual relations leave off ...

The book that would be fashionable must, above all, be obscure, the intelligible is cheap goods for the million only. It must further discourse in a certain pulpit tone – mildly unctuous, not too insistent; and it must follow up risky scenes by tearful outpourings of love for the lowly and the suffering, or glowing transports of piety. Ghost stories are very popular, but they must come on in scientific disguise as hypnotism, telepathy, somnambulism [etc.] ... So are esoteric novels, in which the author hints that he could say a deal about magic, kabbala ... if only he chose. Readers intoxicate themselves in the hazy word-sequences of symbolic poetry.

Nordau, *Degeneration*, pp. 13–14

(iii) TURN-OF-THE-CENTURY GENDER REPRESENTATIONS

(a) Sexual differentiation

Sexual differentiation ... is never complete. All the peculiarities of the male sex may be present in the female in some form, however weakly developed; and so also the sexual characteristics of the woman persist in the man, although perhaps they are not so completely rudiementary. The characters of the other sex occur in the one sex in vestigial form.

Amongst human beings ... there exist all sorts of intermediate conditions between male and female – sexual transitional forms ... [Just as in the scientific investigation of gases, laws about which relate to the 'ideal gas'] we may suppose the existence of an ideal man, M, and of an ideal woman, W, as sexual types, although these types do not actually exist. Such types not only can be constructed, but must be constructed. As in art so in science, the real purpose is to reach the type, the Platonic Idea ... [In human beings] there exist only the intermediate stages between absolute males and absolute females, the absolute conditions never presenting themselves ...

Let it be noted clearly that I am discussing the existence not merely of embryonic sexual neutrality, but of a permanent bisexual condition . . . [and not] merely those intermediate sexual conditions, those bodily or physical hermaphrodites upon which, up to the present, attention has been concentrated.

Otto Weininger, *Sex and Character*
(Heinemann, 1912) pp. 5, 7, 8

(b) Intermediate types

In late years (and since the arrival of the New Woman among us) many things in the relation of men and women to each other have altered, or at any rate become clearer . . . If the modern woman is a little more masculine in some ways than her predecessor, the modern man (it is to be hoped), while by no means effeminate, is a little more sensitive in temperament and artistic in feeling than the original John Bull. It is beginning to be recognised that the sexes do not or should not normally form two groups hopelessly isolated in habit and feeling from each other, but that they rather represent the two poles of *one* group . . . so that while certainly the extreme specimens at either pole are vastly divergent, there are great numbers in the middle region who (though differing corporeally as men and women) are by emotion and temperament very near to each other . . . [This is particularly true of 'Urnings' or 'homogenic' types, who] become to a great extent the interpreters of men and women to each other . . .

The instinctive artistic nature of the male of this class, his wavelike emotional temperament, combined with hardihood of intellect and body; and the frank, free nature of the female, her masculine independence and strength wedded to thoroughly feminine grace of form and manner; may be said to give them both, through their double nature, command of life in all its phases . . . which may well favour their function as reconcilers and interpreters.

Edward Carpenter, 'The Intermediate Sex', in *Love's
Coming-of-Age: A Series of Papers on the Relations of the Sexes*,
(Manchester: Labour Press Society, 1896), pp. 114–115, 133–4

(iv) FEMALE EMANCIPATION – MANLY WOMEN AND WOMANLY MEN

(a) Manly woman

A woman's demand for emancipation and her qualification for it are in direct proportion to the amount of maleness in her . . . Emancipation, as I mean to discuss it, is not the wish for outward equality with man, but . . . the deep-seated craving to acquire man's character, to attain his mental and moral freedom, to reach his real interests and his creative power. I maintain that the real female element has neither the desire nor the capacity for emancipation in this sense. All those who are striving for this real emancipation, all women who are truly famous and are of conspicuous mental ability to the first glance of an expert reveal some of the anatomical characters of the male ... [From Sappho onwards all advocates of women's rights] have almost invariably been ... sexually intermediate types ...

Is it not very remarkable that the agitation for the emancipation of women seems to repeat itself at certain intervals in the world's history, and lasts for a definite period? ...

... It would be premature to found a hypothesis on the data at our disposal, but the possibility of a vastly important periodicity must be borne in mind, of regularly recurring periods in which it may be that there is an excess of production of hermaphrodite and sexually intermediate forms. Such a state of affairs is not unknown in the animal kingdom.

According to my interpretation, such a period would be one of minimum 'gonochorism', cleavage of the sexes; and it would be marked, on the one hand, by an increased production of male women, and on the other, by a similar increase in female men ... [Examples of this may be found in] the 'secessionist taste' which idealised tall, lanky women with flat chests and narrow hips ... [and] the enormous recent increase in a kind of dandified homosexuality.

Weininger, *Sex and Character*, pp. 72–3

(b) Female emancipation and the threat to Imperial man

How are we to account for the fact that among the most highly civilized peoples of the modern world, man, as the human male, with all his physical and other advantages, has contrived, both in the home and in public life, to descend to his present position of apparent equality with, or subordination to woman? And ... why are the privileges or rather responsibilities (political, professional, economic or other), which have hitherto fallen to his lot, now being claimed and steadily appropriated or shared by his womenfolk?

More narrowly described, my problem is to explain how and why the modern Englishman, with the magnificent heritage he has received from his forefathers in the form of the great Empire on which the sun never sets, has become the kind of male who, not only in his sexual, but also in his administrative and Imperial relations, seems no longer able to maintain his supremacy ...

A vast empire can be efficiently administered neither by women, nor by men who have delivered themselves up into the hands of their womenfolk, or ceased to lead and inspire them. It is therefore no mere coincidence that precisely at this conjuncture in our Imperial affairs, when in more than one of our dependencies the cry is beginning to be raised against British rule . . . our womenfolk at home should be claiming an alleged equality with men.

Philip Gibbs, *Since Then* (Heinemann, 1930), pp. 375

(c) 'Modern women . . . razing old foundations of tradition'

[These post-war women] set the pace . . . and the boys can't keep up with them . . . If women become more masculine, men must become more feminine . . . Is [this] going to make a better and more beautiful world, or is it a challenge against Nature itself, a sign of some decadence overtaking humanity because man, enfeebled and overwhelmed, is surrendering his natural rights and privileges? . . . [M]en are losing as women are gaining, and . . . the natural balance of the sexes and their biological relationship are being thwarted by the claims of women who are becoming unsexed, anarchical and rebellious against natural laws, while man, weakly acquiescing in his own destruction, is becoming emasculated, decadent and doomed.

Gibbs, *Since Then*, p. 382

(v) DEGENERATION DESCRIBED

(a) A fin de siècle view

'The clearest notion we can form of degeneracy is to regard it as *a morbid deviation from an original type.*' . . . Degeneracy betrays itself among men in certain physical characteristics, which are denominated 'stigmata,' or brandmarks . . .

In the mental development of degenerates, we meet with the same irregularity that we have observed in their physical growth . . . [Some of] their mental faculties . . . are completely stunted, others morbidly exaggerated . . . For them there exists no law, no decency, no modesty . . . [T]he degenerate does not, perhaps, himself commit any act that will bring him into conflict with the criminal code, but at least asserts the theoretical legitimacy of crime; seeks, with philosophically sounding fustian, to prove that 'good' and 'evil', virtue and vice, are arbitrary distinctions; goes into raptures over evildoers and their deeds; professes to discover beauties in the lowest and most repulsive things; and tries to awaken interest in, and so-called 'comprehension' of, every bestiality. The two psychological roots of [this] moral insanity . . . are, firstly, unbounded egoism, and, secondly, impulsiveness . . . [Other mental stigmata of degenerates are] emotionalism . . . mental despondency . . . pessimism, a vague fear of all men, and of the entire phenomenon of the universe, or self-abhorrence . . . a disinclination to action . . . [a] predilection for inane reverie. The degenerate . . . is equally incapable of correctly grasping, ordering, or elaborating into ideas and judgements the impressions of the external world conveyed to his distracted consciousness by his defectively operating senses. It is easier and more convenient for him to allow his brain-centres to produce semi-lucid, nebulously blurred ideas and inchoate embryonic thoughts, and to surrender himself to the perpetual obfuscation of a boundless, aimless, and shoreless stream of fugitive ideas; and he rarely rouses himself to the painful attempt to . . . counteract the capricious, and . . . purely mechanical associations of images, and bring under discipline the disorderly tumult of his fluid presentations.

Nordau, *Degeneration*, pp. 16–21
[the quotation at the beginning of the extract is from B. A. Morel,
*Traité de dégénérescences physiques, intellectuelles et morales
de l'espèce humaine* (1857)]

(b) Degeneration: a post-war perspective

Degeneracy, in the sense in which I propose to use the word, means either a loss of one or more of the higher characteristics once acquired by a people, or else the occurrence of those characteristics only in a feeble or moribund form. In this sense it may mean either a return to a more primitive stage in the evolutionary ladder, or it may mean a state of individual or national disintegration which interferes with a healthy life or with a full life. Thus a civilized man may be called degenerate, who exhibits barbarian or foetal characteristics, or . . . if his bodily co-ordination or equipment falls below the standard which enables him to look or to function (within the limits of his class) like the cultivated type to which he belongs . . . [he outlines a range of physically degenerative traits].

But these are not degenerate traits confined to one people. They would be degenerate in the savage . . . [T]here is, on the other hand a degeneracy which must be peculiar to a group or a people, in the sense that they may have achieved the standard from which this particular retrogression is possible. Such standards are chiefly concerned with national or tribal beauty, intelligence, stature . . . or other characteristics which constitute a people's pride and possibly its chief weapon of success.

A. M. Ludovici, *Man: An Indictment*
(Constable, 1927), pp. 143–4

(vi) DEGENERATION AND MODERNITY

We have observed the various embodiments which degeneration and hysteria have assumed in our times. We have seen the mental disorder affecting modern society manifesting itself chiefly in the following forms: Mysticism, which is the expression of the inaptitude for . . . clear thought and control of the emotions, and has for its cause the weakness of the higher cerebral centres: Ego-mania, which is an effect of . . . the predominance of organic sensations over representative consciousness; and false

Realism, which proceeds from confused aesthetic theories, and charac-
terises itself by pessimism and the irresistible tendency to licentious ideas,
and the most vulgar and unclean modes of expression.

Retrogression, relapse – this is in general the ideal of [the degenerate
modern artists] who dare to speak of liberty and progress. They wish to
be the future . . . We have, however, seen in all individual cases that it is
not the future but the most forgotten faraway past. Degenerates lisp and
stammer instead of speaking. They utter monosyllabic cries, instead of
constructing grammatically and syntactically articulated sentences. They
draw and paint like children, who dirty tables and walls with mischievous
hands. They compose music like that of the yellow natives of East Asia.
They confound all the arts, and lead them back to the primitive forms
they had before evolution differentiated them. Every one of their qualities
is atavistic, and we know, moreover, that atavism is one of the most
constant marks of degeneracy.

Nordau, *Degeneration*, pp. 536, 555

(vii) LITERATURE, DEGENERATION, (EF)FEMINIZATION, AND THE RACE IN DANGER

Ours may be an age of progress, but it is progress which, if left unchecked,
will land us in the hospital or lunatic asylum. Neurasthenia and brain-
exhaustion are driving the upper classes among mankind post-haste to
Colney Hatch [a well-known asylum]. The causes of our mental disease
are the wear-and-tear and excitement of modern life, and its symptoms
are to be found in the debased emotionalism apparent in so many of the
leading writers and thinkers of our day, who, together with their numerous followers and admirers, are victims of a form of mania whereof the
scientific name is 'degeneration' . . .

Decadentism is an exotic growth unsuited to British soil, and it may be
hoped that it will never take permanent root here. Still, the popularity of
debased and morbid literature, especially among women, is not an agree-
able or healthy feature . . .

Continental influence upon our literature is more apparent now than for
many years past. The predilection for the foul and repulsive, the puling
emotionalism, and the sickly sensuousness of the French decadents, are
also the leading characteristics of the nascent English schools . . .

The pathological novel is beyond question a symptom of the mental
disease from which civilised mankind is suffering. And if the nerves of
humanity at large were in the same state of those of the characters in
erotomaniac fiction, ours would be a decaying race indeed . . .

Along with its diseased imaginings – its passion for the abnormal, the
morbid, and the unnatural – the anarchical spirit broods over all literature

of the decadent and 'revolting' type. It is rebellion all along the line.
Everybody is to be a law unto himself. The restraints and conventions
which civilised mankind have set over their appetites are aburd, and
should be dispensed with. Art and morality have nothing to do with one
another (twaddle borrowed from the French Parnassians); there is nothing
clean but the unclean; wickedness is a myth, and morbid impressionabil-
ity is the one cardinal virtue. Following their French masters, our English
'degenerates' are victims of what Dr Nordau calls ego-mania . . .

Hysteria, whether in politics or art, has the same inviolable effect of
sapping manliness and making people flabby . . .

In no previous age has such a torrent of crazy and offensive drivel been poured
forth over Europe – drivel which is not only written, but widely read and
admired, and which the new woman and her coadjutors are now trying to
popularise in England . . . [Stutfield blusters about the English capacity to
withstand this continental drift into degeneracy.] In this country, at any rate,
amid much flabbiness and effeminacy, there is plenty of good sense and manliness left . . . [however, he dwells long and colourfully on the modern disease.]
Never was there an age that worked so hard or lived at such high pressure,
and it would be strange indeed if the strain upon our nerves were not beginning to tell. In fact, excessive nervous sensibility is regarded by some as a thing
to be admired and cultivated. It is a bad sign when people grow proud of
their diseases, especially if the disease is one which, if left unchecked, will
poison the springs of national life . . . [As far as Stutfied is concerned, women
play a very large part in spreading the 'moral cancer'.] I think it cannot be
denied that women are chiefly responsible for the 'booming' of books that are
'close to life' – life, that is to say, as viewed through sex-maniacal glasses.
They are greater novel readers than men . . . and not a few of them regard
[the new authors] as champions of their rights . . .

But let the Philistine take heart of grace. He is not alone in his fight for
common-sense and common decency. That a large number of really cultivated people whose instincts are still sound and healthy, who . . . cling to
the old ideals of discipline and duty, of manliness and self-reliance in men,
and womanliness in women . . . who, despising the apes and mountebanks
of the new culture, refuse to believe that to be 'modern' and up-to-date is to
have attained to the acme of enlightenment, – all these will be on his side.

H. M. Stutfield, 'Tommyrotics',
Blackwood's, 157 (1895), pp. 833–45 *passim*

(viii) DEGENERATION, DISSOLUTION, AND THE NEW LIFE?

(a) Resurrection

In order, at this point in his Evolution, to advance any farther, man must
first fall . . . In order to know the perfect social life . . . he must learn the

misery and suffering which come from mere individualism and greed; and in order to find his true Manhood ... he must first lose it – he must become a prey and a slave to his own passions and desires ...

Here in this present stage is only the final denial of all outward and class government, in preparation for the restoration of the inner and true authority. Here in this stage the task of civilisation comes to an end ... the bitter experience that mankind had to pass through is completed; and out of this Death and all the torture and unrest which accompanies it, comes at last the resurrection. Man has sounded the depths of alienation from his own divine spirit, he has drunk the dregs of the cup of suffering, he has literally descended into Hell, henceforth he turns, both in the individual and in society, and mounts deliberately and consciously back again towards the unity which he has lost.

> Edward Carpenter, *Civilisation: Its Cause and Cure* (Swan
> Sonnenschein, 1889), pp. 25, 33

(b) Dissolution

But *if* there be no great philosophic idea, if for the time being, mankind, instead of going through a period of growth, is going through a corresponding process of decay and decomposition from some old, fulfilled, obsolete idea, then what is the good of educating? Decay and decomposition will take their own way ...

And Birkin was just coming to a knowledge of the essential futility of all attempts at social unanimity in constructiveness. In the winter, there can only be unanimity of disintegration ... In his private life the same horror of futility and wrongness dogged him ... The incapacity to love, the incapacity to desire any woman ... was a real torture. Never to be able to love spontaneously, never to be moved by a power greater than one's self, but always to be within one's own control, deliberate, having the choice, this was horrifying, more deadly than death.

> D. H. Lawrence, Prologue to *Women in Love*, in *Phoenix II:*
> *Uncollected, Unpublished and Other Prose Works by D. H. Lawrence*,
> ed. W. Roberts and H. T. Moore (Heinemann, 1968), pp. 98–9

(ix) WOMAN, THE FUTURE, AND THE RENOVATION OF THE RACE

(a) Emancipated women, mothering the race

The man of the future will be better, while the woman will be stronger and wiser, to bring this about is the whole aim and object of the present struggle, and with the discovery of the means lies the solution of the Woman Question. Man, having no conception of himself as imperfect from the woman's point of view, will find this difficult to understand, but we know his weakness, and will be patient with him, and help him with his lesson. It is the woman's pride and pleasure to teach the child, and man morally is in his infancy. There have been times when there was a doubt as to whether he was to be raised or woman was to be lowered, but we have turned that corner at last; and now woman holds out a strong hand to the child-man, and insists, but with infinite tenderness and pity, upon helping him up.

> Sarah Grand, 'The New Aspect of the Woman Question', *North American Review*, 158 (1894), pp. 272–3

(b) The woman of the future

[T]he whole conception of a nobler Womanhood for the future has to proceed candidly from [the] basis of her complete freedom as to the disposal of her sex, and from the healthy conviction that, with whatever individual aberrations, she will use that freedom rationally and well . . .

Refreshing therefore . . . is the Spirit of revolt which is spreading among women. Let us hope such revolt will continue. If it lead here and there to strained or false situations, or to temporary misunderstandings – still, declared enmity is better than unreal acquiescence. Too long have women acted the part of mere appendages to the male, suppressing their own individuality and fostering his self-conceit . . .

It has not escaped the attention of thinkers on these subjects that the rise of Woman into freedom and larger social life is likely to have a profound influence on the future of our race . . . [There has been a lengthy period in which women have been sexually selected by economically superior males.] With the return of woman to freedom the ideal of the female may again resume its sway . . . [and] it is possible indeed that the more dignified and serious attitude of women towards sex may give to sexual selection when exercised by them a nobler influence than when exercised by males.

At the last, and after centuries of misunderstanding and association of triviality and superficiality with the female sex, it will perhaps dawn upon the world that the truth really lies in an opposite direction – that, in a sense, there is something more deeplying fundamental and primitive in the woman nature than in that of the man . . .

The Greek goddesses look down and across the ages to the very outposts beyond civilisation . . . and even in our midst from those who have crossed the borderline of all class and caste, glance forth the features of a grander type – fearless and untamed – the primal merging into the future woman; who combining broad sense with sensibility, the passion for Nature with the love of Man, and commanding indeed the details of life, yet risen out of all localism and convention, shall undo the bands of death which encircle the present society, and open for us the doors to a new and wider life.

> Edward Carpenter, *Woman and her Place in a Free Society* (Manchester: Labour Press Society, 1894), pp. 33–40 *passim*

(x) GENDER AND WRITING

(a) 'Modern women's books of the introspective type'

[T]he lady writer has for some years past been busily occupied in baring her soul for our benefit. And not only baring it, but dissecting it, analysing and probing into the innermost crannies of her nature. She is for ever examining her mental self in the looking-glass . . . [her] dominant note is restlessness and discontent with the existing order of things . . . The glory of the woman of to-day, as portrayed in sex-problem literature, is her 'complicatedness' " . . .

What is the purport or origin of all this super-subtlety and microscopic self-examination? Why should people take such infinite pains to make themselves miserable? and why should woman in particular, so 'persistently parade her "scourged white breast" ' for our inspection? Is it simply a symptom of the fret and fever of modern life?

> H. M. Stutfield, 'The Psychology of Feminism', *Blackwood's*, 161
> (1897), pp. 105, 112

(b) 'The feminine note in fiction'

To me the modern history of novelistic literature seems to prove that there is such a thing as a distinctive feminine style in fiction, something which may be good or bad or neutral, according to circumstances, but, at all events, of a type peculiarly its own.

It seems to me to be a fact that a passion for the detail is the distinguishing mark of nearly every female novelist . . . The passion for the detail conflicts in many ways with the general scope of a novel. The subordinate personages are apt to be too highly coloured, the inferior incidents are put, as it were, into the front place, and therefore interfere with the proper perspective of the whole. Recently complaints have been heard that the novel as a work of art is disappearing and giving place to monographs on given subjects, or else individual studies of character. If the complaint be true – and in some respects it obviously is true – the reason is that more and more in our modern age novels are written by women for women. It would be difficult . . . to think of any feminine rival to George Meredith . . . still less . . . to Scott, Thackeray, and Dickens. It is the neutrality of the artistic mind which the female novelist seems to find it difficult to realize . . . if a novelist takes sides, he or she is lost. Then we get a pamphlet, a didactic exercise, a problem novel – never a work of art.

The female author is at once self-conscious and didactic . . . a woman's work is generally the writing of a personal diary. In it she puts all her recollections and her experiences, strongly tinctured with the elements of her own personality. When she lifts her eyes from the page . . . to the big world which is going on around her, she instinctively takes her own view, and lets it colour all that she writes. She has a particular doctrine or thesis which she desires to expound, and therefore A is right because he can be made the mouthpiece of her own tenets, and B is wrong because he represents the enemy ... A woman's heroine is always a glorified version of herself.

W. L. Courtney, *The Feminine Note in Fiction* (Chapman & Hall, 1904), pp. x–xi, xii–xiii

(c) The feminine note in fiction: a woman's view

Is it not too soon after all to criticize the 'feminine note' in anything? and will not the adequate critic of women be a woman?

Mr Courtney, we think, feels something of this difficulty ... Women, we gather, are seldom artists, because they have a passion for details which conflicts with the proper artistic proportion of their work. We would cite Sappho and Jane Austen as examples of two great women who combine exquisite detail with a supreme sense of artistic proportion. Women, again, excel in 'close analytic miniature work'; they are more happy when they reproduce than when they create; their genius is for psychological analysis – all of which we note with interest, though we reserve our judgement for the next hundred years ... At any rate, it seems clear to Mr Courtney that more and more novels are written by women for women, which is the cause, he declares, that the novel as a work of art is disappearing. The first part of his statement may well be true; it means that women having found their voices have something to say which is naturally of supreme interest and meaning to women, but the value of which we cannot yet determine. The assertion that the woman novelist is extinguishing the novel as a work of art seems to us, however, more doubtful. It is, at any rate, possible that the widening of her intelligence by means of education and study of the Greek and Latin classics may give her that sterner view of literature which will make an artist of her, so that, having blurted out her message somewhat formlessly, she will in due time fashion it into permanent artistic shape.

Virginia Woolf, a review of W. L. Courtney's *The Feminine Note in Fiction*, first published in the *Guardian*, 25 Jan. 1905

By 1929 Woolf had become somewhat less tentative in her pronouncements on the feminine note in fiction, though, paradoxically, her views of art seem to be in some respects closer to Courtney's than they were in 1905.

If, then, one should try to sum up the character of women's fiction, at the present moment, one would say that it is courageous; it is sincere; it keeps closely to what women feel. It is not bitter. It does not insist upon its femininity. But at the same time, a woman's book is not written as a man would write it. These qualities are much commoner than they were, and they give even to second- and third-rate work the value of truth and the interest of sincerity.

... The change which has turned the English woman from a nondescript influence, fluctuating and vague, to a voter, a wage-earner, a responsible citizen, has given her both in her life and in her art a turn towards the impersonal. Her relations now are not only emotional; they are intellectual, they are political ...

... The greater impersonality of women's lives will encourage the poetic spirit, and it is in poetry that women's fiction is still weakest. It will lead them to be less absorbed in facts and no longer content to record with astonishing acuteness the minute details which fall under their own observation. They will look beyond the personal and political relationships to the wider questions which the poet tries to solve – of our destiny and the meaning of life.

Virginia Woolf, 'Women and Fiction', *The Forum*, Mar. 1929, repr. in *Collected Essays*, ed. Leonard Woolf, ii (Hogarth Press, 1966), pp. 146–7

(xi) MAN VERSUS WOMAN: MEN VERSUS WOMEN

(a) Womanliness and manliness

Because it is inconvenient to be exposed and thwarted [man] snarls about the end of all true womanliness, cants on the subject of the Sphere, and threatens that if we do not sit still at home ... with shades over our eyes that we may not see him in his degradation, we shall be afflicted with short hair, coarse skins, unsymmetrical figures, loud voices, tastelessness in dress, and an unattractive appearance and character generally, and then he will not love us any more or marry us ... O man! ... you are a very funny fellow now we know you! but take care. The standard of your pleasure and convenience has already ceased to be your conscience. On one point, however, you may reassure yourself. True womanliness is not in danger, and the sacred duties of wife and mother will be all the more honourably performed when women have a reasonable hope of becoming wives and mothers of *men*. But there is the difficulty. The trouble is not because women are mannish, but because men grow ever more effeminate. Manliness is at a premium now because there is so little of it, and we are accused of aping men in order to conceal the side from which the contrast should evidently be drawn.

Grand, 'The New Aspect of the Woman Question', pp. 274–5

(b) This sex which is not one

Women have no existence and no essence; they are not, they are nothing. Mankind occurs as male or female, as something or nothing. Woman has no share in ontological reality, no relation to the thing-in-itself, which, in the deepest interpretation, is the absolute of God. Man in his highest form, the genius, has such a relation, and for him the absolute is either the conception of the highest worth of existence, in which case he is a philosopher; or it is the wonderful fairyland of dreams, the kingdom of absolute beauty, and then he is an artist. But both views mean the same. Woman has no relation to the idea, she neither affirms nor denies it; she is neither moral nor anti-moral; mathematically speaking, she has no sign; she is purposeless, neither good nor bad, neither angel or devil, never egotistical (and therefore has often been said to be altruistic); she is as non-moral as she is non-logical. But all existence is moral and logical. So woman has no existence.

Weininger, Sex and Character, pp. 286–7

(c) Synthesizing women, systemizing man

But the fact of woman remains, the fact that she is relative to man, *synthetic*. Relatively to man she sees life whole and harmonious. Men tend to fix life, to fix aspects. They create metaphysical systems, religions, arts, and sciences. Woman is metaphysical, religious, an artist and scientist in life. Let anyone who questions the synthetic quality of women ask himself why it is that she can move, as it were in all directions at once, why, with a man-astonishing ease, she can 'take up' everything by turns, while she 'originates' nothing? why she can grasp a formula, the 'trick' of male intellect, and the formula once grasped, so often beat a man at his own game? Why, herself, 'nothing', she is such an excellent critic of 'things'? Why she can solve and reconcile, revealing the points of unity between a number of conflicting males – a number of embodied theories furiously raging together ... And let him further ask himself why the great male synthetics, the artists and mystics, are three-parts woman? ...

A fearless constructive feminism will re-read the past in the light of its present recognition of the synthetic consciousness of woman; will recognise that ... it can be neither enslaved nor subjected. Man, the maker of formulae, has tried in vain, from outside, to 'solve the problem' of woman. He has gone off on lonely quests, he has constructed theologies, arts, sciences, philosophies. Each one in its turn has stiffened into lifelessness ... Woman has remained curiously untroubled and complete. He has hated and loved and feared her as mother of nature, feared and adored her as the unattainable, the queen of Heaven; and now, at last, nearing the solution of the problem, he turns to her as companion and fellow pilgrim, suspecting in her relatively undivided and harmonious nature an intuitive solution of the quest that has agonised him from the dawn of things. At the same moment his long career as fighter and destroyer comes to an end [together with] the final metamorphosis of his fear of 'woman'. Face to face with the life of the world as one life he will find it his business to solve not the problem of 'woman' who has gained at last the whole world for her home, but of man the specialist; the problem of the male in a world where his elaborate outfit of characteristics as fighter, in warfare, in trade, and in politics, is left useless on his hands.

Dorothy Richardson, *Ploughshare*, Sept. 1917, pp. 245–6

(d) Woman on the warpath

Whether they are aware of it, or not, the men of today are a little afraid of the women of today; and especially the younger men. They not only see themselves in the minority, overwhelmed by numbers, but they feel themselves swamped by the strange unloosed energy of the silk-legged hordes. Women, women everywhere, and all of them on the warpath! The poor young male keeps up a jaunty front, but his masculine soul quakes. Women, women everywhere, silk-legged hosts that are up and doing and no gainsaying them. They settle like silky locusts on all the jobs, they occupy the offices and the playing-fields like immensely active ants . . . in amazing bare-armed swarms, and the rather dazed young male is naturally, a bit scared . . .

The modern young man is not afraid of being petticoat-ruled. His fear lies deeper. He is afraid of being swamped, turned into a mere accessory of bare-limbed swooping woman; swamped by her numbers, swamped by her devouring energy. He talks . . . rather feebly, about man being master again. He knows perfectly well that he will never be master again.

D. H. Lawrence, 'As if Women were Supreme', *Evening News*, 5 Oct. 1928, quoted from the version reprinted as 'Matriarchy' in *Phoenix II*, pp. 548–9

Index

Printed in the United Kingdom
by Lightning Source UK Ltd.
129822UK00003B/229-240/A

9 780340 562772